NO ORDINARY HEROES

NO ORDINARY HEROES

8 Doctors, 30 Nurses, 7,000 Prisoners, and a Category 5 Hurricane

Demaree Inglese, M.D.

with Diana G. Gallagher

CITADEL PRESS
Kensington Publishing Corp.
www.kensingtonbooks.com

CITADEL PRESS BOOKS are published by

Kensington Publishing Corp.
850 Third Avenue
New York, NY 10022

All Kensington titles, imprints, and distributed lines are available at special quantity discounts for bulk purchases for sales promotions, premiums, fund-raising, educational, or institutional use. Special book excerpts or customized printings can also be created to fit specific needs. For details, write or phone the office of the Kensington special sales manager: Kensington Publishing Corp., 850 Third Avenue, New York, NY 10022, attn: Special Sales Department; phone: 1-800-221-2647.

CITADEL PRESS and the Citadel logo are Reg. U.S. Pat. & TM Off.

First printing: August 2007

10 9 8 7 6 5 4 3 2 1

Printed in the United States of America

Library of Congress Control Number: 2007922605

ISBN-13 978-0-8065-2831-1
ISBN-10 0-8065-2831-1

*To my mother and father, who gave me
unconditional love and taught me that anything
was possible if I worked hard enough.*

—DI

*With love and gratitude to family and friends
who have helped me realize my writing ambitions.*

—DGG

Acknowledgments

This is a true story. I interviewed many people to gather the information necessary to construct an accurate timeline and reliably re-create dialogue, especially in situations where I myself was not present. I would like to express my gratitude to the many medical personnel who submitted to endless hours of questioning: Cheryl Blake, Kentrisha Davis, Yolanda Dent, Marcus Dileo, Carol Evans, Hedy Hartzog, Lakesha Favis, Lillian Ford, Gary French, Robert Gates, Samuel Gore, Michael Higgins, Pebles Jones, Scarlatt Maness, Chuck Perotto, Daphne Powell, Jan Ricca, Brady Richard, Denise Sarro, Paul Thomas, Duane Townzel, and Victor Tuckler. I am also indebted to the security personnel from the Orleans Parish Criminal Sheriff's Office who assisted me: Jim Beach, Gary Bordelon, Robert Brown, William Devlin, Mary Goodwin, Gerald Hammack, Sidney Holt, William Hunter, Chuck Jones, Mary Baldwin Kennedy, John Lacour, Matthew Mills, and John Phillips.

I would like to thank the individuals who furnished photographs for the book: Jim Beach, William Devlin, Samuel Gore, Michael Higgins, John Netto, Jan Ricca, David Skeins, Pam Laborde and Charles Warren from the Louisiana Department of Corrections and Public Safety, and Patrick Garin Photographer. Also, Jarred Zeringue provided the excellent maps that appear in the book.

While I cannot possibly thank all of the incredible security personnel who fought to keep inmates, staff, and civilians safe during our ordeal, I would like to express my appreciation to the Correctional

Center deputies I worked with personally. We owe these brave men and women a great deal, possibly our lives: Danny Boersma, James Brunet, Shandreka Cobbins, Chris Dietz, Patricia Ross, Richard Skyles, Allen Verret, and Lance Wade. I would also like to express my appreciation to Louisiana Attorney General Charles C. Foti, Jr. and Louisiana Secretary of Corrections Richard L. Stalder for their assistance in evacuating everyone from the jail.

I want to acknowledge my friends Tony Guidry and Jerremy Brum, who took Sam Gore and me in after our departure from Houma. Later, they supported me with friendship and a place to bunk when I first returned to Louisiana. I also want to thank Sheriff R. Jack Strain, Jr., for providing me with food and lodging for weeks after the storm.

I will forever be indebted to Jerry Purcell, who opened his home to me for many months while my own house was being renovated. In addition, his technical support was invaluable to me as this project developed.

I would like to thank Joan Tapper, who assisted with shaping and sharpening the narrative, my agent, Tim Wager, who supported this project from its inception, and my editor, Michaela Hamilton, who helped guide this book to publication.

I must mention my longtime friend, Betsey Wilcox, without whom this book would not have been possible. Betsey introduced me to my coauthor, Diana G. Gallagher, and provided encouragement as we struggled to tell this story.

Finally, Diana Gallagher and I were truly equal partners in the writing of this book. Her ideas and experience were essential, and it was both a privilege and a pleasure to work with her.

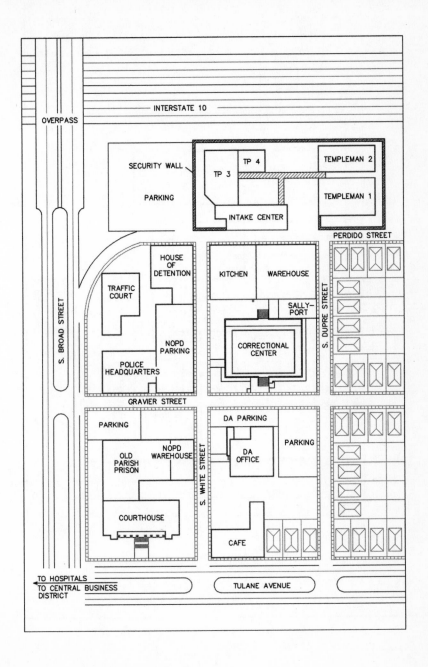

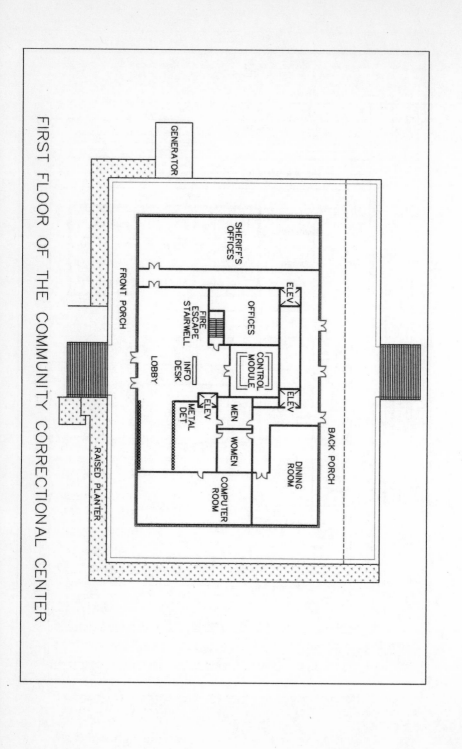

FIRST FLOOR OF THE COMMUNITY CORRECTIONAL CENTER

GENERATOR

SHERIFF'S OFFICES

FRONT PORCH

OFFICES

FIRE ESCAPE STAIRWELL

ELEV

INFO DESK

CONTROL MODULE

LOBBY

METAL DET

ELEV

MEN

WOMEN

ELEV

COMPUTER ROOM

DINING ROOM

BACK PORCH

RAISED PLANTER

Prologue: Wednesday, August 31, 2005

It was late afternoon, and I just wanted a few minutes of downtime. For the skeleton medical staff of the New Orleans jail—thirteen buildings that housed the city's 6,400 criminal inmates—the sixty hours since Hurricane Katrina had hit us had been a nightmare. The ordeals we'd faced made my tour of duty as an air force doctor in Korea seem like summer camp.

Only four days ago my biggest headache as medical director was how to notify the family of an inmate who had died after a long illness. Now I looked across the lobby of the Community Correctional Center, the command center for the jail complex, at the makeshift clinic we'd managed to set up. I wondered how much longer we could hold out. We had handled a stream of life-threatening emergencies that beset the hundreds of deputies and civilians who worked or had taken shelter here. But now hundreds of increasingly rebellious and dangerous inmates had begun to break out of cells on the upper floors. No relief was in sight.

My colleagues were working in the temporary pharmacy that once served as a computer room. In the six years I'd been employed at the jail, I'd never doubted my doctors or nurses, but Katrina had brought out the best in them, a resourcefulness and tenacity I might never have seen otherwise.

All afternoon the cinderblock walls of the building had reverberated with inmates banging and shouting from the floors above, but things seemed quiet for the moment. It was the right time to snatch a few minutes of rest outdoors.

The stench from the restrooms along the back wall made me move faster toward the glass doors that led to the broad, roofed porch. We hadn't had power for two days, but there was ample light coming into the lobby. Still it was tricky to get around the mass of people and the mounds of disheveled clothes, toys, mattresses, and other stuff that marked the spaces they had claimed as their own. My cargo shorts and T-shirt were damp with sweat that never seemed to dry in the New Orleans humidity, and when I rubbed my chin, I scraped a three-day beard that itched in the heat. A breeze outside would be welcome, I thought as I headed for the porch.

The sound of the heavy security door opening behind me stopped me cold. I looked back as Captain Allen Verret and his deputies rushed out from the stairwell that led up to the inmate floors.

"Out!" Verret ordered. "Everybody out, now!" As acting warden, he had total charge of this building, and his voice was so commanding no one would have thought to disobey.

When the last man cleared the door, Verret shoved it closed and locked it.

Only one thing could have put him in such a panic: inmates on the loose.

Verret began barking orders, and the deputies rushed to carry them out. Everyone working in the nearby control room and around the lobby dropped what they were doing and mustered at the information desk.

"Get the civilians out of here!" Verret yelled. "The inmates are coming down. Move these people out of the building—now!"

Confusion stunned the crowd for a moment, but the deputies didn't have to urge anyone to leave. People swarmed through the doors onto the porch. The thick walls buffered the sounds of shouts and pounding in the stairwell, but even so, the noise grew louder and rapidly closer. I moved toward the clinic to warn my doctors and nurses.

"Get your staff outside, Doc," Deputy Skyles called to me. "There're too many inmates coming down. We won't be able to hold them off!" His voice was steady, but fear glinted in his eyes.

"I'm getting them now!" I kept moving, but before I reached the clinic area, the doctors and nurses streamed out of the pharmacy. I urged them on through the doors.

"Outside! Hurry!" Skyles shouted as he turned back to help Verret organize the deputies in the lobby.

Outside, other deputies herded the civilians along the porch, which extended along the sides of the building. I stayed where I could see what was going on inside.

Verret and ten deputies all faced the stairwell door with their weapons raised. Several men had guns. Everyone else had batons or improvised clubs. One female deputy gripped a curling iron to use against the rioting inmates when they broke through the door. I marveled at the courage of Verret and his crew. The threat of violence was real, and they confronted it without reservation.

A few medical staff members came back to find me—close friends all. Their faces were grim, similar thoughts on their minds. The one thing we had all dreaded most was happening: inmates from several floors were scrambling down the stairs. Some of these men were being held for capital crimes like murder and rape. Many had been in jail for decades. None had eaten for days. The security door was the last barrier separating them from freedom— and us.

I'd been in dangerous situations many times in the last few days, but this time I thought we could actually die here. I was scared, but the voice in my head wasn't screaming and I didn't want to run. Instead, a strange calm settled over me. I knew what I had to do.

I grabbed a mop lying against the front glass window and walked over to the porch railing. Placing the handle between two wrought-iron posts, I pulled—hard. The handle broke in two, and I stood back, eyeing the three-foot wooden club in my right fist. Suddenly, I was struck with an unsettling question: Could I actually crush a man's skull?

I looked around. The sight of friends and coworkers, children and seniors, and female deputies armed only with batons gave me my answer. Some were crying. Most were helpless. Everyone was terrified. Yes, doctor or not, I would do whatever it took to protect them. As I walked back into the lobby, one of the doctors, an old buddy named Gary, ran after me.

"What are you doing, Dem?"

"Helping," I answered. "There are eight hundred inmates in

this building. They've been in the dark without food and water for days. If they get through that door, people are going to die."

Gary paused, looked at the deputies, at the door, and back at me. Without saying a word, my normally gentle friend lifted a wooden chair and smashed it against the floor. Picking up a leg, he stood by my side.

Another doctor joined us, carrying a wooden leg ripped from a cot. Two other colleagues grabbed the remaining chair legs. Braced for action, I looked behind me. More than half a dozen nurses—all of them holding flashlights, brooms, or anything else that could be used as a weapon—lined the porch, ready to stop the inmates' advance.

What a way to go. What a crowd to go with, I thought.

Verret's eyes met mine as I stood among the deputies. Gripping his rifle, he nodded in acknowledgment. I nodded back.

Behind the stairwell door we could hear what sounded like rolling thunder as the inmates barreled down the last flight of stairs to the first floor.

BAM! The steel door shook, battered from the rear. BAM! Another blow struck.

My pulse quickened, and there was a rush of blood in my ears. I gripped the mop handle tighter. "Get ready, Gary. Here they come."

Gary swallowed hard, his face pale.

As a third blow shook the door, the breath caught in my chest. I raised my club and waited . . .

Sunday, August 28, 2005

The First Day

Chapter 1

Morning:

Hurricane Katrina is declared a category 5 storm, with winds
at 160 mph.

The eye is still 250 miles from the mouth of the Mississippi
River.

The Superdome opens as a shelter at 8 a.m.

At 10 a.m. Mayor Ray Nagin orders a mandatory evacuation
of New Orleans.

"He died?" I coughed to clear my throat. The phone call from the
jail had awakened me from a deep sleep, and my thoughts were
fuzzy. No wonder, I realized with a glance at the clock on my
bedside table. It was 6:54 a.m. After a Saturday-night foray to a
club on Bourbon Street, I had slept less than four hours.

"Yes, Dr. Inglese," a deputy sheriff said. "At Charity Hospital, half an hour ago."

"I'll be right there." I groaned when he hung up. Next-of-kin
notification was one of my more unpleasant duties as the head
physician at the New Orleans jail.

Swinging my legs off the bed, I rubbed my eyes. Carl Davis,
a violent repeat offender with advanced cirrhosis, had spent the
past two and a half years in the jail infirmary, and though my
medical staff worked hard to give all our inmates excellent care,
his death had been inevitable.

A hot shower washed away the remnants of Bourbon Street

dirt and smoke, and I checked a mirror. My close-cropped hair needed barely any attention, but beneath my dark, thick eyebrows, my eyes kept trying to close. The stubble on my square jaw could stay. I hated to shave.

By the time I put on green scrubs and went to the kitchen, I was almost awake. Except for a few packets of instant grits, my cupboards and refrigerator held few promising prospects for breakfast. My house had just gone on the market, and the realtor was starting to show it. I didn't have the time or patience to clean the kitchen on a moment's notice.

It wasn't that I wanted to leave town. I had put a lot of time and effort into this house. A hundred years old, near Tulane University, it had hardwood floors, ceiling medallions, elaborate moldings, a veranda, a slate courtyard, gardens—all the elegant charm of historic New Orleans, plus two newly renovated floors, the result of hours of my free time over the past eighteen months. But I no longer wanted to spend my weekends and evenings working in the yard or making repairs. A condo was much more practical for a thirty-nine-year-old single man with two jobs and an active social life, and I eagerly wanted to move into a new place I'd found on the river.

The condo, close to the gym where I worked out almost every day, was also near my favorite restaurants and the park where I ran—and a quick ten minutes to my haunts in the French Quarter. And it didn't hurt that the condo provided an excellent view of the Mardi Gras parades. When it came to being a doctor, I took my work seriously, but I also loved New Orleans and its lively party scene.

I wolfed down a bowl of grits and listened to the latest weather report. Tracking the progress of Hurricane Katrina had engrossed the entire city over the past few days. But because New Orleans had a two-decade history of bad storms swerving away at the last moment, most residents retained a devil-may-care attitude that was at odds with the increasingly serious predictions and the hurricane's current path. Despite the morning's sun, Katrina was still bearing down on New Orleans, and it had just been upgraded to a category 5—potentially catastrophic.

It was only about three miles and a ten-minute ride to my office at the Community Correctional Center. But I hadn't bothered to fill up my Mercedes yesterday, foolishly assuming I'd have all day today to do that. Instead, I took the patrol car I used for official business, but its gas gauge, too, hovered near empty. Procrastination was one of my bad habits. Though I made sure everything at the jail ran like clockwork, I tended to put off mundane personal tasks, like paying house bills and filling gas tanks.

As I drove down the oak-lined roads of my uptown neighborhood, I was struck by how deserted it was. No one was out on the porches that wrapped around the gracious Victorian homes. The boisterous Tulane students who normally clustered on the streets were absent. Even more worrisome, every gas station I passed was closed and boarded up.

I caught a glimpse of the Broad Street pumping station, which kept below-sea-level New Orleans dry in ordinary weather. Katrina would undoubtedly give those pumps a real workout over the next few days.

A twinge of panic pierced my fatigue. I couldn't have known an inmate would die, but I was beginning to regret going out last night. A more prudent man would have gotten gas and gone shopping instead. Too late now, I thought, as I turned onto Tulane Avenue, a main city thoroughfare, which led right past the jail complex. Notifying Carl Davis's next of kin and preparing the necessary reports had priority over gas and hurricane supplies.

Since Davis had died of natural causes, telling his family might be easier than when I had to explain an unexpected or violent death. He had cirrhosis of the liver, an incurable disease, and the inmate's condition had deteriorated steadily despite aggressive medical treatment. That didn't mean, however, the family would take the news calmly. After six years at the jail, I hadn't been able to alter the public misconception that inmates were given inadequate care. That belief was too entrenched to dislodge.

Maybe the hurricane would keep the story off the front page, though. Newspapers and television routinely presented a skewed account when reporting the death of an inmate, ignoring critical facts that exonerated the medical staff. The New Orleans jail booked 105,000 arrestees per year and averaged only eight deaths, one-third the national average. The low death rate was even more impressive considering the nature of our jail's population. Most of the inmates came from an impoverished, drug-using, inner-city environment, and almost all had medical problems: 5 percent had HIV, 20 percent latent tuberculosis, and 29 percent hepatitis. A quarter of the inmates suffered from mental illness, and 70 percent had drugs in their blood at the time of booking. The homeless and indigent lacked primary care, and some deliberately committed minor crimes to get access to the jail's medical services.

I was proud of what we'd accomplished. In 2000, Charles C. Foti Jr., the sheriff of Orleans Parish for thirty years—later Louisiana's attorney general—had hired me to reorganize and improve the jail's medical department. I instituted many new programs, including screening and treating inmates for communicable diseases, which significantly curtailed the spread of infections throughout the city. Just last September, in 2004, the National Commission on Correctional Health Care had recognized the jail for providing outstanding medical care at a low cost. Unfortunately, most of the public hadn't noticed.

Bad publicity plunged to the bottom of my things-to-worry-about list as I parked across the street from the Correctional Center's glass-fronted entrance. Its towering ten stories underscored the building's importance as the command center for the thirteen buildings that made up the jail. Slamming the car door, I ran up the front steps and took the elevator to Medical Administration on the second floor.

Paul Thomas, the director of nursing, stepped out of his office as I walked through the door. "What are you doing here so early?"

"Carl Davis died at Charity Hospital an hour ago." I walked past the bathroom and into my office, one of seven spartan rooms that opened off the center hallway. Fluorescent lights lit the corridor, which ended at a small barred window. My office was like most of the others: a computer stood on a cheap pressed-wood desk that took up much of the stained tile floor.

"Like you don't have enough to do today." Paul paused, his burly frame filling my doorway.

"I have to notify Davis's family before I do anything else." I sank into my desk chair and looked up. "Did the mayor order a mandatory evacuation?"

"Not yet, but he will," Paul said. The soft-spoken fifty-two-year-old was the department hurricane fanatic and de facto alarmist. Whenever a tropical depression was upgraded and named, tracking charts went up on his office wall. He logged on to weather websites, made meticulous contingency plans, and kept everyone in Medical Administration advised of course changes and projections. The downside of Paul's obsession was his insistence that every new storm would be the one to finally ravage New Orleans.

"I decided to bring the nurses in at three instead of six," he said. "If we don't get everyone here early, some of them might not show. This storm's a bad one, and people are starting to panic."

The gravity of the approaching storm made my windowless cinderblock office seem smaller and more cramped than usual. I called a deputy in the Communications Division, which relayed calls and information throughout the jail complex, then talked to someone in the Special Investigation Division. SID deputies handled the detective functions of the sheriff's office, and they were already looking for Carl Davis's next-of-kin.

I began collecting all the records pertaining to his illness, treatment, and death, including a download from Charity Hospital. The massive, free-care medical center stood a mile and a half down Tulane Avenue past the courthouse. Staffed by the Schools of Medicine at Tulane and LSU, the facility was a Level 1 trauma center. That was where we sent inmates who were too sick to be cared for in the jail's infirmary.

As the hospital record printed out, I called the infirmary, where Davis had been housed. Every inmate had a medical chart, containing doctor's notes, X-rays, lab results, and medication records. I would need the complete file to conduct a thorough case review. Two hours later—with periodic interruptions by Paul to let me know of Katrina's worsening outlook—I had all the necessary paperwork on Davis, but SID had still not located any family member. Assuming they had evacuated, we postponed the notification until after the hurricane.

On my way out of the building, I ran into Captain Allen Verret, the associate warden of the Correctional Center. A barrel-chested man of forty-three, with a mustache and brown hair flecked with gray, he had the calm, assured presence of a born leader. He instilled confidence and treated his deputies with the same respect they felt for him.

"How's it going?" I asked. The Correctional Center warden— each building in the jail complex had its own—was away on vacation, and Verret was in charge.

"It's been a busy couple of days. I barely had enough time to see my wife and son off to Mississippi and pack a bag for myself." Verret's manner was off-hand, but deep worry lines creased his face. He was obviously preoccupied with serious matters.

"I don't really believe all this," I confessed.

"You're not the only one," Verret said. "I just came from a meeting with the sheriff and his officers."

Verret told me he and several others had voiced serious reservations about keeping the inmates at the jail. I had raised similar concerns myself yesterday, and I certainly wouldn't have been shy about arguing had I been invited to the meeting. I could be insistent and even headstrong when pressed.

But now that Jail Administration was certain that Katrina would hit, they felt there was no longer time to evacuate almost 7,000 prisoners. In addition to the usual 6,400 inmates, the facility had taken in 374 prisoners from neighboring St. Bernard Parish, which was considered more likely to flood.

"We don't have enough food, water, flashlights, and batteries stored in the warehouse," Verret continued. "If we're here longer than a couple of days . . ."

"We're as prepared as possible in Medical," I assured him. We'd been implementing our disaster plans for a couple of days. "The clinics have been stocked with supplies, and the nurses will pass out extra meds just in case."

"Good." Verret nodded. "Jim Beach wanted to distribute food and water to all the buildings before the storm, but Administration decided to wait."

As the director of Food Services, Major Jim Beach was responsible for providing 20,000 meals a day to the prisoners. On a routine day, three cooks and two dozen inmate workers prepared breakfast, lunch, and dinner in the kitchen, then transported the food—one hot meal and two cold ones daily—to each of the jail buildings, where deputies and inmates carried it to the tiers, as the barracks-like cells were known. The hurricane would undoubtedly create problems, and Beach was trying to anticipate them.

As I left Verret and walked outside, Paul Thomas's latest bulletin weighed on my mind: "The Mayor just ordered a mandatory evacuation of the city. This is going to be brutal."

Katrina was the worst storm to threaten the Louisiana coast in recorded history. There was nothing more I could do to prepare at the jail, and I still had to gas up two cars, buy food and water, and pack.

Chapter 2

As I drove away from the Correctional Center, I used my cell phone to call the St. Tammany Parish Jail, where I held a second job as medical director. The smaller facility was forty-five miles north, close to Lake Pontchartrain, which put it at considerable risk. The staff there had a well-thought-out hurricane plan, and with only one building to cover, preparations were proceeding on schedule.

Next I contacted Sam Gore, the doctor who had overseen Carl Davis's treatment in the infirmary. Not surprised by the patient's death, his matter-of-fact tone masked the sympathy he felt for all those in his care. "Did you tell his mother?"

"No, his family probably left town," I explained.

"That's what the sane people are doing," Sam quipped. "Lisa and the kids are already gone. I've got some last-minute things to take care of, but I'll see you soon."

Sam and I had been friends since our residency at Keesler Air Force Base in Biloxi, Mississippi, a dozen years ago. Later we were stationed together again at Andrews AFB, near Washington, D.C. I grew used to his unflappability; he addressed all situations—good and bad—with the same unemotional detachment. He didn't shout. He didn't raise his voice. In fact, there was little about Sam that made him stand out in a crowd. About five-foot-ten and average weight, he looked like the best friend of the main character in a TV sitcom. His most prominent physical characteristic, a dark brown cowlick, stuck up just like Harry Potter's. But his mental toughness, and our many years together, had taught me to rely on him without question. I would do anything for close friends and colleagues. And I expected them to respond the same way. True to form, Sam had readily agreed to work throughout the storm.

When Sam hung up, I dialed Gary French at his house, a quarter mile from Lake Pontchartrain. I'd known him for years, too, ever since he had been my medical student at the Andrews AFB hospital. When I became medical director at the New Orleans jail, Sam and Gary were the first doctors I recruited.

If Sam was stoic, Gary was not. Thirty-five and five-foot-nine, he had the sturdy build of an ex–high school wrestler and the disposition of a born pessimist. During the buildup to a crisis, Gary always appeared frantic, but when hell broke loose, he was focused, steady, and got the job done. When I had asked him to work during the storm, he'd balked at the idea of staying in the city during a category 5 hurricane. However, despite his reluctance, I wasn't worried. He always came through.

"Made up your mind yet?" I asked when Gary answered his phone.

"I'll be at the jail."

I smiled. "The hurricane wouldn't be the same without you."

"I know I'm going to regret this," Gary muttered, then added, "At least Allen's gone. He took the dogs to stay with his family in Arkansas."

I was glad that Sam's family and Gary's roommate had already evacuated. The normally bustling city streets were empty of traffic, virtually deserted. Obviously everyone had headed to the interstate, and even with contraflow in effect—using all the lanes to send cars out of New Orleans—traffic on the highway would be bumper to bumper.

"Do you have food and water?" I asked Gary.

"I bought supplies three days ago, but I haven't done anything to hurricane-proof the house. And I don't know what to do with my car." A nervous tremor crept into Gary's voice. "What are you doing with yours?"

I hadn't decided yet. My normal way of dealing with those

kinds of decisions was to logically work out a plan, then, at the last moment, go with my gut. I told Gary to be at my house at two. I'd have figured something out by then.

I hung up and turned onto my street. Barely a breeze ruffled the neighborhood's majestic oaks or disturbed the lush, carefully tended landscaping around Greek Revival and Victorian mansions. What would happen to those gardens, I wondered, in 150-mile-an-hour winds?

I pushed that thought to the back of my mind, when I realized that though I had taken a different route home, I still had not seen a single open store or gas station.

Chapter 3

Midday:

Katrina's sustained winds reach 175 mph, with gusts of 215 mph.

The eye is 225 miles from the mouth of the Mississippi River.

The Superdome now contains 10,000 evacuees and 550 National Guardsmen.

The National Weather Service warns that the effects of a category 4 or 5 strike will be catastrophic.

Katrina Advisory #23 predicts a storm surge of eighteen to twenty-two feet.

The ride back to my house finally pushed me into action. The sight of my neighbors' expensive 100-year-old homes, all of them vacant and too quiet, shuttered and boarded up with cheap plywood, sharpened my sudden sense of dread. I hadn't even bothered to tape the glass in my own house. I had a lot to do, and limited time. I parked and raced inside, frantically trying to decide where to begin.

The silence depressed me, so I turned on the TV in the den. The weather map appeared on almost every channel, with the menacing arrow of Katrina ready to strike at Louisiana's heart. Going upstairs to the bedroom to pack a bag, I realized I hadn't done laundry in days. I grabbed a pile of dirty clothes, rushed down to the basement, and threw in a load. Then I checked my kitchen.

The cabinets were still empty, and the refrigerator contained only a package of chicken breasts, two slices of American cheese, a jar of relish, and two bottles of Ketel One vodka—not exactly ideal hurricane provisions. The jail kitchen would provide meals, but how long could it feed 7,000 inmates plus hundreds of deputies and the family members who would undoubtedly seek refuge in the steel-and-concrete buildings? It was common for employees to bring their families and pets to shelter during storm alerts. They also brought their own food and water as a precaution, but I was miserably unprepared.

Delaying what might be a futile search for a store with supplies, I started packing and finally prepped my house. First I filled all three bathtubs with water, then I ran around securing my valuables. I moved the chairs and sofas away from windows and took important papers and several artworks—cherished paintings my father had done—to the second floor, along with old family furniture that came from my grandmother. They'd survive if the roof blew off the third floor or if the ground floor flooded.

While I waited for another load of clothes to dry, I called my parents, who had recently retired to South Carolina. I kept the conversation brief, just long enough to assure them that I'd be safe at the jail. After all, it was a massive structure with generators and access to a warehouse full of food. I doubted I'd have any trouble riding out the storm.

As for planning for any medical emergencies at the jail, Paul Thomas and I had exchanged half a dozen phone calls on Saturday, coordinating our disaster plan and the staff needed to carry it out. We had designated thirty nurses out of seventy total as essential medical personnel and notified the seven physicians who had volunteered to stay at the jail of their assignments.

When it came to hurricane response at the jail complex—a sprawling assortment of old and new buildings that spread over some five city blocks near the central business district of New Orleans—the procedures were well established and well practiced. Most officers had been at the jail twenty or thirty years and took shelter there two or three times each hurricane season.

The Correctional Center, as always, would be the heart of the operation. The ten-story building—twelve if you counted the basement and the roof—served as headquarters for the Sheriff's Office, which included all the jail structures. The Center's main-floor lobby contained a waiting area, computer room, and control room, where the sheriff's deputies monitored building security. Upstairs, the inmates lived in tiers, multicell dormitories on four floors, with an administrative floor in between each of them for offices, classrooms, the central phone system, and a medical clinic. A core group of doctors and I would be stationed in the Center.

The surrounding neighborhood resembled a quilt pieced together with multistory prisons, garages, open parking lots, court buildings and legal offices, seedy bail bond businesses, mechanic shops, and warehouses. One edge of the area—which could be a confusing jumble even to those who worked in the jail complex—was bordered by modest houses of one and two stories.

The back of the Correctional Center faced the jail's warehouse and vast kitchen, which was already ratcheting up preparations to feed inmates, employees, and their families during the coming storm.

On the block beyond that stood the Intake Processing Center, where prisoners were normally brought in or released from custody. Arrests and bookings were unlikely during the hurricane, but I had made sure Dr. Marcus Dileo and several clinic nurses would be there, just in case.

From the rear of Intake a fenced, roofed walkway formed a long T, whose arms stretched in both directions to the newest jail buildings—four massive steel and concrete structures with bars across every window. Inside, the vast hallways were interrupted by thick, sliding security doors.

Templeman 3, with 1,200 prisoners in its four stories—a mix of maximum-security prisoners and newly arrived inmates—was on the left, along with the much smaller Templeman 4. I had assigned Dr. Larry Caldwell to cover those buildings.

At the right end of the walkway stood Templeman 2 and Templeman 1, where the infirmary was located. Sam Gore, as usual, would be in charge of its 200 seriously ill patients.

Surrounding all these interconnected buildings, adding its own air of menace, was a twenty-foot wall of smooth poured concrete topped by curls of razor wire.

The Old Parish Prison, New Orleans' original jail, was in the other direction—down the block and around the corner from the front steps of the Correctional Center. Attached to the grand parish courthouse, the Old Prison had a gray concrete exterior punctuated by small square windows that added to the building's dank, sterile atmosphere. All of the jail's facilities held different classifications of inmates—male, female, juvenile, federal or state prisoners, or municipal offenders. The Old Prison had the worst of the worst; it housed the red-banders, maximum-security inmates named for their colored plastic wristbands. The Old Prison would be staffed by nurses, who could call for a doctor from the Correctional Center, if necessary.

There were several other jail buildings as well: the House of Detention, across the street alongside the Correctional Center, loomed twelve stories. Among other things, it housed a psychiatric unit, which would be overseen by Dr. Shamnugan Shantha. The women's prison, Conchetta, was a converted hotel a few blocks away; also on the outskirts of the complex was Templeman 5, so new that no prisoners had transferred there.

The assignments were made; the doctors and nurses knew when to report. Before Katrina's next move, though, I still had my own preparations to finish. I had time for one more phone call, this time to my grandmother. At eighty-six, she lived alone in the Pittsburgh suburbs and still had a razor-sharp mind. Gram had been anxiously watching the news. She wouldn't have a moment's peace until the danger to her precious grandson was past.

She knew though that I could handle myself. My seven years in the air force had included a year on a "remote" tour in Osan, Korea. Right out of residency training, I'd found myself as the only air force internist in that country, as well as chief of medical services and the leader of a disaster casualty team. Because of the time difference between Korea and the States, I could count on little help from more experienced physicians in the United States. Those months taught me to work independently, shoulder responsibility, be decisive, and take command of personnel. I was confident I could reach back to those experiences and handle whatever emergencies Katrina threw at me.

Ironically, it was because of the air force that I'd first grown to love this city. When I got some rare time off as a resident at the base hospital in Biloxi, I'd escape to New Orleans, and it wasn't long before I had a large network of friends here. The place had captured my heart. I still couldn't believe that the free-and-easy city that I now called home faced destruction. Another glance at the TV brought that reality home. I still needed gas, water, and food. I grabbed my car keys and headed for the door.

Chapter 4

I got in my Mercedes and started looking for supplies. The first gas station I saw had closed, and my fuel gauge was now below E. I could feel myself beginning to panic: I was going to run out of gas *now*. Then, a mile and a half down the road, I could make out perhaps two dozen cars waiting to fill up at an open gas station–convenience store. I pulled up to the end of the line and prayed that the pumps wouldn't run dry before it was my turn.

Since moving to New Orleans I had eased right into the local attitude toward hurricanes. The last big storm to hit Louisiana was Andrew in 1992, and before that you had to go all the way back to the sixties, with Betsy and Camille. "These storms are never as bad as the weatherman predicts," was the refrain I heard all over town. In the last few years that had held true—and attempts to put the population on alert had woefully backfired.

The evacuation for Hurricane Ivan, in 2004, had been a disaster. Weather experts and municipal authorities had wanted the people of New Orleans to stop ignoring hurricane threats, and a large portion of the population had heeded the advice and evacuated. There had been just one small catch: the powers-that-be had not bothered to open all lanes on the interstates to outgoing traffic until after the cars had slowed to an intolerable crawl. The ninety-minute drive to Baton Rouge took eight hours; Houston ended up being a twenty-four-hour trip.

Only a couple of months ago, Hurricane Dennis had been projected to hit New Orleans. Everyone on staff at the jail had taken extraordinary precautions. Deputies, families, doctors, and nurses had all arrived prepared to ride out the storm for three days. While we slept, the hurricane had made landfall on the Florida Panhandle and we didn't get a drop of rain.

But I was coming to believe this time would be different. Katrina couldn't be ignored. And as a member of the jail's disaster planning committee, I'd read too many reports with dire predictions: If Katrina came close, the whole city would flood. A fifteen-foot storm surge would stop the pumps that protected New Orleans. If the storm actually hit the mouth of the Mississippi, fifty to a hundred thousand people could die. After the storm, the city wouldn't have power or water for weeks. Anyone who stayed could die from dehydration—or, if they drank floodwater, they'd get dysentery and die from that. Despite my own tardy response to Katrina's threat—and much as I liked to kid around with my friends—I'd spent the last thirty-six hours convincing as many as possible to get out of town.

The gas was still flowing as I pulled into the station. Next to me, the other customers rushed around, barely acknowledging anyone else as they talked on cell phones and filled their tanks. After using the pump, I went into the mini-mart to see if anything edible remained. During Ivan, tons of Spam had been available at the last minute, but now there wasn't a single can left.

I tried to ignore the people shoving past me in the aisles and filled a cardboard box with beef jerky, canned ravioli, spaghetti with meatballs, Vienna sausages, breakfast bars, and the last single jar of peanut butter. As I reached for it, another shopper gave me a scathing look, but she didn't say a word. The bread was gone, but someone mentioned that the French bakery on Magazine Street was still open. After I paid and got some cash from the ATM, I drove straight to the bakery and bought three round loaves.

With two problems solved, I turned my attention to what to do with my car. I called a friend, who suggested the Canal Place parking garage. So many residents were driving out of the city, surely there would be spaces. I had a plan worked out by the time Gary arrived at my house. His first words were true to his pessimistic outlook.

"I just know my house is going to flood," he said. "And even it if doesn't, I'm sure one of the trees in my yard will fall on my new roof. I cut away some of the branches, but I don't think that's enough." Gary paced between my couch and TV. Frowning, he ran his hand over his closely cropped brown hair. "A category four could flatten everything."

Hating to focus on the possibility that everything I owned could be destroyed, I shook off the bad feeling. "Let's go," I said, palming the keys to the patrol car.

My parking plan was simple. We'd use the patrol car to shuttle first Gary's Honda then my Mercedes to the garage. Afterward, we'd return to my house, pick up our food, clothes, and bedding, and head for the jail.

The Canal Place lot, however, was jammed full, as were the next two places we tried. Apparently, a lot of residents had a similar idea; New Orleans citizens, it seemed, were waking up and belatedly trying to shelter their vehicles from the elements. I felt the same way. My Mercedes was brand new, and I hated the thought of flying branches and debris marring its spotless pewter finish. I needed advice from someone who *really* knew the city. I signaled Gary to pull over and wait while I called Mike Higgins.

A native of New Orleans, and an excellent psychiatrist, Mike Higgins was a good soul in an unconventional package. Thirty-five with a shaved head, he was an athletic, wiry 150 pounds. Shy around strangers, among friends he became talkative, with a biting sense of humor. A stickler for following rules, Mike terrorized the nurses with phone calls about lapses. He had already worked at the jail for some time when I took over the medical department, and I made him director of psychiatric services almost immediately. When I reached Mike on the phone, he was at a garage on St. Charles Avenue with plenty of open spaces. We'd meet there, and I'd drive everyone to the jail in the patrol car.

"Are Moby and Georgie with you?" I asked before hanging up, referring to his two dogs. Mike might have been a hardass with the nurses, but he positively doted on his animals. As for me, I was allergic to them. I wouldn't refuse Mike a ride, but I hoped they weren't along.

"They're in my office." Mike knew the dogs caused me discomfort, and he made an effort to minimize my contact with them. But he also went out of his way to see that Katrina would do them no harm.

When Gary and I got to the garage, we found Mike on the fourth level by his parked pickup. Brady Richard, head of Medical Supply, was there too. "REE-chard," he'd say, when he was introduced, emphasizing the Cajun pronunciation of his name. Brady had grown up on the Bayou, and he greeted us in his thick accent. "Y'all ready for this?"

"As ready as we can be." I noticed that Brady hadn't shaved. Not only did he and I sport similar military-style haircuts, he, too, had an aversion to razors, and most of the time he walked around with two or three days of dark stubble.

Nobody cared if Brady looked a little scruffy. Outside of work, his life centered around his extended Louisiana family, his dogs, and the area's most popular hobbies—hunting and fishing. He probably wouldn't shave again until after the hurricane.

As everyone was piling into my patrol car, my cell phone rang. It was Sam Gore. He had already unloaded his things at the jail, but he was resigned to leaving his car outside unprotected. I told him to meet us at the garage.

We waited for him by a cement wall that overlooked the city panorama of skyscrapers, with their acres of glass. Would all those windows shatter in the face of 150-mile-an-hour winds? The sidewalks that bordered the banks, law firms, and office buildings of the central business district were empty, though the sun was still shining and few clouds broke the blue of the sky. Except for the doomsday weather reports and the deserted streets, there was nothing to indicate that a storm of unprecedented intensity was headed our way.

When Sam pulled in, he locked his car and slid into the backseat of the patrol car with Gary and Brady. Five minutes later, we were at the jail. I let Mike and Brady out at the Correctional Center, and dropped off Sam at Templeman 1. Gary stayed with me while I stopped at the maintenance yard and filled the patrol car with gas before heading home to shuttle my Mercedes and get our stuff.

Back at the house, Gary and I listened to the weather as we loaded supplies into the patrol car. The National Weather Service had just issued a special warning about the massive devastation that would accompany a category 4 or 5 storm.

"It's going to be worse than I thought," Gary said.

I knew by now the storm probaby would not veer off and miss New Orleans. "At least we'll be safe in the jail."

Gary wasn't reassured. "With a storm this big, I'm not sure it'll matter where we are."

The first drops of rain fell as we got back on the road. By the time we neared the Superdome, the sprinkle had become a steady drizzle.

"Look at that!" Gary exclaimed.

I glanced to the left. The scene at the massive stadium, home to the New Orleans Saints, could only be described as mind-boggling. An enormous line of people stretched down the ramp, wrapped around the building, and continued down the street. I saw mothers trying to keep track of three or four kids, and old men and women in wheelchairs. Thousands waited to enter the shelter, all of them with suitcases, coolers, and whatever else they had managed to carry from their homes. People looked dazed. It would take hours to get everyone inside, and it was raining.

"It's like Noah's Ark," Gary said. "They're lining up two-by-two to get away from the flood."

"That flood destroyed the world," I reminded him.

Chapter 5

That afternoon, while I was busy prepping my house and scouring the city for supplies, Captain Allen Verret and his deputies were readying the Correctional Center for the coming onslaught. By midafternoon they had everything under control except for securing the sallyport, the gated loading zone at the back of the building.

After taking inventory of supplies and equipment, Verret had dispersed flashlights, batteries, rain gear, and olive-green work clothes to the hurricane contingent of thirty-five deputies stationed in the building. Because more than a hundred people would take shelter in the building, he ordered staff to haul new prison mattresses out of storage, then modified security routines to permit easy movement between administrative floors. He hated having to prop open the steel doors to the fire escape stairwell—it ran the entire height of the building, including the floors that held the inmate tiers—but for now it would be too difficult to monitor the many people going up and down.

"Skyles!" Verret called. "Maintenance is on the way with the pumps. Get the crew and meet me in the sallyport."

"Right away," the deputy said, striding away. Thirty, tall, and a solid 270 pounds, Richard Skyles was ex-military with experience in handling explosives. He never flinched in dangerous situations, and Verret could always rely on him.

The captain took the elevator to the basement and walked

outside through double steel doors. The sun was still shining, but a few white clouds were beginning to gather.

The sallyport was a short, wide driveway that descended from the street into the basement of the Correctional Center. Sandwiched between that building and the warehouse, the steep drive was bordered by concrete buildings on both sides. A retractable gate halfway down the drive allowed deputies to securely load and unload inmates and supplies. Vans and delivery trucks pulled past the retracted gate and parked in front of the heavy doors Verret had just stepped through. Deputies did not open those doors until the retractable gate was closed and locked.

Verret scanned the concrete walls on either side. Securing the sallyport was necessary whenever a major storm threatened the city. In a heavy rain, the roads around the Correctional Center flooded. The basement end of the sallyport was six feet below street level. Unless deputies blocked off the entrance, street water would pour down the steep decline, forming a pool and flooding the basement. Even mild flooding would be catastrophic.

The Center's outside generators had been raised several years ago to protect the machinery from flooding. The preventive measure was well-intentioned but had failed to take into account two vital facts: the power was channeled through the electrical room in the basement, and the additional height wasn't enough to save the generators from a fifteen-foot storm surge. Verret had often wondered what "genius" architect had put the generator relays several feet below street level in a city that flooded, but that didn't matter now. He had to cope with the problem as it existed.

When Skyles showed up with five other deputies, Verret put them to work hauling large steel posts and metal plates from their storage area at the bottom of the sallyport. The deputies carried seven of the four-foot posts up to the street and inserted them into anchors spaced across the driveway. The men sweated heavily in the August heat, and they gladly took a break when a maintenance truck arrived pulling a trailer with two diesel-powered pumps bolted to it.

Verret stood at the top of the drive, directing the truck between two of the metal posts. The sallyport didn't have a roof, and the pumps were needed to remove the rainwater as it accumulated. The driver parked at the top of the drive, just behind the posts.

Next, Verret and his men carried six steel plates—eight feet by four feet—up the drive. It took three men to carry each one. The deputies carefully slid each plate into grooves on the steel posts and then sandbagged the joints.

After two hours of backbreaking work, Verret and his men finished the job. The assembled structure formed a steel wall from the Correctional Center to the warehouse, a temporary dam to keep flood water out of the sallyport.

"I'm glad that's over," Skyles said, wiping sweat off his face.

"Yeah, but we still have to get the pumps ready." Verret stretched to work a kink out of his back.

The deputies attached two long suction hoses to the pumps on the trailer and extended them down into the deepest part of the drive. Next they connected two outflow hoses and draped them over the steel dam to drain into the street.

As Verret followed his men back into the basement, he glanced over his shoulder. When the sallyport began taking water, they would have to come back out to start the pumps. It wouldn't be easy in a driving rain and punishing winds.

In the meantime, there were other, less complicated, but still critical preparations to be done. Verret sent deputies to remove tree branches, secure loose objects, and stack sandbags on the back porch. They distributed pillows and prison mattresses to civilians and set extra mops, buckets, and towels by the front and rear doors.

Then he went to check in with his deputies on the tiers. The inmate housing units had televisions, and Verret knew the prisoners would be following Katrina's approach closely. Security was always on the acting warden's mind, but there was no way to anticipate what the hurricane would bring . . . or when. They needed to be prepared for anything.

Chapter 6

Evening:

The National Hurricane Center warns that Katrina is
"potentially catastrophic," and the levees may be
"overtopped."
Some 36,000 evacuees crowd into the Superdome.
Mayor Nagin orders a 6 p.m. curfew.

The sight of so many people waiting to get into the Superdome
had a sobering effect on Gary and me, and we both tried to hide
our uneasiness as we unloaded the patrol car in front of the Correctional Center.

"We'll have to make three trips, maybe four." Gary stared at
the stuff piled in the trunk and picked up a carton of bottled
water.

"We have all night." I lifted two boxes of food and led the
way up the two dozen front steps.

"This water is really heavy," Gary said, panting when we
reached the wide porch that surrounded the building. The first
floor was twenty feet smaller than the nine stories above, and large
cement columns supported the upper stories, creating an overhang
that formed a ceiling for the porch.

"Don't complain. It's good exercise." I halted as two grade
school boys ran past me, laughing and shrieking. When an elderly man walked around the corner, the boys stopped to pet his
small dog.

Here we go again, I thought. Every time we had a hurricane alert the deputies brought spouses, children, or parents to shelter at the jail. That was understandable; unlike most houses in New Orleans, these buildings were made to withstand the weather. But the thought of all those civilians made me uncomfortable. I worried for their safety. I didn't like the idea of inmates sleeping in such close proximity to children and their animals. Cats in cages were bad enough, but some of the families even brought pet rabbits!

It looked like fifty to a hundred people had already arrived. They would probably number close to two hundred in the end, and if the storm was as bad as predicted, we might have some neighborhood residents, too, before long. Several people gathered on the porch, watching and waiting as they did before every storm.

Inside, civilians and their belongings crowded the lobby. It looked like a flea market free-for-all with grocery bags, cases of water, suitcases, electronic gear, toys, pet carriers, and bedding stashed along the walls. People of all ages sat on the fixed plastic chairs where family members waited to see inmates on visiting days. Kids and teenagers sprawled on the floor. They played cards and board games, listened to radios, or just talked. For many, conversation and laughter were ways to take one's mind off the storm.

Gary followed me across the lobby and through a metal detector to the elevator. We had too much to carry up the stairs. When the elevator door opened on 2, I was surprised to see people sitting on the floor of the large foyer. They were sorting through supplies, arranging pillows and blankets, and plugging TVs and game systems they had brought from home into whatever outlets they could find.

The hubbub of noise and activity was muted when we entered the door to Medical Administration. I put the food on a chair in my office, while Gary stashed the water in the cramped filing room down the hall.

"Hey, look who's here." Mike stood by his office. The psychiatrist had piled boxes in the open doorway to keep his dogs inside. One of the animals barked. "I bet Dem just can't wait to give you boys a big hug."

"Let's skip the hug." I glanced over the barrier. As long as I didn't get too close, my eyes wouldn't start watering. Moby, a black-and-auburn English bulldog, was short and solid with a squashed face. The bearded collie, Georgie, resembled a small sheepdog, taller with long gray-and-white hair. They were making themselves right at home.

"Maybe it's a good thing you brought them," I said. "If the storm is as bad as they say, we can always eat them."

"I'd sooner eat you," Mike replied indignantly.

"In fact, we should change their names. Let's call them Lunch and Dinner." I loved to bait Mike.

He rolled his eyes. Mike enjoyed verbal sparring with his friends, and he could take it as well as he could dish it out. Neither of us missed a chance to zing the other.

Paul called out from Mike's office, ready as always to pass along the latest warnings and bulletins. "The mayor just set a six p.m. curfew. There's almost no chance Katrina will miss us."

He and Brady were glued to a television on Mike's desk. We hadn't used the TV since 9/11, when we were all riveted to the news coverage. Now the set was tuned to the Weather Channel.

Gary and I made a few more trips to finish unloading the patrol car, then I drove it to a raised parking lot two blocks away and jogged back in steadily falling rain. But the wind wasn't bad, and I didn't even bother to change my damp clothes when I returned to Medical Administration.

The mood there was surprisingly light. None of us had actually been through a hurricane of significant size before. Despite numerous threats, previous storms had all veered off at the last minute to wreak their havoc somewhere else. Even now we still had a hard time accepting that Katrina would be different, though the predictions of 160-mile-an-hour winds and double-digit storm surges pouring out of the radio and TV were starting to grate on me.

Dire forecasts aside, we talked and joked while we inventoried our supplies. I looked around the group. If someone didn't know us, I had to admit it might be hard to tell us apart. All of us were white, with short dark hair, predominantly in our thirties, mostly ex-military, and in good physical shape. But when it came to personalities, our differences emerged.

I was the extrovert, perhaps due in part to the same Italian heritage that accounted for my Roman nose and my last name, Inglese. My nickname, Dem, was short for my middle name, Demaree, the result of a whimsical impulse on my parents' part.

Mike, a clean freak, was almost obsessive about what he ate. He opened a large tub of low-fat bagel chips, took a handful, and passed the container. Then he pulled low-fat crackers and no-added-sugar peanut butter out of a grocery bag.

"Do you ever eat anything that's *not* low-fat?" Paul asked.

"Ha!" Brady laughed heartily. "He even brought low-fat dog food for Moby and Georgie."

Gary grinned. "Are you sure you want to go on *The Amazing Race* with this guy, Dem?"

Every Tuesday, Mike, Gary, and I got together to watch the reality TV show that pitted teams in round-the-world competitions that were part treasure hunt and part *Fear Factor*. When the call went out for contestants for the upcoming season, Mike and I had dressed in scrubs and recorded an audition video inside a jail cell. We thought our comical introduction and clever repartee—and the fact that the show had never featured physicians, let alone jail employees—might do the trick. We hadn't heard back . . . yet.

"Looks like we have plenty of food." Gary closed the cooler he had brought and pushed it aside.

"And water," Brady added.

Among us, we had nearly twenty gallons. Paul had found more bottled water and a half-case of Gatorade in the file room. That would be more than enough. Once the storm had passed over, we expected to be back at home within a few days, back to normal.

"Did everyone bring batteries?" Paul asked.

We all had some, mostly Ds for flashlights.

After we finished our inventory, I went into my office. In spite of the mounting tension, the calm professional in me took over the moment I sat at my desk. I picked up the phone to check in with the physicians at Intake and Templeman. At the infirmary in Templeman 1, Victor Tuckler, a moonlighting ER physician from Charity Hospital, had reported an hour early for his 7 p.m.–to–7 a.m. shift.

"Landfall at dawn," Paul announced, sticking his head in my doorway for a second before ducking back out. We could expect Katrina to come ashore in less than twelve hours.

Victor might be staying longer than usual tomorrow, I thought, but, with 7000 inmates to care for, I could use the extra help. Templeman 1 and 2 housed 1,500 general population inmates, along with the 200 seriously ill infirmary patients. During the emergency, Sam and Victor could look after them all.

Gary and I could handle the 800 inmates housed at the Correctional Center. Some were immigration detainees who spoke only Spanish, but Gary was fluent. He had spent two years as a Mormon missionary in the Dominican Republic.

Mike came in and perched on the edge of my desk. "Dr. Shantha brought her son, Vinnie, here on her way to the Psych Unit in the House of Detention. He's staying in an office on the second floor, near the guys in the Communications office."

I nodded approval. Vinnie was nineteen, and he'd be more comfortable with us than at the building where his mother had charge of the jail's most serious mental patients, psychotic inmates · and patients with suicidal and homicidal tendencies.

Paul appeared in the doorway again. "The clinic nurses are putting together a week's worth of pills for the inmates who're on medications. If we lose power or have a problem, the patients will be set."

Brady barged in past Paul. "Sam just called wanting more IV fluids for the infirmary. I'll take what he needs from Medical Supply and bring some to the other clinics, too."

"Wait a minute." Paul left without explanation and immediately returned with a dozen handheld yellow radios. He looked at Brady. "I got a bunch of these from the warehouse and was just getting ready to pass them out. Can you take them to the clinics? Then we can talk to each other if the phones go down."

After everyone left, I concentrated on my paperwork, including the case review of Carl Davis's death. The paper records on my desk had gone limp in the oppressive humidity, a side effect of the faulty second-floor air-conditioning. Water stains marred the ceiling, and paint was peeling off the wall. Every building in the jail—all of them steel and cinderblock structures—showed signs of age; the Correctional Center had leaky plumbing, too. Despite the dismal decor, I had never regretted my decision to become medical director. The past six years had brought satisfaction that far exceeded the difficulties.

We'd improved the health care tremendously, adding laboratory services, treadmill testing, and X-ray imaging to the clinics. In addition we had increased the numbers of doctors and nurses, hiring well-qualified full-time providers, despite the lack of recognition, poor salaries, and less than appreciative patients . . . dangerous patients.

Of course, we'd never actually had to face a hurricane like Katrina. Whatever lay in store, we'd have to deal with it. My office was quiet, and putting aside thoughts of inmates, sheltering civilians, and possible emergencies, I turned my attention back to the medical records. I wanted to finish them before dinner.

Chapter 7

An hour or so later, Gary opened my office door. "C'mon, Dem. We're late."

"And this could be our last meal," Mike added.

"It's probably not a good idea to tempt fate, Mike." Gary frowned.

"I like living dangerously." Mike met Gary's anxious gaze with a mischievous grin. He knew that would get a rise from Gary.

"Since when is a no-fat-no-exceptions diet living dangerously, Mike? I want all the calories I can cram in tonight." I cast a side-long glance at Gary and added my own barb. "Just in case it *is* our last meal."

Several new people had joined the families camped in the foyer outside of Medical Administration, and the security door by the elevator was propped open. The hallway beyond it led to another security door that opened into the fire escape stairwell. The inmates on the tiers upstairs were quiet. They had just eaten dinner and were probably watching TV and wondering how their own families were faring.

But here downstairs, the growing number of children added a level of high-pitched noise that grated on taut nerves, especially in the cement-walled stairwell where the acoustics amplified sound. As we walked down to the lobby, three teenagers—a boy chasing two squealing girls—burst through the doorway below and raced up past us.

"It's going to be a long night," Mike muttered.

When we got to the first floor, we headed down a hallway past the sheriff's office. In a wide corridor at the rear of the building, the kitchen staff had set up tables with metal serving pans, disposable plates, and plastic utensils.

Gary stared into an empty chafing dish. The pan was coated with dried tomato sauce. "We really are too late."

"Have a sandwich," I said, picking up a plate. There were several racks holding turkey, cheese, and loaves of bread. I made three sandwiches for myself, then moved out to the back porch where dozens of people were watching the rain. The wind wasn't bad yet. It could have been New Orleans on any stormy summer night.

Almost everyone stood under the protection of the overhang, but a few stalwart souls scattered across the thirty feet of tiled porch that wasn't covered. A wrought-iron railing ran along the perimeter with a break at the rear steps. The kitchen and warehouse stood across a narrow courtyard.

I spotted Paul and walked over. "This isn't too bad."

"Just wait. The wind isn't even tropical storm force, yet," Paul explained. "It's going to get a lot worse."

Sitting down beside him, I pondered the many twists and turns my life had taken to bring me to this moment: sitting cross-legged on the porch of a New Orleans jail, eating turkey sandwiches and watching the first stages of a major hurricane. It seemed surreal.

It brought me back to a hair-raising helicopter ride in Korea when I was transporting a heart patient over rice fields, through a thunderstorm, dressed in body armor. I remembered wondering what choices I had made—me, a kid from an upper-middle-class family in Pennsylvania—that had brought me to such a bizarre and dangerous situation. That night I had no idea what was around the corner. Katrina's dangers were just as serious, and again I couldn't imagine what was in store.

Chapter 8

About 8 p.m., Gary, Mike, and I went back upstairs to Medical Administration. Paul was already there, standing in the hallway and staring over the dog barricade at the TV in Mike's office. He was intent on the latest, ever more serious weather bulletin.

"Do you guys want to play cards?" Mike reached over the piled boxes to scratch his bearded collie behind the ears.

"I'm ready." I grabbed a chair from my office and pulled it into the hall.

"Just so you know," Paul said, "I brought some packages of turkey and cheese up from downstairs. They're in the fridge in the file room."

"Good thinking." The kitchen had left trays of sandwich supplies in the hall downstairs for late diners.

Gary carried an unopened carton of copy paper out of the secretary's office and dropped it to use as a table. We pulled our chairs around the box, and I shuffled the cards.

"Has anyone gotten a call out on their cell phone?" Mike asked. "I've been trying for an hour, but either the circuits are busy or"—he mimicked the computerized message voice—"'Your call cannot be completed at this time.'"

Everyone from New Orleans—in the city, on the highway, and beyond—was probably trying to contact loved ones.

"We might not have *any* cell phone service before long," Gary said. "Transmission towers were knocked out all over Florida in the hurricanes last year."

I had called my parents on my office phone before going down to dinner. They were relieved to hear from me, but not reassured. After watching cable news coverage for days, they were sure New Orleans faced total destruction. I didn't want to add to their stress and downplayed my own concerns—with the caveat that phone calls might not be possible after the hurricane—at least for a few days till essential services were restored.

"Use the jail phone," Gary said. "I couldn't reach any Louisiana numbers, but out-of-state area codes go through."

"Anyone hungry?" Brady walked in holding the handles of a steaming pot. He had a hot plate in medical supply a few floors above us. "This is the best jambalaya in town."

"I just ate," I said quickly. His shrimp, sausage, and rice casserole was a staple in Louisiana, but it didn't appeal to my palate. I was a firm believer that vegetables, meat, and rice should be separated in distinct piles and not mixed together. Besides, Brady's Cajun cooking always had a kick.

"Hurry up and eat, Brady," I said. "Paul doesn't want to play, so you're our fourth for canasta."

"I can eat and play cards at the same time." Brady set the pot down on a counter in the hall. "Help yourselves whenever you're ready."

Playing canasta relaxed me. My grandmother had taught my whole family to play, and the connection to her took the edge off my anxiety. The game also distracted us from Katrina—which was coming ten miles closer every hour—and worries about how it would affect the jail and its inmates.

Forty minutes later, Paul burst from his office. "The radios don't work."

Brady put his cards down. "The yellow ones I just took to the clinics?"

Paul nodded. "I called Templeman 3, and I couldn't raise them. Then I tried Detention and couldn't get them, either. I couldn't reach anyone outside of this building."

"So they work here?" I asked.

"Yeah. Talking to nurses here won't be a problem, but staying in contact with the other clinics probably will be." Without another word Paul turned and went back into his office. A minute later, he came out carrying two metal trashcans and strode down the hall to the sink.

"The wardens have police radios," Mike said. "We can get an urgent message in or out if we have to."

I dealt another hand, trying to block out Paul's increasingly loud commotion.

He furiously scrubbed the trashcans. We ignored the thuds, scraping sounds, and metallic clanks until he lined the containers with trash bags and started filling one with water from the sink.

"What the hell is he doing?" Brady asked.

If Paul heard, he didn't let on. He filled one can, then started on the second.

"What're you doing?" Brady repeated.

"Storing water in case we need it," Paul answered.

Mike's eyes widened. "I'm not drinking water from a garbage can."

"You'd rather die of thirst?" Paul looked at Mike expectantly. "These cans are clean. Besides, the water isn't even touching them. It's in the bags."

Mike folded his arms. "Don't care."

"When your dogs need water, you'll be glad we have it." Paul wasn't put off by Mike's stubborn stance. "And when we lose water, we can use it to flush the toilets."

"I'm more worried about losing power," Brady said. "No power means no elevators and no air-conditioning."

The air-conditioning system on the second floor barely kept the humidity and temperature tolerable, but it helped. The thought of losing it in a Louisiana August wasn't pleasant. Something else occurred to me. The doors to hundreds of inmates' cells were also powered by electricity. What would happen if they couldn't be opened . . . or shut? How would the prisoners react to being trapped? Or what if they got loose? A hint of anxiety made me hungry again.

"Think I'll make another turkey sandwich." I stood up.

Mike squinted at me with a critical eye. "Don't you think you're fat enough?"

"Not for a hurricane." I was beginning to reach back to what

I had learned in air force survival training. At a solid 180 pounds, I was fit and athletic, but I didn't want my muscle mass to be lost to starvation rations. If things got as bad as they were predicting, we might end up without food for days. I was going to build up my body's reserves, just in case.

"Let's take the dogs out," Brady said to Mike. "I'm startin' to go a little stir-crazy."

Apprehension, even with good reason, wasn't programmed into Brady's bayou mind-set. He was energetic, enthusiastic, and ready for anything—sometimes to the point of recklessness. Walking Moby and Georgie probably eased his tension. Gary and I decided to go with them.

When Mike opened the Medical Administration door, he paused before going through. "Oh, my God."

I looked out and gasped, too. In the last hour the crowd had not only doubled but had also dug in, like misplaced people in a refugee camp. Civilians now sprawled on prison mattresses all over the foyer floor. Islands of pale green plastic demarcated the territory each family had staked out. Somehow, we managed to navigate the packed floor to the security door without stepping on anyone.

Down in the lobby, more people jammed in, watching Katrina's opening salvo. The windows and doors had not been boarded up yet. Streetlights and lights from the DA's office across the way illuminated the parking lot and road, and the pine trees along the street bent in heavy gusts of wind. Although the porch overhang afforded some protection from the storm, most of the onlookers stayed inside.

Mike and Brady took the dogs around to the back porch, where the building provided better protection from the driving wind and rain. I wasn't ready to let the storm get the best of me just yet, and when Gary couldn't dissuade me from getting a better view, he joined me out front.

The wind battered two tall trees near the front steps. A large branch broke and fell off as we watched. The rain blurred the outline of the Old Prison behind the police mechanic shop to the right, creating a ghostly aura around the structure. Small houses in the other direction looked gray and forlorn.

As we turned to go back inside, Captain Verret walked out. "Do you need anything for Medical?" he asked.

"An airlift to Chicago," I joked. I told him again that Gary, Mike, and I would be in the Correctional Center to respond to any medical problems that might arise. So far the only glitch was the limited range of the yellow radios.

When another blast of wind rocked Gary back a step and pelted us with rain, we went in. Verret held the door open for some deputies who carried sheets of plywood out of the lobby.

Mike, Brady, and the dogs passed us on their way back upstairs. With the hurricane's landfall still hours away, they wanted to get as much rest as possible. Gary and I should have taken the hint, but even on less than four hours' sleep, I couldn't resist one more look at Katrina's first attack.

A large group of spectators had gathered on the back porch. The storm was growing steadily in strength, and gusts whipped streams of leaves around the corners of the building. The young oaks lining the street swayed, and the heavy rain began to flood the small courtyard between the onlookers and the kitchen.

Gary and I watched the storm unfold for nearly an hour. When a burst of wind tore a glass-and-metal light fixture off the porch overhang, showering glass on the spectators, we decided to turn in. Even if Katrina surprised us—as Ivan did, with less than an inch of rain—we'd still have a busy day tomorrow.

When we walked back through the lobby, the anxiety I had suppressed all night surfaced. A disturbing sense of claustrophobia set in as Verret and his deputies secured the last sheet of plywood over the front windows, shutting off the outside view. I felt as closed in as the 800 inmates locked upstairs. *Now we're all prisoners of the storm.*

Monday, August 29, 2005

The Second Day

Chapter 9

Early morning:
At 2 a.m. Katrina makes a slight turn north.
The storm is 150 miles in diameter, with winds of 155 mph
  and advancing at 10 mph.
Around 3 a.m. the 17th Street Canal levee is breached.
City power is lost, forcing jail buildings to switch to
  generator power.
By 5 a.m. Katrina's eye is 90 miles from New Orleans, with
  winds of 150 mph.
At 6:10 a.m. Katrina makes landfall in Plaquemines Parish,
  Louisiana, as a category 4 hurricane.

In the early hours of Tuesday morning, Gary and I finally went
up to Medical Administration. The smell of dogs was overpowering, and there was no room on the floor of my small office to
stretch out. Every other bit of space was occupied by sleeping
staff.

"Why don't we go to my office?" Gary said. He held up his
keys. As the jail's director of infection control, Gary's desk was
several floors above.

We carried our bedding, Gary's cooler, some food, and water
up a few more flights of stairs. Although we were bone-tired, we
didn't regret the move. There was plenty of space in the large windowless room where Gary and eight medical assistants worked.
And, as a bonus, Infection Control had excellent air-conditioning.

Gary even found a gift basket of Sugar Daddy candy, Clark Bars, and KitKats on an assistant's desk.

"It *is* an emergency," Gary said, unwrapping a Clark bar before he plugged in an electric pump and inflated his air mattress.

There was another welcome discovery. Infection Control had an unexpected cache of water—a five-gallon jug in the water cooler.

"Gary, how many other offices up here have water coolers?" I asked, unrolling the floor mat that I had slept on in Korea.

"I don't know. Let's go look. We might need the supplies." Gary followed me out.

We searched several administrative floors and found a number of unlocked offices with two partial and two full five-gallon jugs. We also found more bottled water and Gatorade in office refrigerators. If circumstances ever became desperate, the water stash up here might be a lifesaver.

We set our cell phone alarms for 6 a.m. and crashed. The glow of computer screensavers around us added an eerie image to the scene. As we dozed off, an intense drama began to unfold downstairs.

Captain Verret carried two sandwiches as he walked out the rear door of the Correctional Center onto the back porch. He had to remember to thank the kitchen staff for leaving the turkey and cheese trays in the hall. His deputies were too busy to eat on a schedule. He himself hadn't even had time to change out of his wet work clothes. That was probably just as well. He'd be soaked many more times before the night was over.

Hugging the back wall, Verret stared at the mounting storm. Katrina was still offshore, but the wind was already breaking off tree limbs and shattering unprotected glass. Branches, papers, trash cans, and shingles shot past the building and disappeared into the howling night. Sheets of water resembling panels of frosted glass sliced a path down the street, tearing the leaves off trees.

He had hustled the last of the late-night gawkers inside an hour ago, before the storm turned deadly. Now anyone who stepped too far away from the building risked being impaled by once-harmless objects that the hurricane had transformed into missiles. Staying close to the wall, Verret moved around the corner, toward a more protected side of the Center. He paused and looked down at the street twenty feet below the porch, where the pouring rain was creating a rushing river. Trash and other floating debris sped by like small boats on a storm-tossed sea.

Kind of how I feel, he thought. Verret had acted as warden many times before, but never during a major emergency. He couldn't afford to make a mistake. Too many people—inmates, families, and staff—were counting on him. And other officers, including Sheriff Marlin Gusman, would be scrutinizing every decision he made.

Deputy Skyles appeared and interrupted his thoughts. "It's really coming down now," he said.

Verret glanced at his watch: It was 2:36 a.m. "Is there water in the sallyport?"

"Almost a foot," Skyles answered evenly.

Verret nodded. The basement floor stood only two feet higher than the sallyport. The water hadn't reached the doors yet, but it would—soon. "Guess we'd better start the pumps."

Verret, Skyles, a crew of deputies, and a few inmates assigned to the work detail went out the basement doors to the sallyport. Wind and rain assaulted the men as they trudged through the twelve inches of water, up the driveway to the trailer that held the pumps. The machines pull-started like lawnmowers, and it took several tries to engage the pumps. Verret made sure water was being sucked up and then drained through the hoses draped over the dam wall before ordering the men back toward the building for the final phase of flood-proofing.

Verret closed and locked one of the basement doors, and Skyles and two men bolted a large steel plate in front of it. The other deputies lined the bottom with sandbags. Then they placed a second plate next to the remaining open door. The group moved back into the basement, leaving one of the inmate workers—a small, agile man—outside.

The same crew had been through this unusual drill a month earlier during preparations for Hurricane Dennis. The inmate worker still in the sallyport slid the free steel plate across the open doorway, bolted it into place, and sandbagged the bottom. The plates were two feet shorter than the actual doorway, which left a gap at the top when the doors were open. Inside, Verret stood on a chair, reached over the plate, grabbed the inmate's outstretched arms, and pulled him through the gap and into the basement. Once the inmate was safe, Verret closed and locked the second door.

It wasn't an elegant system, but it worked. If the sallyport continued to fill with water, the steel plates and sandbags would keep the basement dry—at least for a while.

Chapter 10

Back on the first floor, Sergeant Patrice Ross, a short, thin black woman, was keeping watch over the civilians in the lobby. As Verret came back upstairs, he ordered her and some other deputies to keep the area mopped. He knew from previous storms that water would soon be blowing in under the front doors.

As he walked away, the lights flickered and went out.

"We just lost city power," Ross said from the darkness.

Verret tensed—until the generators kicked in and emergency lights came back on.

"That's it for the air-conditioning," Skyles said.

Verret nodded and said a silent prayer that the barrier in the sallyport would hold.

"What are we doing about feed-up?" Skyles ran his hand over a damp buzz cut that was so short he looked bald. "You know what the inmates are like if they miss a meal."

"Let's get through the storm first," Verret answered. "Then we'll worry about it."

Breakfast was still a couple of hours away, and Verret wasn't ready to think about 800 hot, hungry inmates yelling, banging on bars, and probably stopping up toilets in protest, if their meal arrived late. They'd be fed, but not on time. Without elevators, the inmate workers would have to carry food up the stairs to the tiers, and that would take several hours in the ten-story building. And with so many kids running wild in the stairwell, it was dangerous to let the workers move about too freely. He'd have to clamp down on the kid problem—after the hurricane.

"If they miss breakfast, there's going to be trouble," Skyles kept at it.

"They'll live," Verret answered dryly. "With Katrina coming, we've got bigger worries than breakfast."

At 5 a.m. Verret's radio stopped working. The relay towers that bounced the radio signal throughout the city must have gone down, he guessed. That meant the New Orleans Police Department had lost radio contact, too. The police used the same system, and the loss would seriously impede their ability to evacuate the city, enforce the curfew, and respond to emergencies.

An hour later, the front lobby of the Correctional Center was swamped with water that rushed under the front doors with each gust of wind. Puddles had accumulated in front of the information desk, and people were tracking water up the stairwell. Sergeant Ross and two deputies worked feverishly with mops and towels, trying futilely to sop up the flood while some civilians attempted to push their belongings out of the way. Other people tried to sleep, but one or two curious souls had gotten up and were peering through the gaps in the plywood sheets over the doors to see what was happening outside.

"We've got to sandbag the outside of the doors," Verret told Skyles. The captain's skin felt cold and clammy under his wet work clothes, and he grimaced at the thought of going out onto the back porch, where the heavy bags were piled. He didn't relish another drenching, but the job had to be done.

Skyles went for a flatbed cart, and as Verret started toward the rear of the building, a deputy slipped in the stairwell and almost fell. "Keep the stairs dry," Verret called over to Ross. "We don't want any accidents."

Skyles met him at the back doors and held them open, while Verret pushed the plastic-bottom cart outside. He tried to keep a firm grip on the metal handle, but as he cleared the door, the wind almost yanked the cart from his grasp.

Skyles quickly picked up a sandbag and dropped it on the cart to weigh it down. "That's one." The deputy yelled to be heard. "How many more?"

"Twenty should do it," Verret shouted back. The jet-engine roar of the wind pounded all other sound into oblivion.

The hurricane was much stronger than an hour before. Oaks along the street were bent in half, and with gusts whipping around the corners, the back porch was no longer shielded from the raging tempest. Both men fought to stay on their feet as they loaded sandbags onto the cart.

When they were done, Verret waved toward one side. "That way!"

The wind was at their backs as the two men pulled the weighted cart to the corner. After they turned onto the side porch, they had to walk bent over into the wind. The rain felt like needles piercing Verret's skin.

"Get ready!" Skyles shouted as they neared the front porch. The full force of the storm hit them as they came around the building.

Verret clung to the cart, drenched and battered by Katrina's power. He watched as the storm hurled shrubs, lawn furniture, and street signs down the road. The street and parking lot between the Correctional Center and the district attorney's office were covered with water, but this was no placid lake. The ferocious gale churned the water into froth, creating white-capped waves that reminded Verret of the ocean. The water had already flooded the cars parked on the street. If it kept rising, the sheriff's patrol cars parked on the higher ground of the DA's lot would be lost, too.

"Let's move!" Verret's words were buried in the hurricane's roar, but Skyles understood. Fighting the wind, they struggled to pull the loaded cart along the front of the building. Verret's muscles screamed with each step.

Across the street, the top of a tall pine snapped off and careened into the darkness. The tall sweet olive trees that flanked the front steps of the Correctional Center had been ripped from the ground. Saplings and bushes inside a cement planter that skirted the building had been shredded.

The screech of tortured metal rose above the storm's howl. Verret glanced back as the wind ripped tin roof panels off the police mechanic shop and spiraled them high into the air. Whole sections of the roof hovered for a moment before riding the next

squall. On the corner, a utility pole snapped at the base and toppled into the water.

"My God!" Skyles exclaimed.

Verret suppressed the same fear he heard in his deputy's voice.

Sheets of water washed across the porch, and Verret urged Skyles
to keep going. When they reached the front doors, the captain
grabbed a door handle to steady himself. Holding on to it with
one hand, he pulled a sandbag off the cart with the other. Soaked
by the rain, the two-foot-long bag was even heavier than normal.
Like a soggy brick, Verret thought, pushing the sandbag against
the door with his foot. Skyles used a similar method, dragging
bags off the cart and shoving them into position.

They worked slowly but without breaking rhythm, until the
last bag was jammed in place against the doors.

"That's all we can do!" Skyles hollered.

I just hope it's enough, Verret thought as they began retracing
their steps, both of them holding on to the empty cart as they
made their way toward the side of the building.

The wind slammed into their backs, pushing them relentlessly,
forcing them to speed up. Without the sandbags, the cart was at
the mercy of the hurricane. Halfway to the corner, a powerful
gust viciously yanked it forward, dragging the men along. Verret
lost his footing on the slippery porch and fell to his knees. Skyles,
still holding the handle, was flung into the air. The cart and the
deputy crashed down onto Verret, savagely twisting his arm. Trapped
underneath, Verret swore, certain he had broken a bone. His arm
hurt like hell, and the pain intensified as the wind swept the men
and the cart into the Center's wrought-iron railing.

When Skyles rolled off him, Verret pulled his arm free and
crawled away from the cart. Grabbing the railing with his good
arm, he tried to stand. Another brutal blast hammered him back
to his knees.

Suddenly, hands gripped him from behind.

"Are you all right?" Mike Higgins shouted, pulling Verret to
his feet.

Verret glanced at the psychiatrist and nodded as Brady Richard
helped Skyles to stand. He didn't know why the two men from

Medical were outside, but they all risked being swept off the porch if they remained.

"Let's get out of here!" Yelling, Verret stumbled to the back of the Correctional Center. No one spoke further until they were safely inside.

"Don't think I'm not grateful," Verret said, "but what the hell were you two doing out there?"

Brady shrugged. "Just taking a look."

"Good thing for you," Mike added.

Brady agreed with an exaggerated nod. "I thought for sure that railing was gonna give."

I'm lucky it didn't, Verret thought, rubbing his arm.

Mike frowned. "Is your arm okay?"

"I'll be fine," Verret grumbled. He hoped it wasn't broken. Katrina had just made landfall. The worst was yet to come.

Chapter 11

Morning:

At 8 a.m. Katrina's storm surge causes the Industrial Canal
   to overflow.
Flooding in the lower Ninth Ward is six to eight feet deep.
Katrina's eye passes east of New Orleans at 9 a.m., with
   125-mph winds.
At 11 a.m., ten feet of water flood St. Bernard Parish.

Captain Verret was exhausted. He'd changed his clothes, and his
arm still throbbed, but he couldn't sleep with the hurricane raging. He looked into the dining area near the back doors, where
Skyles was watching storm reports on television with Captain
Danny Boersma, another of his deputies.

"It's bad, but the eye's passing east of the river," said Boersma,
who carried his muscular five-foot-eleven-inch frame with the
cocky confidence of a member of the sheriff's motorcycle division. "They're saying it could have been worse."

"The wind's still 125 miles an hour. That's as strong as an F2
tornado," Skyles said.

"But it's almost over." Boersma shrugged. "Still, it might be
days before we get city power back."

It really could have been worse, Verret thought as he walked
outside. His eyelids felt heavy, and he hoped a blast of air would
revitalize his weary mind and body. With all the windblown leaves,
trash, and other debris it was difficult to see. Something struck

his ear. Wincing at the sting, he turned his back to the storm just as something exploded in the sallyport.

Verret rushed to the edge of the porch overlooking the sunken driveway. "Oh, my God . . ." His breath caught in his throat when he realized the sallyport dam had ruptured. One of the steel plates was gone, and water from the street was surging through the breach. It hadn't reached the basement doors yet, but it was rising fast.

Verret ran, bursting through the back doors straight to the dining area. "Skyles! Boersma! The sallyport's flooding!"

Skyles jumped up, knocking over his chair. The blood drained from his face.

"Round up as many big guys as you can find and meet me back here in five minutes." Verret didn't wait for a response.

He raced out to notify Sheriff Gusman, who was sleeping in his office in the Correction Center. He alerted him to the emergency. When Verret returned, Skyles and Boersma were waiting with five other deputies.

Verret said bluntly, "We've got to repair the dam before water gets into the basement."

Seven solemn faces nodded. They knew the generators would shut down if the electrical room flooded: no generator, no power—no control over the jail.

"The sheriff doesn't want us to go. He thinks it's too dangerous"—Verret paused—"and it is. But I don't have a choice. I could use some help, but this is strictly a volunteer operation."

Not one man opted out.

The deputies' courage inspired Verret as he led them outside. It wasn't in his nature to defy authority, but he had been at the Correctional Center in 1995 when a bad storm flooded the basement and the building lost all power. If that happened again with the Center full of wives, kids, and elderly family members, it would be troublesome at best. If 800 inmates with nothing to lose escaped, it could be deadly. He really *didn't* have a choice.

Though it was well after dawn, a gray darkness hung over Verret and his men as they battled the wind on the side porch. When they neared the front corner, he shouted a warning. At the turn, the storm attacked with a deluge of rain. The gale lancing across the front porch was strong enough to send even a heavy deputy flying. Clasping hands, the men formed a human chain to keep from being carried off.

With Verret in the lead, the linked squad descended the front steps. Verret halted at the water's edge, fifteen feet from the submerged sidewalk. The deputies crouched and clung to the banister.

Verret scanned the intersection to the left. The road was the most logical route to the sallyport, but the flood was nearly three feet deep. It was impossible to see through the water to the asphalt. Verret remembered stories of people falling into open manholes and drowning during bad storms. He didn't know if the tales were true, but he had no intention of finding out. He shifted his gaze to the side of the steps, where he knew a cement planter ran along the front of the building and back down both sides. Two and a half feet high, the top of the planter was only a few inches under the surface of the water.

Making an instant decision, Verret climbed over the banister. As he balanced on the planter's edge, a violent burst of wind whipped by, almost blowning him down. Fortunately, Boersma clasped his arm, holding him until he regained his footing. Once he firmly anchored himself, Verret helped his men onto the planter, one at a time.

They were above the flood, but nothing shielded them from the storm. The frenzied wind struck at an angle, smashing the deputies against the building's front wall. The planter's muddy soil shifted under their feet, and with each forward step they slid backward a little. Holding on to each other, they clutched at whatever support they could find: cracks in the cement, broken trees in the planter, and the porch railing above. Every inch of ground gained seemed an Olympic feat.

Before making the turn at the corner, Verret paused. A sane man would go back, but Verret knew this was a defining moment in his life. Did he have the strength and courage to lead his men forward? He pushed on.

As the eight men moved along the side of the building, the wind savaged them from behind, lifting them off their feet. The deputies clawed their way forward, clinging to the rough concrete wall till their fingertips bled. Shards of wood and glass pelted their backs. Splintered shingles became shrapnel. But every man knew the stakes. They all kept going. At the end of the planter, the men were forced to wade into the flooded street. Verret went first, without a word or hesitation.

"Where in the hell's the trailer?" Boersma shouted when they reached the sallyport.

The deputy wasn't kidding, Verret realized with a quick glance toward the dam. The trailer holding the pumps had disappeared, and the water in the sallyport was now level with the flood in the street. The lower end of the driveway was under nine feet of water. Its surface rippled with small waves.

The trailer is still in the sallyport, Verret thought. Water rushing through the breach must have pushed it to the deep end of the driveway. Before they could search for the pumps, however, they had to repair the dam. The basement doors and sandbags wouldn't hold for long, and every minute brought them closer to catastrophe: flooding of the electrical room.

The water at the top of the drive was three feet deep. Ducking under, the deputies felt for the missing steel plate. After a few tries, Boersma surfaced with the free end of one of the pumps' drainage hoses.

A few minutes later, Skyles yelled, "Found the plate!"

Three deputies wrestled the heavy plate back into position between the steel posts. Boersma and another man retrieved submerged sandbags that had shifted and wedged them against the seam.

With the dam restored, Verret was ready to tackle the trailer. "Now we have to get the pumps."

"How?" Boersma asked.

"We'll use the hoses to pull the trailer up the driveway," Verret said.

"Do you know how heavy that rig is?" Skyles exclaimed.

"We need those generators," Verret insisted. He grabbed Skyles squarely by the shoulders. "Are you with me?"

"No retreat, no surrender!" The ex–army man shouted, responding to Verret's intensity.

With the hurricane howling around them, the two men made

their way into the churning water following the drainage hose down into the sallyport until they could no longer stand.

"The trailer must be right below us," Skyles sputtered, treading water.

Taking a deep breath, Verret dove. For the first time in hours, the storm sounds were silenced. He couldn't see in the murky water, but he groped until he touched machinery. Running his hands over the pump, Verret searched for another hose. When his lungs begged for air, he kicked upward. As he broke the surface, rain again sltung his skin and the hurricane-force wind shrieked in his ears and battered his face. He gasped, taking in water and coughing.

"Any luck?" Skyles asked, surfacing beside him.

"Yeah, it's right below." Verret dove again.

After the third dive, Skyles came up with a hose. He swam the end back to the men on the street and then returned to the submerged trailer. Fifteen minutes later, they had located all three missing hoses.

Exhausted, Verret and Skyles swam back to the road and leaned against the dam. The men took a moment to catch their breath. Then they joined the other deputies and took up positions, two men to a hose. They planted their feet in the swirling flood and paused for just a moment.

"On three!" Verret shouted. "One! Two . . . three!"

With teeth gritted and muscles straining, the men pulled. The trailer didn't budge. Verret shouted again. The men hauled on the hoses, but there was still no movement. When a third attempt failed, the men waited.

"This just isn't going to work," said a deputy, flinching when a crushed beer can blew into his shoulder.

Verret stopped to think, then turned to Skyles again. "If we push the trailer while they're pulling, we might be able to move it."

"That's enough, Verret," one of the deputies snapped. "It's over. There's nothing more you can do."

Verret ignored him. "Skyles?"

"I'm just waiting for you," Skyles said.

Verret had passed the point of reason. Refusing to give up, he and Skyles swam madly back to the trailer.

As Verret and Skyles dove, Boersma shouted. "Ready . . ."

Under the water, Verret and Skyles pushed the back of the trailer. It shifted forward a few feet. Then they surfaced for air.

"Damn, this is going to work." Skyles grinned.

Again and again, the men dove, and the trailer slowly inched forward.

Spurred on by Verret's relentless determination, the deputies pulled, pushing their physical limits until the heavy trailer finally reached the top of the steep drive.

Aching and spent, Verret swam to the dam and hung on the edge. Skyles gripped the steel plate with both hands, too breathless to talk.

Boersma raised the ends of the suction hoses. "What about these?"

Verret realized the intake hoses had to be dropped back in the deep end. He groaned and held out his hand.

"Give me one," Skyles said wearily.

When Verret and Skyles returned again, the deputies helped them over the top of the dam. The two men collapsed against the warehouse wall, content to observe while the others struggled to start the waterlogged pumps. Twenty minutes passed before one pump engaged and water began pouring from the outflow hose.

Fifteen minutes later, Boersma gave up on the second pump. "I'm done. We'll just have to hope that one pump is enough."

Verret was too tired to argue.

It took every last shred of energy to make the trek back around and into the building. Verret just wanted to sleep. But first, he had to report to the sheriff. And he needed to check with his deputies on the tiers. Only then would he fall into bed. At least the building was safe, for now.

Chapter 12

Afternoon:

Katrina weakens as it moves inland into and across Mississippi, with winds of 95 mph.

At 1:45 President George Bush declares Louisiana and Mississippi emergency disaster areas.

City officials confirm the breach in the 17th Street Canal levee.

The Coast Guard initiates rescue operations.

Governor Kathleen Blanco mobilizes the Louisiana National Guard.

At 5 p.m. the jail's Templeman 1 and 2 buildings lose generator power.

"That's the last patient, Dr. Inglese," Nurse Audrella Mazant said with her characteristic smile.

I smiled back at the wiry black nurse whose dedication and efficiency far exceeded her size. "If you need me, I'll be downstairs."

All morning Gary and I had been seeing patients in the Correctional Center's second-floor medical clinic. Although we'd canceled routine inmate appointments because of the storm, the clinic's two tiny exam rooms had been busy for the last few hours as we treated minor problems and complaints, mostly from civilians.

On my way down I passed Captain Verret in the stairwell. He had pulled an all-nighter and looked it.

"You still up?" I asked.

"Not for much longer," Verret replied, heading up toward an empty room on the second floor where the deputies were bunking.

The stairwell steps were slick, and the air smelled of wet concrete. I grabbed the banister for support. Only the emergency lights were on. At least the generators are working, I thought.

The lobby was crowded. People were up and moving after the stormy night, and the front doors were open again. Spirits had lifted, and the hum of conversation filled the room. A few people had ventured outside to see Katrina's aftermath. I wondered how the inmates were faring on the tiers upstairs.

I pushed through the crowd, anxious to survey the damage myself. I'd taken a look a few hours earlier, but the howling wind and torrential rain had hidden the extent of the destruction. Now, though it was still raining hard, the wind had slowed. As I stepped onto the front porch, I was stunned by the scope of the hurricane's power.

Flood water surrounded everything and rose to the fifth step of the Correctional Center. Parked cars stood in water that reached up to their door handles. Every tree in sight had lost limbs or been uprooted, and surviving branches had been stripped bare of leaves. Roofs had been sheared off nearby houses. Nothing had escaped unscathed.

"Can you believe this?" I said, joining Mike and Brady by the railing.

"Look at Cheryl's van." Brady gestured across the street at a flooded blue minivan that belonged to one of the medical assistants. "This is worse than I thought."

"Yeah, look at the houses over there," Mike said, pointing to the side. "There isn't a roof left. Those poor people have lost everything."

"Dr. Inglese." Sheriff Gusman called from behind me.

I turned as he lowered his walkie-talkie. A good-looking, polished black man in his forties, the sheriff was usually dressed impeccably in a suit and tie. It was strange to see him in a black T-shirt, red shorts, and rubber wading boots.

"Yes, sir?" I asked, moving toward him.

"Old Parish Prison just called. They have an inmate down, and he's unconscious. Go see if you can help."

"Do we know what happened?" I asked. "His vitals?"

"He hit his head. That's all I know."

I glanced at the water outside. The entrance to the Old Prison, attached to the courthouse, was two blocks away. I was not thrilled with the prospect of walking through the flood, especially with the rain still coming down.

Apparently, the sheriff guessed my thoughts. "I'll call for a truck to take you over," he quickly added.

"Just give me a minute," I said with obvious relief. "I'll be right back."

I ran up to my office, where I had left my suitcase. Even with the hall window and emergency lights, I needed a flashlight to find my flip-flops. I didn't want my only tennis shoes getting wet.

Slipping the flashlight into my pocket, I unwrapped a breakfast bar and chewed as I raced back downstairs.

A sheriff's office flatbed truck rolled slowly down the street by the time I reached the front porch. Massive tires kept the cab and engine above the three-foot flood. Although the driver pulled as close to the front steps as possible, there was no way to avoid stepping in water before I climbed into the passenger's seat. Changing into flip-flops had been a good call. We hadn't even left the Correctional Center, and my feet were soaked.

The deputy kept the truck in low gear as we crept along the street to the intersection. I stared out the windshield at the devastated houses to my left. People stood on porches and second-story balconies, yelling and waving their arms for help. I felt for them, but there was no time to stop. A patient with a serious head injury was waiting for me in the Old Prison clinic.

I snapped out of my medical mind-set the moment we turned the corner. I was used to flooding around the Correctional Center. It happened every time we had a heavy rain. But I was completely unprepared for the scene before me.

Water stretched endlessly in all directions. Homes, businesses, everything in view was swamped. As I digested the sight, another shock jolted me. The truck's engine began grinding.

"We have a problem, Doc," the driver said.

My stomach tightened when I looked forward. Smoke was pouring from under the hood.

The deputy set his jaw, shifted, and kept on driving, steering the truck toward the courthouse, more than a block away. As the truck lumbered forward, I watched out the side window. Sewage, trash, and other debris floated on the water. Nothing would keep me from getting to my patient, but I did *not* want to wade through that foul flood.

Chapter 13

The truck finally broke down twenty feet from the courthouse steps. I climbed down and waded over to the stately building, then sped across the inlaid marble floor of the lobby, to the corridor that led to the Old Prison. The medical clinic was downstairs, on the building's ground floor, and I ran down the steps as fast as I could in my flip-flops and soggy cargo shorts. The building had lost all power, but light from an overhead window lit the damp hallway, which was already beginning to flood. I paused for a moment when I realized I was going into a maximum-security prison with no electricity, but I pushed on. Sandbags protected the offices on either side of the hallway from the ankle-deep water. A damp, musty smell clung to the cinderblock and steel walls.

A second later I burst through the clinic door into total darkness, turned on my flashlight, and shouted, "Jan!"

"Dr. Inglese?" Jan Ricca, the nurse in charge, called back. The beam from her flashlight blinded me as she stepped around a corner. Five-foot-six with short red hair, glasses, and freckles, Jan looked like an Irish angel in green scrubs. "I'm glad you're here. We've got a man down in the back."

"That's why the sheriff sent me," I said, following Jan past metal desks, storage cabinets, and the station where another nurse and a medical assistant were busy at work. In the windowless examination room a big husky black man dressed in orange prison scrubs was stretched out on the table. He was motionless with his eyes closed and looked to be in his twenties. "What happened?"

"He was on the tier, and he fell and hit his head," Jan explained. "At first, he seemed to be okay. He was able to walk to the clinic with a deputy, but after he got here, he passed out. His name is Williams."

"Any vitals?" I slipped my flashlight into a pocket to free up my hands.

"His last blood pressure was low—fifty-nine over palp," Jan said, "with a pulse of eighty-six."

This man's in big trouble, I thought. Immediate loss of consciousness was common with a head injury, but losing consciousness a short time *after* the injury was potentially serious. My mind sifted through possible explanations. One stood out: the potentially fatal brain swelling that occurs in some cases of head trauma or brain hemorrhage.

"This might be cerebral edema." I felt the same rush of adrenaline I used to experience when I worked in a hospital intensive care unit. "We're not going to lose this guy," I said, as much to reassure myself as Nurse Ricca.

Conditioned by years of training, I set my fear aside and focused. I fired questions at Jan. "Any medications? Allergies? Any significant medical history I need to know about?"

"No," Jan said. "Nothing."

"Well, his airway's intact, and he's breathing on his own." I paused to measure the inmate's respiratory rate. "Eighteen a minute. Do we have IV access?"

"No, Dr. Inglese." Jan followed my actions with her flashlight. Around us the darkness was absolute.

The patient still hadn't moved.

"Get me another set of vitals."

Jan handed me her light and wrapped the blood pressure cuff around the patient's limp arm. I couldn't make out his plastic ID wristband, but I knew Williams was a red-bander. All the inmates in the Old Prison had been charged with crimes that ranged from armed robbery to rape and murder.

"His pulse is still eighty-six," Jan said, "but his blood pressure is eighty-nine over sixty."

"That's better." I used Jan's flashlight to check the patient's pupils. They were round, equal, and reactive to light. So why isn't he awake? I wondered, handing the light back to Jan.

"Mr. Williams, can you hear me?" I gently slapped his face in an attempt to rouse him. Williams moaned but did not open his eyes.

"Do you know what he hit his head on?" I asked.

Jan shook her head. "No."

"He walked here under his own power?" I was looking for confirmation.

"Yes, and he was talking," Jan said. "He only became unconscious after I started to examine him."

"I doubt we have to worry about cervical spine injury, since he walked down from the tier. Did he complain of any neck pain?"

"Not to me," Jan replied.

I ran my hands over the inmate's face and head, feeling carefully for the characteristic crunch of shifting bone. There was no evidence of bleeding or laceration on his scalp. I had to rely on touch as much as the faint beam from Jan's flashlight. A CAT scan could have provided the information I needed, but Katrina blocked the way to the nearest hospital. If I was going to help Williams, I'd have to trust my instincts and make do with whatever limited examination I could perform in the dark. In Korea, I had learned to function without state-of-the-art technology. I never imagined I'd need those skills again, but then I'd never been in the middle of a hurricane in a jail.

"No spinal fluid in his nose." I shifted my attention from the man's nostrils to his ears, looking for other signs of a skull fracture. There was no blood anywhere.

Williams groaned again, moving his arms and legs, and I suddenly remembered that medical staff was never left alone with a red-bander.

"Where's the deputy who brought him to the clinic?" I looked at Jan as I finished checking Williams's neck for misaligned vertebrae.

"He went to see about another sick inmate," Jan explained. "He should be back soon."

Not soon enough, I thought. Williams was lying quietly again, but that didn't eliminate the threat. He could be a multiple murderer with nothing to lose if he killed again. I glanced out through the treatment-room door.

The other nurse's flashlight created a play of shadow and light on the walls. She was packing medications and supplies into boxes, in case the clinic had to be evacuated.

Williams grunted. With his improved vitals, he should be awake.

"Mr. Williams!" I spoke loudly and motioned Jan to move her flashlight beam so it didn't shine directly onto the man's face. "C'mon, open your eyes."

The patient obeyed, squinting in the dim light.

"Can you hear me?" I asked.

"Yeah," Williams mumbled.

His response was encouraging, but I still had to ascertain his mental status. "Do you know your name?"

"Albert Williams."

"What day is it?" I asked.

"Monday."

"What's going on outside?" I continued.

"There's a hurricane." The man's voice got stronger with each answer.

"Do you know where you are, Mr. Williams?"

"The Old Prison."

Satisfied that the inmate was conscious and oriented, I turned to Jan. "Start a large-bore IV and get some fluids into him."

"I can try, Dr. Inglese, but . . ." Jan hesitated. She was obviously uncomfortable voicing her reservations, but facts couldn't be ignored. "It's dark, and everything is wet. This isn't the best place to put in a line."

She had a point. Under normal circumstances, the medical clinic in each jail building handled only minor ailments and injuries. Patients with more serious problems were sent to the infirmary, the acute-care clinic in Templeman 1. Life-or-death cases went directly to local emergency rooms.

"Why not just get him to the hospital?" Jan asked.

"Because there's a hurricane outside," I countered, more sharply than I intended. "No one's going anywhere without a boat, and the sheriff won't put medical staff or deputies at risk unless it's absolutely necessary."

"A boat?" Jan sounded surprised.

Her reaction stopped me cold. I suddenly realized that, without windows in the medical clinic, the nurses here had no idea what conditions were like outside.

"Everything's flooded," I explained. "There's water everywhere—as far as you can see. And it's deep. Even if we could transport Williams, the hospitals may not be open. You'll have to keep him here, at least until the hurricane's over and we have more information."

"Here?" Jan looked appalled. "But we don't have power, and when you're gone, we won't even have a physician."

"And we're in the middle of a major disaster," I said. "We'll have to make do the best we can."

Jan sighed, then shrugged in resignation. "I guess we don't have a choice." As practical as she was pleasant, she didn't waste energy fighting battles she couldn't win.

I turned back to the patient. "You doing okay?"

"Yeah." Williams slowly sat up.

"Feeling dizzy?" I asked. "Any headaches? Neck pain?"

The man shook his head. "No, Doc."

"That's good." I motioned to Jan, and we stepped away from the exam table. "He's got a concussion but doesn't seem to be really hurt. Just keep monitoring his level of consciousness and vital signs. He should be all right."

The man was feeling better. Which might be a problem. Even my muscular build and seven years of military training wouldn't hold off someone as big as Williams. If he decided to run, I probably couldn't stop him. I hadn't found a shank—a homemade knife—when I examined him, but you never knew. Many Old Prison inmates concealed them.

"You better lie down, Williams," I said, pulling the flashlight out of my pocket. It wasn't an ideal weapon, but I gripped it firmly and added, "Any sudden moves might give you a bad headache."

Williams stared at me through narrowed dark eyes. The effect was chilling.

"You don't look like no doctor," Williams said, shifting his gaze to my shorts and T-shirt.

I used my doctor voice to support my authority. "Lie down."

The inmate paused, then nodded. "Whatever you say, Doc."

I breathed easier when he stretched out and closed his eyes.

"Got another one for you, Doc," said a voice from behind. "This guy says he's sick."

I turned to see a deputy standing by the nursing station with a tall, thin, black inmate. The young prisoner swayed as though he was about to fall.

"Bring him in, Deputy," I said, "and come keep an eye on Mr. Williams."

"Is he going to be all right?" the deputy asked as we switched places.

"He'll live." I wasn't so sure about the new patient. It took a minute for me to find his chart in the dark. The eighteen-year-old kid had been arrested and screened just yesterday, and he had denied having any medical problems. But the youth now had a high fever and body rash, and his overall wasted appearance strongly suggested HIV.

"He should be in the infirmary," Jan said as I finished the examination and wrote orders for both patients.

"If the flood gets much higher, the infirmary will be under water," I said. "He's better off here for now, with or without an IV. Keep giving him Gatorade—and Tylenol for the fever. At least we can make him more comfortable."

"We'll do what we can," Jan replied.

Anxious to get back to the Correctional Center, I gave Jan a final instruction. "If there's a change in either patient's condition, call me."

"Call you?" Jan raised an eyebrow. "Our phones aren't working. Most of the time there's no dial tone, and if we do get a connection, it doesn't last. I haven't heard from my husband and son since last night. I can't call you."

"Then find an officer with a radio and have them call." Everyone at the jail was dealing with the same failing systems. I caught Jan's eye. "You've got this under control, right?"

"We're good," she said with an uncertain smile. "If the water rises, we'll probably have to evacuate to a higher floor, though. We have a lot of packing to do. No sense leaving anything behind we might need later."

The clinic was in good hands with Jan, but the broader implications of the Old Prison situation were more troubling. Katrina had barely passed over, and Jan already had two patients. God only knew what was happening at the other ten clinics, I thought as I walked out.

Chapter 14

As the door to the clinic closed behind me, I headed back to the stairs. The water in the dim corridor was above my ankles now. If it kept rising at the present rate, it would top the sandbags and flood all the first-floor rooms. The stairs to the second floor were already slick with moisture.

I returned to the courthouse lobby and made my way outside to the large porch, where I could look at the devastation. It seemed worse than it had an hour ago. The city of New Orleans had become a shallow sea. Water flowed through broken windows in nearby buildings. Eddies swirled around the truck that I had come in. But the deputy who had driven me over had abandoned the stalled vehicle, and he was nowhere to be found. I would have to walk back. My stomach knotted at the very thought.

As I started down the steps, a gust of wind slashed at my T-shirt, nearly knocking me over. I managed to stay on my feet, but we were still on the edge of the hurricane. What would happen, I wondered, if a stronger back band smashed through while I was wading back to the Correctional Center. I could be swept away. That thought stopped me dead at the edge of the filthy water.

A plastic milk container floated by. And worse yet, sewage, trash, and debris from damaged buildings and cars filled the flood water. Any cuts and scratches would be open invitations to infection. But walking back was my only option.

I breathed out several times—quickly, like a sprinter preparing to run—and then eased into dark, groin-deep water with my stomach churning and my teeth clenched. The water was cold, and I shuddered, as much from disgust as the chill. Holding my arms out to the sides and keeping the flashlight in my hand, I moved forward along the sidewalk. The water would be six inches deeper if I stepped off the curb.

Sporadic gusts and stinging rain added to my distress, though I was more attentive to floating garbage than the weather or even where I put my feet. As I stepped sideways to avoid a wire trash container, I slipped off the curb. Panicked, I struggled to keep my balance before I fell completely into the cesspool. Grabbing a street sign for support, I recovered my footing, but two steps later I stumbled again. Finally, the thought of being dunked in sewer water was so revolting that I stepped down onto the street. The water was deeper, but I thought the road would be more clear of debris. Relaxing a little with each step, I got to the corner and turned left.

Suddenly, something under the water grabbed my leg. I tried to shake my foot free but couldn't. Several yards ahead, I saw a downed power pole. I froze. The cross beams were studded with transformers, and all the wires were in the water.

My foot was tangled in a power line. Oh, my God, I'm going to die, I thought, paralyzed. For a few terrifying seconds, I fully expected to be fried by a jolt of electricity. When a moment passed and I was still breathing, I realized the wire wasn't live. Even so, I could hear my heart pounding above the wind.

I tried lifting my foot instead of shaking it, and the cable fell away. However, I wasn't out of danger yet. The street was evidently as littered with obstacles as the sidewalk. Stepping wide of the tangled cable, I opted for the middle of the road.

Things crunched underfoot, and I had visions of my flip-flops punctured by shards of glass or metal debris. In fact, I was surprised I hadn't lost them by now. Sheets of corrugated metal roofing and twisted business signs were half submerged, reminding me that sharp hidden objects could slice me at any time. Every step sent another shiver of dread up my spine.

This is unbelievable, I thought with a glance back at the run-down buildings in every direction. On my right, a man and a woman stared at me from an apartment above a corner restaurant. I had to be a comical sight, strolling through waist-deep water in a white T-shirt with my arms spread wide. Still, their intense gaze was unnerving, as though they were watching a horror movie and waiting for some terrible calamity to claim its next victim.

Then I remembered—manholes.

There were at least four, maybe as many as six, manholes at the intersection. I had read somewhere that the heavy covers came off during floods. At any given moment, I could drop through one of the openings and drown.

Slowing my pace to a crawl, I tested the way ahead by carefully scuffing first one flip-flop then the other along the asphalt. I was ready to halt the instant I no longer felt solid ground.

Spotting the office of the district attorney ahead on the right, I thought I could save myself some time and trouble by cutting through the building. Still wary, I angled toward the sidewalk. When I stubbed my toe on the curb, I didn't swear. At least the maze of manholes was behind me.

Relieved, I slogged up an incline toward the office entrance. The water was only ankle high at the door, and I smiled when I knocked on the glass. A security guard stationed inside the building looked at me and shook his head "no."

"I'm a doctor with the jail!" I yelled.

The guard shook his head again.

"I'm with the sheriff's office!" I shouted.

The guard ignored me.

Frustrated, I banged on the door. The man inside didn't seem to care that I needed help, and after a moment, I gave up. Given the lack of electricity, Old Prison nearby, and my outlandish appearance, I couldn't blame him for not letting me in.

Sighing, I looked back the way I had come. My gaze lingered on the coroner's office, on the side of the courthouse, and I wondered how long it would be before the bodies inside started to smell. The Old Prison with its barred windows looked even more dismal than usual in the pelting rain. The roof of the police mechanic shop was gone. A few remaining panels creaked and groaned in the last throes of the hurricane.

I had come more than halfway back to the Correctional Center.

A wide landscape planter for trees and ornamental shrubs ran the length of the DA's office. Its cement wall rose two feet above the water level, and it was twelve inches wide on top—more than enough for me to balance on. I jumped onto the planter and quickly advanced another twenty-five feet to the corner of the DA's building, where a lower planter ran along the front.

I jumped down onto it and started to make my way in ankle-deep water. After three steps, however, I noticed small red islands floating inside and around the cement planter. The surface of the water was actually undulating. Curious, I leaned over for a closer look and gasped. Fire ants!

Mike Higgins had told me to watch out for fire ant flotillas. He'd said the insects huddle together when they get wet and float on the water. I'd thought he was joking. He wasn't.

And I was allergic to fire ants. One bite and I'd swell up like a balloon. Multiple bites might very well kill me.

This was too dangerous. I eased back to the corner of the DA's building and waded away from the planter. A snake swam by. There were water moccasins in the area, but I didn't have a clue how to identify them. The snake seemed as anxious to avoid me as I was to avoid it, but after that, I scanned the surface of the water even more carefully. Mike had also passed along his grandfather's old hurricane advice: "Always keep an ax in the attic," and "Where there's water, there's 'gators."

I was willing to bet that the old man hadn't been kidding, either.

As I finally made my way across the district attorney's parking lot and neared the Correctional Center, I realized I had an audience. Mike, Gary, and Brady were all on the front porch laughing—at me.

"How's the water?" Mike called out.

"Gross?" added Brady.

As I trudged up the front steps, all I could think of was getting a shower. I hoped the building still had running water.

"How's the patient?" Gary asked, concerned as usual about any inmate's health.

"A concussion, but he's awake and alert now. It was my walk back that was the problem. You weren't kidding about fire ant flotillas, Mike. They really do clump together in water."

"Told you," Mike joked in a condescending tone.

"Between the ants and the downed electric lines, it's a miracle I made it back alive."

"Alive and a mess," Brady added.

"And God knows what you caught in that filthy water," Mike exclaimed with a grimace. He gasped when he realized his mistake.

"How about a welcome home hug, Mike!" Opening my arms, I stepped toward him.

Mike held up his hands to fend me off. "Do *not* touch me, Dem. I mean it!"

I lunged, forcing him to jump back.

"What's it like out there?" Gary asked. "Seriously."

"Bad—worse than you can imagine," I answered. "There's water everywhere you look. The city is in big trouble."

Smiles faded. Saturday night we had all been worried about getting through the hurricane. Now that the storm was almost over, the danger should have been past.

But our ordeal had just begun.

Chapter 15

Leaving my friends on the porch, I went to find Chief William Hunter, second in command of the sheriff's office and a close personal friend of mine. I knew he had the keys to the sheriff's shower—the only shower in the building that wasn't on an inmate tier. Chief Hunter sat at his desk in his crowded first-floor office. His small Jack Russell terrier lay restlessly in a kennel on the floor near his feet.

"I need to use the sheriff's shower, Chief!" I had to yell to make myself heard over the yapping animal. "I had to walk back from the Old Prison!"

"Shut up, Lucky!" The chief glared at the dog and handed me the keys. "Don't forget to bring those back, Doc. They're the only set I have."

I raced up to my office and grabbed my toiletry kit and some clean clothes, then hurried to the shower room, which was also on the second floor. At least the Correctional Center still had some lights and running water, and the water was *hot*. The tension eased out of my muscles as I scrubbed grime and who-knew-what-else off my skin. All things considered, we were in good shape for having just weathered a category 4 hurricane. Yes, the flooding was extensive, but we had generator power, food, and water.

No one would die of thirst waiting to be rescued.

Thirty minutes later, clean and refreshed, I went back downstairs to brief Sheriff Gusman on the patients I'd seen. He was on the front porch, surveying the damage. As I walked toward him, a frantic cry diverted my attention.

A short, heavyset black woman in a blue dress was wading down the street through chest-high water. Arms raised over her head, she called out as she approached the Correctional Center. "Help me! Someone, please, help me."

My first impulse was to jump in after her. However, as I started down the steps, I remembered a cardinal rule of water safety: never jump in after a drowning person. I paused and took another look, reassessing the situation. The woman could walk, so clearly I'd be able to stand without difficulty.

It seemed safe to go after her, but as a precaution, I scanned the crowd for backup. My eyes fixed on the first familiar face. "Brady, I need some help."

Without hesitation, Brady bounded down the steps to join me at the water's edge.

Trying to avoid wading through the flood in the street, I climbed onto the planter next to the front steps. The water inside it reached just below my knee. If the woman kept moving toward us, Brady and I would be able to intercept her without getting completely soaked again.

With Brady close on my heels, we moved along the length of the muddy planter toward the woman. Mindful of submerged obstacles, I watched each step. I didn't like what I saw. I pointed. "Brady, look."

"Oh, my God, there's a turd in the water." Brady's eyes widened with horror.

For the second time that day, I regretted wearing flip-flops.

"Help me!" The woman shouted. "Please, help me!"

"Come over here, and I'll get you." I waved, urging her toward me. She stopped fifty feet away.

With a resigned sigh, I jumped off the wall of the planter into waist-deep water. "This way!" I yelled, moving toward her.

The woman did a slow about-face and started walking back the way she had come. "Help me," she cried again.

"Ma'am, wait!" I started after her.

"She's been doing that all afternoon," said a deputy up on the porch behind me.

"Doing what?" I snapped my head around.

"She comes down calling for help," the man explained, "and leaves as soon as anyone goes after her."

"Any idea why?" I asked, wet and annoyed. I needed another shower—for nothing. I hadn't even been able to help the woman.

"She lives in one of those apartment buildings." The deputy gestured to the side. "Her father's in a wheelchair, and she can't get him down from the second floor."

"What's she going to do if she does get him down?" Brady scanned the water that covered every street, driveway, and lawn as far as we could see. "Unless they've got a boat, they're not going anywhere."

I hated to turn away from someone in trouble, but I didn't know what else to do. Her father would be better off waiting on the second floor until a fully equipped rescue team arrived.

At least I still had the key to the sheriff's shower. I focused on using it again as we waded through the foul sludge and back up the steps. Only Brady's lower legs had gotten wet.

"Mike!" Brady exclaimed to the psychiatrist, who was still standing on the porch. "There are turds in the water."

Mike looked at me. "Is he joking?"

"No joke," I said. "I almost stepped on one."

Mike was revolted at the thought. It wouldn't have surprised me if he had deliberately chosen psychiatry to avoid touching patients or their body fluids.

Intent on soap and hot water again, I hurried upstairs for another set of clean clothes. I was beginning to worry that I hadn't brought enough.

It was just past five when I joined Brady, Mike, and Gary for dinner. Paul, who had spent the afternoon tracking the weather and flood news, was there as well. The kitchen staff had gotten one meal up to the inmates, and for the civilians and deputies, they had cordoned off a section of the back porch and set up tables. Spaghetti, ravioli, and turkey sandwiches were on the menu. It was much earlier than my usual dinner hour, but I was famished.

Mike grinned as I took a paper plate off the stack. "Did you wash your hands?"

"I took another shower, Mike," I assured him. "But I think we might have more to worry about than a few germs."

"That's for sure." Gary piled turkey and cheese on his plate. "I've never seen flooding like this, not even around this building. The water's almost up to the windows on Cheryl's blue van."

I knew firsthand that the water was still rising, much faster than normal. It had gone from groin- to waist-deep in a couple of hours.

"The flooding's all they're talking about on the radio," Paul said. "The whole Ninth Ward is under water."

"What about the pumping stations?" I asked as we moved away from the serving tables.

"The pumps aren't working," Mike said. "But they're not broken, either. Whoever was in charge evacuated without leaving anyone behind to turn them on."

"Unbelievable." Gary shook his head.

"Unforgivable," Paul agreed, glancing at the crowd lining up to get dinner. "A lot of these people live in the Ninth Ward."

Everyone in the Correctional Center was feeling the stress, but we all handled it differently. A few people on the porch stared blankly, eating without interest. Others laughed and talked as though nothing extraordinary had happened over the last twenty-four hours. Some individuals took out their frustrations unfairly on the kitchen staff. Boredom, worry, exhaustion, and fear did not excuse their offensive behavior.

We could hear a middle-aged woman loudly berate a kitchen deputy. The ravioli wasn't hot enough, she groused, and there was no more soda.

"What's her problem?" Gary scowled. "This is a jail, not a five-star restaurant."

"A jail that didn't *have* to let these people take shelter. You'd think they'd be grateful." Incensed and indignant, Mike spat out the words.

The woman's attitude was unconscionable. The kitchen staff had managed to serve up hot food a few hours after a major hurricane, but their dedication was lost on her. I had witnessed several similar outbursts since breakfast. The kitchen workers had handled the incidents firmly, but graciously. The deputy serving the ravioli apologized, too, and just shrugged when the woman left in an angry huff. His courtesy and competence far exceeded any reasonable expectation.

"Verret looks exhausted," Mike said.

Not surprising, I thought as I followed Mike's gaze across the porch. Verret had only slept a couple of hours since yesterday morning. Now, instead of grabbing a hot meal while he had the chance, the acting warden stood by the railing above the sally-port, staring down.

"He looks worried," Gary said.

"And that worries me." Mike ran his hand over his shaved head.

Curious, the four of us went over to take a look. As we leaned over the railing, the source of Verret's anxiety was immediately apparent. The flood in the street had risen higher than the sally-port dam, and water was spilling over the top faster than the pumps could remove it. A pool had formed by the basement wall, and it deepened as we watched.

"This can't be good," Brady said.

"It's not," Verret said, his tone blunt and ominous. "If the water—"

A thunderous boom cut him off.

"What was that?" Gary asked, visibly shaken.

"The basement doors just gave way. Water's getting in," Verret said. "We've got about an hour before the generator goes."

Verret bolted back into the building.

Chapter 16

Early evening:
Communication breakdowns throughout New Orleans hinder
rescue and relief operations.
Rooftop rescues take place, along with widespread looting.
The breach in the 17th Street Canal levee widens.
Female inmates from Templeman 4 are evacuated to another
building.
First-floor inmates from Templeman 1, 2, and 3 are being
moved to higher floors.
Generator power in most jail buildings is lost.

Verret ran back into the lobby of the Correctional Center, wishing he had a radio. Service had become increasingly unreliable,
working one minute and cutting off the next, and he had stopped
carrying one. Now he needed strong men who wouldn't flinch in
a crisis, but he didn't have time to look for the people he usually
relied on. He didn't have to—Skyles and Boersma were talking
to the deputies sitting at the information desk.

Verret yelled as he ran toward the stairwell. "Skyles! Boersma!
The basement's flooding!"

No further explanation was necessary. The two men followed
him down the stairs.

Bursting into the basement, Verret looked around the cavernous
room. The pressure of the water rising in the sallyport had ripped
the metal plate away and pushed one of the doors open. Water

poured in. A handful of deputies and inmate workers were already piling sandbags across the doorway to try to block the flood.

Verret's gaze darted to the electrical room, which was a step higher than the basement floor. Within minutes, the rising water would hit the generator relays inside.

"Get those inmates out of here," Verret ordered.

Deputies and inmates stopped working and rushed toward the stairs as Verret strode toward the open door. One departing deputy looked back as Verret, Skyles, and Boersma each hoisted a sandbag.

"Verret, you probably shouldn't stay, either." The deputy glanced at the water spreading relentlessly across the cement floor. "There's no way to stop this now."

"We've got to try something. If we sandbag the electrical room door, we might buy a couple of hours." Verret carried a sandbag across the basement and dropped it against the sill. Skyles and Boersma put down two more.

The three men worked quickly, speaking little as they stacked sandbags in front of the electrical room.

The water, though, continued to rise. Skyles stood back. "It's almost up to the door."

Verret pushed another bag into place.

"It may not be long before it hits a live circuit." Skyles paused, as if waiting for a response, then went on. "I don't want to get electrocuted."

"Just keep going," Verret insisted. He saw his two deputies exchange a worried glance, but he wasn't ready to surrender.

As the acting warden picked up one more bag, Skyles fixed him with a hard stare. "Let it go, man. It's over."

Verret glared back with stubborn determination.

Skyles grabbed the captain's arm. "Just let it go."

Verret watched the water flowing in through the basement door. Nodding in resignation, he dropped the sandbag where he stood and walked toward the stairwell. This time, there wasn't anything more he could do.

Chapter 17

At 4 p.m. generator power had kicked in at the jail infirmary. Dr. Sam Gore took a break from the afternoon grind of patient care and headed out to the covered T-shaped walkway that linked the Templeman buildings with the Intake Processing Center.

The infirmary had only one small window that looked out on a cement exercise yard and a few slit-like openings near the ceiling, so there was no way to tell what was happening outside. All afternoon, when there was a little free time, members of the medical staff had gone outside to check on the progress of the flood.

As Sam peered through the chain-link fence that enclosed the walkway, he could see the water in the street slowly creeping toward the building, though the rain had finally stopped. At noon it had been thigh high around the cars parked across the way. Now the autos were covered. Too bad for Eddie Williams, Sam thought. The slim black infirmary nurse had parked his car on the street, and it was a lost cause, along with several vehicles belonging to officers on duty at Templeman.

Too bad for the officers, too, he said to himself, though at the moment his sympathy was mixed with annoyance. In the last few hours Sam had talked to the warden and other high-ranking officers several times about evacuating the infirmary patients to a higher floor. However, "We're not evacuating," was the only response he'd gotten. Well, if the water got any higher, they'd have no choice, and moving people and supplies in dim generator light and without an elevator would be no picnic.

Sam turned back, passed through the massive sliding steel doors that guarded the entrance to Templeman 1, and started down the wide cinderblock hallway toward the infirmary. A few Special Investigation Division deputies were approaching, dressed in full riot gear—Kevlar vests, with shields and shotguns.

"Hi, Doc," one called out as Sam moved over to let them pass.

The doctor nodded in acknowledgment. He knew the SID deputies had already responded to several emergencies in the building during the afternoon. Inmates on the upper tiers were banging on walls and bars, setting fires to sheets and toilet paper, and fighting. At one point the infirmary staff had been rattled by the sounds of gunfire within the building. Later they were told the shots were rubber bullets.

Sam passed the warden's office—he could see the squat figure of seventy-three-year-old Chief Rudy Belisle huddled with a couple of officers—and when he got to the end of the hallway he could hear the infirmary patients acting up, too. There were eight infirmary tiers opening off the corridor. Inside each tier, bunk beds lined the walls and metallic picnic tables were bolted down in the middle of a central living area.

I can't blame them for being anxious, he thought; they should have been moved hours ago. Still, the noise was unsettling. As he walked into the infirmary, though, Sam's mood lightened. All around the acute-care unit, which resembled a three-bed mini-emergency room, he saw the staff cheerfully busy, preparing for a move that was certain to come, even if no one was sure when. He had laid out an evacuation plan days ago, identifying the second-floor gymnasium as a location for a makeshift infirmary and compiling lists of what needed to be moved.

Lillian Ford, the nurse in charge, was overseeing the work with her usual good humor. An outgoing black woman, she was efficient and friendly, but the well-prepped staff didn't need much direction.

Duane Townzel stacked patients' charts and put supplies in boxes, acting with the focused calm one would expect from a member of the sheriff's office Search and Rescue team. The muscular nurse, a good-looking black man of forty-six, had been an EMT and could always be counted on in a crisis.

Meanwhile, Tracy Nichols, a four-foot-eight dynamo, was speedily packing up medications and the one-page records that catalogued each patient's drug regime. The nurse seemed unfazed by the situation, as she always was.

A half dozen other nurses performed similar tasks. To one side, Victor Tuckler carefully cleaned a patient's wound and applied a bandage. Decisive yet soft spoken, the moonlighting ER doctor had been stranded at the infirmary when Katrina hit. His competence and caring personality made him a welcome addition to the staff.

Scarlett Maness looked up and heralded Sam's entrance with a typical smart-ass remark. "Well, look who's back," said the nurse, a large five-foot-seven woman with hair the color of her name. "Where are your booties, Dr. Gore?"

Sam chuckled. Earlier in the day, at the height of the storm, he and Victor had been called to the House of Detention to patch up an inmate who'd fallen and cut his head. Victor had had the foresight to bring black wading boots and a yellow slicker to the jail. Sam, however, had to make do by cutting a hole in a garbage bag and draping it over his green T-shirt and khaki shorts, borrowing a hat, and donning Lillian Ford's too-small pink rubber boots. Scarlett had teased him mercilessly about his appearance, getting a laugh out of everyone. But he had to admit it was a ridiculous get-up. He'd probably never live it down.

Lillian walked over. "Have you talked to the warden recently, Dr. Gore? Is he going to move the patients?" She and Sam had worked together for years, and their normal conversation was usually full of banter, but at the moment the head nurse was seriously worried. "There's water in the exercise yard," she added, "and it's getting close to the back door."

"I spoke to them a half hour ago, and they still insist there's no need to move," Sam said.

"Well, what the hell are they waiting for?" she sputtered. "We needed to move *before* we lost city power. Now the elevators don't work. We'll never get the med carts up the stairs."

The heavy carts were the size of a dishwasher and held all the patients' medications. Lillian was right about getting them to the second floor.

Scarlett chimed in, "I told Major Crane we needed to move two hours ago, but he wouldn't listen to me. All that officer would say is, 'Nobody is moving!' At least he took the list of the sickest inmates, though."

Sam thought about the most seriously ill patients. Fifteen names were on the list—several wheelchair-bound inmates, a dialysis patient, one with severe lung disease, a few with advanced AIDS, and a female inmate who was nine months pregnant. As he contemplated the difficulties of getting them upstairs, Scarlett broke his train of thought.

"Oh, my God. Look at that shit," she said, wrinkling her nose and calling attention to the unpleasant smell and the chunky brown water beginning to flow upward from the grill drains in the infirmary floor. The sewage system was starting to back up, as it often did during bad storms.

"Oh, not now," Lillian said. "This is disgusting."

"It's in the hall, too," said Chuck Perotto, who had just stepped out to check. Fifty-nine, bald, with a round cherubic face, Chuck was a highly trained registered nurse, and his compassionate manner put patients at ease. He had lost one foot in a traffic accident as a child and walked with a prosthesis, but he refused to let that stop him.

"Well, that tears it," Sam said. "I'm not waiting any longer. Let's get everything together and start carrying stuff upstairs to the gym. We're getting the hell out of here."

It was what everyone was waiting to hear. The staff shifted into high gear. Hefting boxes and bags of supplies and juggling flashlights, Sam, Victor, and some of the nurses made their way along the wet hall to the stairwell that led up to the second floor. They moved rapidly, spurred on by the sounds of inmates yelling and banging in the background.

The gymnasium was some thirty feet long by thirty feet wide, more of an exercise space than a real gym. It had a tile floor and small windows where the walls met the fourteen-foot ceiling. There were plenty of electrical outlets but no sink, just a spigot for a hose connection. Somehow they'd have to make do.

Trying to keep the supplies organized and accessible, Sam told the others where to put the boxes, then led them back downstairs for more. With each trip the nurses tracked filthy water into the gym, contaminating the space. Sam made a mental note to bring extra bottles of alcohol up; they'd need them to clean things off later.

When he got downstairs, other nurses were still working feverishly. They grew increasingly nervous as the brown sewage-laced flood rose around their feet. Within a half hour, it was six inches deep; water was now coming in through the back door, too. There was no longer any time for jokes.

Denise Sarro, who had been checking the blood sugar levels of diabetic patients, walked into the infirmary and immediately started helping Scarlett empty the medication carts. A plump strawberry blonde with a pixie cut, Denise was hardworking and forthright with suggestions.

"Let's put the meds in trash bags," she said in a voice that could be heard across the room. "The bags will keep everything dry . . . and we can float them out if the flooding gets too bad."

By now the water in the hallway was rising quickly, flooding the tiers and panicking inmates, who could only scream louder and bang on whatever was handy—bunk beds, walls, metal tables.

The sounds carried into the infirmary, and Scarlett stopped the doctor when he walked by.

"Dr. Gore, I feel so bad for the patients," she said. "We have to do something."

"You're right," Sam said. "I'll take care of it." He signaled a deputy in the hall and got him to open one of the tiers. Each tier had a double set of doors, like an airlock, and with the inmates so agitated, the deputy would only let the doctor go past the first door. Through a window in the second, however, Sam could make out two dozen patients packed against the barrier, straining to see and be heard. They had been lighting fires, and the smoke veiled their bodies. Their heads looked as though they were floating in space.

Sam, a man who rarely raised his voice, shouted for the men to quiet down.

"Listen," he screamed. "Wait a minute. Shut up! Be quiet and let me talk." He kept at it until he heard inmates inside passing the message: "Everyone be quiet. Listen to the doctor."

In a few minutes the yelling had died down. "Stay calm," Sam told the men, straining his voice to make himself heard through the door. "We're going to get you out of there." Finally he could hear the word passed to inmates at the back of the tier.

One by one, at each of the eight tiers, he repeated his actions. By the time he had finished, the water throughout the first floor of the building was over a foot deep. In the tiers it reached almost to the bottom of the bunk beds. For the handicapped patients, some of them paralyzed, Sam knew the threat was dire.

The inmates in wheelchairs were sitting in water up to their knees. Those confined to beds would soon be lying in the filthy flood, unable to get up. The water is full of sewage, Sam thought to himself. The risk of infection for AIDS and cancer patients and diabetics—for anyone with an open wound—is enormous. And if the water overtook their beds, some could drown. He had to get them out of there.

Sam rushed down the corridor to the warden's office, where Chief Belisle was talking to one of his officers. An extremely heavy man, Major Andy Crane was sweating and pale as he consulted with his boss. The two men looked up as the doctor walked in.

Just at that moment, the emergency lights went out—the generators in the Templeman buildings had failed.

Chapter 18

"That's the end of the power," Major Crane said grimly, in a deep southern drawl, flicking on a flashlight as the doctor again made his case.

"We've got to move the patients now," Sam said. "The water is up to the bottom of the beds, and the handicapped inmates are going to drown if you don't do something. You've got to evacuate the inmates—now."

Accepting that he had no other real choice, the warden gave in. As Belisle dispatched Crane to round up several deputies and inmate workers, Sam headed back to tell his staff the news.

The infirmary was dark; only a little light filtered in from the high windows, and Victor and the nurses worked by flashlight in near silence. They knew what had to be done. Much of the inventory had been prepackaged days ago. Now they were simply trying to make sure everything was covered.

"What about the refrigerated meds?" Chuck asked. "We almost forgot those." He opened the refrigerator door and had to scramble as the drugs floated out into the flooding room. He stuffed the meds in a couple of trash bags.

"Take some bottles of alcohol with you," Sam told him.

Eddie Williams and Duane Townzel were gathering bandages, sutures, and other wound-care supplies.

"I'm putting all the diabetic records in one bag," Denise announced, "and taking them upstairs."

"Lillian," Sam interjected, "what about stethoscopes and blood pressure cuffs?"

The head nurse nodded.

"Tracy," Sam said. "Take an EKG machine and a defibrillator. They run on batteries. And Eddie, get all the penlights from the supply cabinet. Someone get more IV fluids and tubing."

Nurse Pebles Jones heard him and went to get the items. Scarlett gave her a hand.

The group shuttled supplies on carts through the still-rising water, down the pitch-black, reeking hall. The wet, slippery steps in the stairwell made carrying the boxes and bags terrifyingly difficult. With their hands full, the nurses had to rely on penlights they held in their mouths, biting down on the switches to keep them lit.

As the staff continued to move boxes and bags to the gym, the deputies finally arrived to evacuate the infirmary patients. Sam went with them and watched as Security opened the doors to the handicapped tier, bracing themselves for a riot. But relieved at finally getting out, the inmates remained surprisingly calm.

Beginning with a 400-pound paraplegic, a couple of deputies tried to lift the patient into a wheelchair that could barely contain him. It took four men to move the inmate, who screamed with fear and pain when they brushed open sores on his back and buttocks. Those sores are going to get soaked with sewage, Sam realized as the wheelchair splashed in floodwater. How he wished they had done this earlier.

The deputies wheeled the gargantuan man to the bottom of the stairs, then tried to carry the wheelchair up with the patient in it. Straining under the weight, the deputies almost dumped the man into the water. The inmate screamed again and struck out with his arms.

"Wait a minute," Sam called. "This isn't going to work. It's too dangerous."

"What about a laundry cart?" one of the younger deputies suggested. He groped his way down the hall and came back with a large gray, wheeled Rubbermaid bin. Once again four deputies strained to pick up the inmate, clumsily depositing him in the bottom of the cart. With great effort six deputies slowly carried the cart upstairs.

"Where are you taking him?" Sam asked a senior deputy.

"Everyone's going to the third floor. We'll put the men in the big storage room above the gym, where you're going," the deputy said. "And we'll take the women to a holding cell outside the general medical clinic."

A small third-floor clinic handled routine medical care for the Templeman 1 and Templeman 2 buildings, and there were already three nurses up there. It was a good place for the women patients.

Duane, Victor, and Eddie came back to help the deputies, who took the rest of the handicapped patients up the stairs a few at a time by flashlight. They pushed those in wheelchairs through the water to the stairwell, then passed them up a chain of deputies. Some inmates had to be carried from their beds. Others made the trip in the laundry bin. The inmates on crutches trudged down the dark hall on their own, under the watchful eyes of the deputies, and managed to hobble or hop up the slippery stairs. Scarlett and a few other nurses had also returned to assist.

"The other tiers should go faster," Sam said when the handicapped tier was almost emptied.

"Let Security do it, Dr. Gore," Scarlett said in her usual forthright manner. "It's not safe. There's two feet of water in the hall, and there are red-banders in those tiers. They're not cuffed, and all kinds of things are floating around that they can grab for weapons."

She was right, Sam thought. He couldn't take chances with the medical staff. Just last year, he himself had been stabbed while treating one of the inmates.

"Okay," he said. "Let's get whatever else we can and get to the gym." He and the nurses made one final sweep of the infirmary, gathered up their personal items, and headed up to the second floor.

Despite all their efforts to keep things clean, the space was wet with sewage, and without a sink there was no way to really clean it up. Using flashlights and penlights, the staff went to work, laying out the equipment they would need first.

I just hope there are no real emergencies before someone gets us out of here, Sam thought as Lillian sent Denise up to the third-floor clinic with some meds and records. Who knew how soon inmates and deputies would come in for care. And there were also families sheltering on Templeman's upper floors. They might need the infirmary, too.

Moments later, as if on cue, a deputy came in supporting a young, black female. "Doc," he said, "she needs some help. She thinks the baby's coming."

Mary Lebeau was nine months pregnant and having pelvic pains.

Victor immediately ran over and set the woman on one of the few dry spots on the floor. Scarlett pulled down the woman's scrubs and held a penlight, while the ER doctor started a pelvic examination. How are we going to manage? Sam wondered as he watched the scene with mounting anxiety.

The patient moaned. Scarlett gave the girl a stern look and declared, "Mary, you are *not* having your baby here!"

For the first time in hours, Sam laughed out loud. They'd get through this somehow.

Chapter 19

Evening:
Sandbagging of the 17th Street Canal levee fails.
Inmates in Templeman 3 begin to riot and break out of
  flooded cells.

"Dr. Inglese!" Sheriff Gusman called as Gary and I walked into the Correctional Center lobby around six o'clock. The sheriff was standing just outside the front doors, holding his walkie-talkie. "We've got another inmate with a head injury."

"The Old Prison patient or someone else?" I wanted to be sure I understood him correctly.

"Someone else—at the House of Detention," Gusman explained. Another man had fallen, struck his head, and wasn't fully conscious. Dr. Shantha, a psychiatrist, was the only physician stationed at Detention. For an injury like this, I had to go, and Gary volunteered to come with me.

"I sent for a boat," the sheriff added as he turned back inside. "It'll be here in a few minutes."

I was glad I didn't have to wade over to Detention, but I wasn't going to lose another set of dry clothes. Gary and I ran upstairs to Medical Administration. He put on sandals while I changed back into my wet cargo shorts and flip-flops. We were on the front steps of the Center five minutes later, just as our boat pulled up. The rubber orange craft had inflatable sides and a solid bottom and could carry six people. Gary and I boarded without getting more than our ankles wet.

The deputy who was driving throttled up the outboard motor, turned right at the corner, and steered up the street. Detention stood directly across from the kitchen, and the driver pulled up to the jail's ground-floor entrance.

As Gary and I stepped out, I told the driver to wait for us. If the patient's condition was serious, we'd have to take him to the infirmary.

The first floor of Detention, several steps up from street level, was flooded with muddy water, ankle-deep and filled with trash. At least the old building still had generator power. There was not a soul in sight as we walked down the peeling, cramped hallway.

Gary suddenly halted and peered anxiously at something floating in the water. "Is that a rat?"

"Yeah, that's a rat." I laughed.

Groaning, Gary moved on. "I can't believe I'm wearing sandals in this muck."

"You'll get used to it," I said. "Trust me."

We hurried up to the second-floor clinic, a giant room packed with desks and with a tiny exam room in the back. Yolanda Dent, the tall black nurse on duty, led us through to a man sitting on a bench.

"This is Terry Jordan," she explained. "He's a psych patient who fell earlier today. Dr. Gore and Dr. Tuckler came over from the infirmary a few hours ago and stitched up his forehead, but he's still confused. He nearly passes out when we stand him up."

I bent over the patient. "How are you doing?"

"Okay," the thin, black inmate responded with a blank stare.

"Do you know where you are, sir?"

"Jail," he answered.

"What's your name?" I asked.

"Elvis."

"What's your name?" I asked again, startled.

"Elvis."

"Who am I?" Now I was concerned.

"My daddy."

Straightening up, I looked at Gary. "This guy is completely disoriented." I turned to Nurse Dent. "Do you have vitals?"

"Blood pressure's one-ten over sixty-two," she told me, "with a pulse of one-twenty."

"Head injury, tachycardia, confusion," Gary said. "I hope this isn't a bleed, because we won't find a neurosurgeon tonight."

"Get me his chart and med records." I wanted to know the inmate's history and what medications he was taking.

As Nurse Dent handed me the records, a male nurse assigned to the psychiatric unit at Detention walked into the clinic.

"Do you know this guy?" I asked him, paging through the patient's chart. "He hit his head and thinks he's Elvis."

"That's normal for him," the nurse answered. "He's psychotic. Yesterday he thought he was Kurt Cobain."

"Wow, he's on pretty big doses of thorazine." As I studied the record, a thought struck me. "Did you give out medications prior to the storm?"

The psych nurse nodded. "Some patients got a week's worth, but psych patients only got enough for a day or two, depending on their illness."

"Mr. Jordan, where are your pills?" I asked.

The inmate pulled out an *empty* medication packet.

"If he took two days of thorazine all at once," I said to Gary, "that would explain the somnolence, rapid heart rate, and passing out when he stands."

"That's probably *why* he fell earlier," Gary added.

By the time I had finished my evaluation, I was confident there was nothing seriously wrong with the patient. I gave additional orders to the staff, and Gary and I turned to leave.

As we headed toward the stairs, one of the building's officers intercepted us. "The warden sent me to get you, Doc. One of the deputies is having a heart attack."

Chapter 20

Colonel William Short, the warden of the House of Detention, was on the radio when Gary and I entered his office. He looked up when the call ended, his expression grave.

"What's going on?" I asked.

"A deputy with chest pain," Short answered. "That's all I know. The signal kept breaking up."

"Where is he?" Gary asked.

"At the Albertson's on Jeff Davis and Tulane," he said, referring to a supermarket ten blocks from the jail. "You've got a boat. Go see what you can do."

"If this really is a heart attack," I said, "we might need some backup—medications, equipment. I'll need a way to call for help."

"Take this." The warden handed me a radio. "Call me if you need anything."

Gary and I stopped back in the clinic and grabbed some drugs and a responder bag containing basic first aid supplies. Then we headed to the boat.

When I told the driver where we were going, he was dumbfounded.

"Driving a couple blocks between buildings is one thing," the deputy said. "Driving a mile through these neighborhoods is nuts. The streets were littered with trash and debris *before* the storm. Who knows what's under the water now; we could run into anything. It's dangerous to be out there, and it's getting dark."

"Then we'd better hurry," I said, stepping into the boat. I tried the radio as we pulled away from Detention. "Colonel Short, do you copy?"

No answer.

I tried the radio several more times, but all I got was static. Disgusted, I set the radio in the bottom of the boat.

Gary voiced my feelings. "Guess we're on our own."

"Keep a lookout for junk in the water," the driver said. "I don't want to crash."

Gary stared intently ahead. But as we pulled away, I felt the familiar rush of adrenaline once more. Yes this was a risky trip, but in some ways it appealed to the action junkie in me, the one who loved to scuba dive, rock climb, and go caving for fun. I calmed myself and focused on the water in front of us.

The driver went slowly to avoid running into anything that could overturn the boat or rip a hole in the rubber sides. Despite his care and our vigilance, we kept colliding with submerged objects, sometimes gently, other times hitting with a solid impact. As daylight dimmed, our anxiety increased.

Downed trees and utility poles made some flooded streets impassable, forcing us to backtrack and detour more than once. The arduous journey took much longer than we had anticipated, and the sky grew darker, increasing our sense of imminent danger. We barely said a word as we braced for the next impact.

The tension was worsened by the bizarre alteration of once-familiar terrain in the twilight. Car roofs broke through the water, forming small islands in the sea. Many neighborhood houses had no roofs, and walls were ripped away. The incessant thrum of the outboard motor scored the macabre scene with an eerie cadence.

No one was visible, and the buildings were devoid of light, but we were not alone. Every so often, someone hollered or waved from a roof or window, pleading for help. With a deputy in distress, we couldn't stop. We pressed on.

As we passed the sheriff's office mechanic shop, several deputies called out to us from a second-story window.

"You need to get to Albertson's. Deputy Wallace's having a heart attack, man! He's dying!"

"You've got to get him," another man yelled.

"We're on our way!" The boat driver shouted back.

Up till now, my attention had been focused on navigating the treacherous waters, but as we approached our destination, my thoughts shifted back to the deputy in trouble. He had made it through the hurricane and was still on the job. Now *our* job was to reach him quickly and provide the best care possible.

But how exactly were we going to do that?

Gary and I could certainly give him rudimentary care in the field. However, if this were truly a heart attack, the man would need in-depth medical intervention. I didn't know if Templeman 1 still had generator power, but the infirmary there wasn't equipped to handle a full-blown heart attack. Deputy Wallace would need a real hospital.

And as far as I could tell, the whole city had no power. Not a single light brightened the gray twilight around us. Surely the nearby hospitals had emergency generators, but who knew how those institutions had fared in the storm and the flooding?

As the driver pulled into the supermarket parking lot, the water got shallower as we neared the building. In front of the store I saw a deputy in camouflage pants and a black T-shirt, flagging us down. He had parked his patrol car on the sidewalk, and no one else was anywhere in sight.

"That must be him," Gary said as the boat bottomed out. "At least he's standing."

I shared Gary's sense of relief. We'd had no idea what the deputy's condition would be. From the reports, I expected him to be on the ground, perhaps even unconscious.

"What's the matter, Deputy Wallace?" I climbed out of the boat and waded through a few inches of water to the sidewalk, which was dry.

"I've got some pain in my chest." The man winced. "I get this way when my pressure's high. I go see Dr. Gore in the infirmary, and he gives me medication." Wallace was animated, speaking fast, and pacing as he talked.

Gary raised an eyebrow but didn't say anything.

"Do you have a cardiac history?" I asked, taking equipment from the responder bag.

"Yeah." The deputy nodded. "High blood pressure."

"Have you ever had a heart attack?" I took his pressure. It was moderately elevated and so was his pulse. His lungs were clear.

"No, just chest pains when my pressure gets up. You know, when I get too excited." The deputy began collecting equipment and supplies from his patrol car. "My blood pressure might be too high, so I thought you could take me to the infirmary to get me checked out."

Gary's jaw tightened as we exchanged incredulous looks. The man was vigorously lifting heavy cases from his vehicle's trunk. He showed no distress and had no shortness of breath. He was probably having a panic attack.

The whole situation was a classic example of people overreacting in a disaster. As Deputy Wallace's story was repeated from one person to the next, what had begun as simple chest pain was transformed into a near-death scenario.

"I can't believe we came out here for this," Gary muttered.

Me either, I thought. The boat driver, Gary, and I had taken a serious risk navigating the dark, flooded streets, and we had wasted valuable time and resources responding to a nonexistent emergency. Still, the deputy had a history of high blood pressure, so we decided to take him back to the infirmary just to be safe.

"Do you have flashlights?" the driver asked as the three of us piled into the boat with the deputy's supplies and several guns from his vehicle.

"Sure do." I pulled my flashlight from my pocket.

Gary flicked on his beam as the driver headed toward the infirmary. Spotting underwater hazards was even more difficult now that the darkness was complete, and minutes seemed like hours, until at last the boat scraped bottom a few feet from the Intake Processing Center. From there a walkway led to the Templeman buildings.

Telling the driver to wait, Gary, Deputy Wallace, and I dropped into waist-high water and waded to the street-level entrance. Inside, the huge, newly paneled lobby was knee-deep in water. During normal operations, the area would be crowded with people waiting for friends and family to be released from custody. Now the space was ghostly silent. A massive deputy with a flashlight sat behind the long reception desk in front of dozens of partly submerged chairs.

"Dr. Inglese, what are you doing here," asked Deputy Keller, a 500-pound man I knew well. He frequently asked me for medical advice.

"Taking a deputy to the infirmary," I answered.

Deputy Wallace checked his firearms with Keller, and we made our way to the back of the Intake Center and the roofed, chain-link-enclosed walkway.

As we strode down the outdoor corridor in tense silence, water sloshed against our legs and trash bobbed on its surface. Stacks of trays laden with bread, cheese, and turkey had been abandoned along the route. As we turned right into the walkway toward the infirmary, my flashlight stopped working. I moved closer to Gary to share his light, and something skimmed by my leg. I flinched, hoping it was nothing more sinister than an empty bread wrapper.

The darkness inside Templeman 1 was absolute, hard evidence that the generators here were down. The sour odor of sewage tainted the air. Gary cautiously flashed his beam in front, guiding us through a mass of garbage and foam chairs floating on the water. At last we reached the infirmary and pushed open the door.

Gary panned his flashlight across the room, but there was no one in sight. The unit was flooded, dark, and completely deserted.

Chapter 21

We stood in the infirmary doorway, wondering where everyone had gone. I hadn't been in touch with the unit since noon, but Sam Gore was intelligent and resourceful, and the infirmary nurses were all extremely capable. No matter what had happened, I knew Sam and his crew could handle it. A moment later a deputy came by and told us the staff had moved the infirmary to the gymnasium on the second floor.

As we walked to the stairs, I stuffed my useless flashlight in my shorts pocket, freeing my hands to grab the railing. Gary took the lead with his light, but he moved too fast, leaving Wallace and me blind in the dark stairwell.

"Gary!" I yelled. "Wait!"

"What?" Gary turned the beam on us.

"You're going too fast."

"Sorry," Gary said. "I just want to get out of here as soon as possible."

"So do we, but we need to *see*," I said sarcastically.

Gary waited until we reached the second floor, then we made our way down the damp cinderblock hallway.

The scene in the gymnasium was chaotic, yet calm. Piles of medications, records, and equipment lay scattered all over the room. Doctors and nurses were seeing to half a dozen patients, an eclectic mix of inmates, deputies, and family members. The medical staff was relying on flashlights and penlights to see what they were doing.

"This looks like a war zone," Gary said.

Straight out of World War I, I thought. The floor was wet, and patients were lying on the ground, some on blankets, but most on hard tile. The staff worked with quiet diligence, seemingly oblivious to the primitive conditions.

Sam walked over as I guided Deputy Wallace to a vacant space on the floor.

"What have you got?" Sam asked.

"Hypertension and chest pain. Possibly a heart attack, but more likely a panic attack." I quickly summarized the deputy's case. "He says he knows you."

"Yeah, I've treated him." Sam bent to examine the man.

"Do you have a cardiac monitor?" I asked.

Sam laughed. "Are you kidding? We don't have lights. We don't have anything. Go take a look. I've got this covered."

All around the gym I saw salvaged equipment—thermometers, stethoscopes, blood pressure cuffs, IV kits, and an EKG machine. I spotted Victor Tuckler near the door, but before I could go speak to him, Duane Townzel rushed in, carrying a female deputy in his arms.

"Deputy having an asthma attack!" Duane shouted.

Victor responded immediately, with Chuck Perotto right behind him.

The patient's breathing was labored. Suddenly her eyes rolled back and she passed out.

"Grab an ambu-bag, Chuck!" Duane yelled.

"Wait," Victor said as Chuck reached for the resuscitation mask. "She's still breathing on her own."

Leaving the ambu-bag, Chuck picked up a blood pressure cuff before Victor had to ask. They were all accustomed to dealing with medical emergencies. Seeing they had the situation under control, I continued my inspection of the temporary infirmary.

Denise Sarro had just finished taking vitals on another female deputy, who sat holding a baby.

"What's wrong with them?" Gary asked as we approached.

Denise was almost always cheerful, but her usually startling laugh was absent tonight.

"They're both dehydrated," she said in a subdued tone. "But

the baby's worse. Poor thing's listless and bleeding slightly from the mouth. Dr. Tuckler doesn't think it's too serious, though. He just ordered some fluids."

I followed Denise across the room, where she retrieved a bag of IV fluid from a cardboard box. Everyone in the gym looked tired, but Denise seemed particularly worn out.

"You look exhausted," I said.

Denise sighed. "I was up most of the night with the patients. The storm had them pretty rattled, especially one of the seizure patients. Whenever she gets upset, she fakes a seizure for attention."

"Pseudo-seizures?" I asked.

Nodding, Denise continued. "I'm usually pretty understanding, but last night I'd had enough. After her third call for help, I told her, 'This is ridiculous. You get back into bed now! I have work to do.' After that, I didn't hear from her again."

Sometimes, being stern was the only way to manage problematic patients. "Hope tonight's better," I said.

I walked back to Sam and Deputy Wallace. The faint lighting gave the doctor a crazed look. With his disheveled clothing and prominent cowlick, he reminded me of Jack Nicholson in *The Shining*.

He drew me aside and spoke in a low voice. "I think you're right about Deputy Wallace, Dem. This is a panic attack. His pressure's a little high so I gave him some atenolol, but it isn't his heart. He's come in with anxiety problems before."

"Thought so." I frowned. "Gary and I weren't too happy about going all that way in a boat to treat a case of nerves."

"It's the same here," Sam said. "We're seeing more deputies than inmates. There have been a few sick people, but mostly guys with garbage aches and pains . . . definitely not emergencies. The nurses have done a great job sorting out the ones who really need help."

"When did you move the infirmary?" I asked. Settling in to hear the story, I took a seat on one of three foam chairs lined up along the gym wall. Their square bases and rectangular backs were hardly stylish, but no one could dismantle them and use the pieces as weapons. Inmates made shanks out of any hard material they could find.

"Around five, when the water started coming in." Sam took two bottles of water from a bag and handed me one as he filled me in. "By the time we finished, the water was above our knees."

"It's deeper than that now," I said, trying to imagine the scene. Sam's description of the move was staggering, but he was characteristically modest.

"The deputies and nurses did most of the work," he finished. He reached up to smooth his cowlick. The tuft of dark hair sprang up again the instant he cupped his hands behind his neck.

"Well . . ." I said, "you did a hell of a job."

"The trip was really hard on some of the patients," Sam added.

That was undoubtedly an understatement. Some of the infirmary patients were recovering from surgery. Others were afflicted with terminal diseases. Like Carl Davis, I thought, recalling the inmate who had died of cirrhosis yesterday morning. Only one day ago? I felt as though I had been trapped in Katrina's grip longer than thirty-six hours.

"How's the third-floor clinic doing?"

"It's fine," Sam said.

I briefed him on the other medical clinics. "The Correctional Center and Detention are okay, too, but I'm really worried about the first-floor clinics in the Old Prison, Conchetta, and Templeman 4. They must be flooded by now."

"The female inmates in Templeman 4 and the nurse there are all okay," Sam said. "They were moved to Templeman 2."

"Any word about Templeman 3?"

"Chuck and Victor went over earlier to see someone vomiting blood." Sam turned to Chuck, who was still with the asthmatic deputy. "Chuck! You busy?"

The deputy was awake, sitting and talking with Victor.

Chuck walked over to join us. "What can I do for you?"

"How's the deputy?" I asked.

"She's doing much better." Chuck explained, "She had a panic attack that set off her asthma."

"This is getting ridiculous," I said. "We need the deputies to get a grip and hold it together. This could get a lot worse. How are things at Templeman 3? Dr. Gore said you treated someone over there?"

"I did," Chuck nodded. "He's fine. We left him with Dr. Dileo."

"Dr. Dileo?" I sat back. "You mean Dr. Caldwell."

"No, Dr. Dileo," Chuck repeated. "Dr. Dileo and the Intake Center nurses were all evacuated to Templeman 3 several hours ago when Intake flooded."

"So there are two doctors there now?"

"Right." Chuck nodded. "Dr. Dileo and Dr. Caldwell."

I turned to Sam. "I should relocate Dileo to Detention. Then Gary and I will have one less building to cover."

"Sounds like a plan," Sam agreed, "but you'll have to go over there and tell him yourself. The phones aren't working."

Gary was treating a deputy who had just walked in complaining about sore feet. The man had been standing in water for hours, evacuating prisoners to higher floors, and he probably had an infection. Gary was needed here for a while.

It looked like I'd be making the trip to Templeman 3 alone.

Chapter 22

I picked up a penlight on my way out. By the time I fumbled to the bottom of the dark stairs, though, I regretted not borrowing Gary's flashlight. There was one positive aspect to my near-blind trek. I couldn't see all the garbage around me. Soggy remnants of unmade turkey-and-cheese sandwiches had spread across the water in the corridors like thick pond scum, and gobs kept sticking to my bare legs.

My spirits improved when I left Templeman 1 and stepped out into the walkway. Air flowed through the chain-link fencing, and the view of the night sky was a welcome contrast to the claustrophobic atmosphere in the gym, where the tension was magnified by oppressive darkness and cramped quarters. Out here the water was also less cluttered.

A deputy guarded the massive steel-and-glass doors to Templeman 3. The thin penlight beam alerted him to my approach, and he looked me up and down when I stopped at the entrance. His suspicion was justified. A lone man wandering the flooded jail in a dirty T-shirt and wet cargo shorts was a cause for concern, until he recognized me.

The deputy inserted a large steel key in the lock and slid the door open. "Sorry about that, Doc. I didn't know it was you for a minute there." Most of the deputies recognized the medical director on sight, though I did not know all 1,100 jail employees by name.

"Not a problem." I smiled as I walked through the cinderblock hallway that was similar to the entrance in Templeman 1. Before going upstairs to check on the clinic, I went to the warden's office. I didn't want to wander around the jail in the dark without letting the warden know I was there.

Chief Gary Bordelon bent over his desk. In his mid-fifties, with gray hair, a round face, and an understated confidence, the warden was reviewing building plans with Major Chuck Jones, his second in command. A flashlight on the desk dimly lit the dark room.

Their backs were to me, and I spoke to announce my presence. "Chief, how's it going?"

"What are you doing here, Doc?" Bordelon glanced over his shoulder.

"I came to check on the clinic. How are you doing?"

Bordelon looked at me, down at the water, and back at me. "No electricity, no phones, and the whole first floor is flooded. I'd say we're not doing so well."

The warden now faced a security and a logistical nightmare, I realized. The receiving tier for new arrestees was on the first floor of Templeman 3. People who did not bail out of jail immediately were held there until they went to court. However, court hadn't been in session for three days due to the storm. Everyone arrested since Friday afternoon was still on the tier, and the cells were probably packed to overflowing.

"How many inmates do you have on the receiving tier?" I asked, curious.

"Three hundred and four," Major Jones said.

"Plus three hundred St. Bernard inmates in our first-floor gymnasium," Bordelon added, "which is flooded, too."

The officers' unruffled composure was impressive, considering they had 750 inmates in cells that were filling with water. They had to evacuate, but safely moving that many men in the dark was a major undertaking.

"We moved everyone we could to the second and third floors," Bordelon continued, "but without power, every door has to be opened manually, and some of them won't open."

"Why not?" I asked.

"They're old . . . the water," Jones explained. "Or inmates tried to kick their way out and knocked the doors off track."

"What are you going to do?"

Bordelon motioned to a crowbar and a sledgehammer lying on a nearby table. "We're going to get them out."

The two men were in the thick of a crisis, and I didn't want to interfere. I told Bordelon I was going to the clinic and turned to leave.

"Be careful out there, Doc," Bordelon said evenly. "A few of the St. Bernard inmates climbed through the gym ceiling and got out to the roof of Templeman 4."

The warden's words brought me to a halt. "There are inmates loose in the building?"

Bordelon shook his head. "No, they're trapped on the roof. They're contained, just not secured."

"I'm glad you cleared that up," I mumbled sarcastically. "I feel so much safer now."

As I picked my way through the dark corridors and up the stairs, I could hear inmates yelling and banging on metal doors on the tiers above me, the first signs of a prison riot. The sounds of potential danger were inescapable, made even sharper by my unfamiliarity with the building. As the medical department had grown over the last couple of years, I'd spent more time at my desk doing administrative chores than in each of the clinics. Now I felt like I was trying to find my way through a maze where a wrong turn could have disastrous consequences.

My nerves settled down when I entered the second-floor clinic, where flashlight beams lit the room. There were no patients, and Dr. Caldwell and the clinic nurses were packed into the space with Dr. Dileo and the Intake Center staff. They were talking, cracking jokes, and laughing.

The Templeman 3 clinic had dealt with routine medical problems all day, and the staff had distributed medications for several days to the inmates. More than enough personnel were present to handle emergencies, so I asked Marcus Dileo to go to Detention. The doctor responded with his characteristic amicability. A short man of nearly fifty, Marcus was usually the first to step in and volunteer for any assignment. Though he'd have to walk through flooded streets to get to Detention, he didn't complain.

I retraced my steps to the temporary infirmary, where Gary had just finished treating the deputy with sore feet. There was no further reason for him to stay there. Sam had Victor and enough nurses to take care of both Templeman 1 and 2. I needed Gary to help me cover any emergencies that might arise elsewhere in the jail complex.

Going back downstairs and through the darkened halls again was easier with Gary's flashlight, but we were caught off guard when Chief Belisle intercepted us. He was extremely worried about one of his officers—a man having chest pain. From the weary look on Gary's face, I could tell we both had the same thought: not another panic attack!

We found Major Andy Crane sitting in a chair outside the warden's office. The 450-pound officer was straining to breathe, and his puffy face was coated with sweat.

"Describe the pain, Major," I said.

"Burning, squeezing." Crane placed his hand on his sternum, "Right here."

"What's your cardiac history?" I asked, taking his pulse. His heart was racing.

"High blood pressure, ventricular fibrillation or atrial. I'm not sure." The big man struggled to breathe.

Gary met my grim stare. This was no panic attack. This time, the emergency was real.

Chapter 23

Time was critical. If Major Crane *was* having a heart attack, each minute meant more lost heart muscle. Or worse, he could die at any moment from an abnormal heart rhythm.

I sprang into action. "We have to get him upstairs."

Gary's eyes were open wide with concern. Then he nodded. Moving the hugely overweight patient through flooded hallways and up stairs would be difficult and dangerous, but we both knew there was no other option. The additional strain on Crane's heart could be deadly, but we needed the oxygen, medications, and equipment in the temporary infirmary. Bringing those items to the patient wasn't feasible. Nor was treating him properly while he was seated knee-high in water.

Leaning forward, I tried to reassure the distressed officer. "You'll be all right, but we have to get you to the infirmary."

"Okay, Doc." Crane's voice was hoarse, and he groaned as we helped him up. Gary and I held him under his arms and walked him to the stairs.

Crane gasped with every step. Knowing that the exertion might trigger a fatal heart rhythm, I cringed every time he breathed. When we reached the stairs, I needed both hands free. I shoved my penlight in my mouth, held the railing with one hand, and pulled Crane up, while Gary pushed from below.

It seemed like hours, painful hours, till we got to the top of the stairs. Sam came running as soon as we lumbered through the door of the makeshift infirmary. "What's wrong?"

"Chest pain, shortness of breath, tachycardia . . . a possible heart attack," I explained as Gary and I helped the man hobble to an open space on the floor.

Still in pain from the exertion, Crane lay down, and we opened his shirt. Chuck rushed over and began taking vitals while Sam placed an oxygen mask over the patient's nose and mouth.

"Scarlett! Get me aspirin and nitroglycerine!" I waved to Nurse Maness and then turned to Gary. "Grab a bottle of water from that backpack by the wall."

Chuck called out Crane's vital signs. "BP, one-ninety over one-ten. Heart rate, one-twenty and irregular."

Scarlett handed me the medications.

Gary returned a moment later. He twisted off the cap of the water bottle and held it while the patient washed down the aspirin.

I waited until Crane had swallowed before slipping a nitroglycerine tablet under his tongue. "He's got a history of atrial fib, Sam."

"Anything else you can tell us, Major?" Sam asked.

I sent Scarlett to get the EKG machine while we reviewed Crane's medical history in more depth, including his current medications and allergies.

Sam had to be alarmed by Crane's symptoms, but he didn't show it. His even tone and calm demeanor had a soothing effect on the patient. "How are you doing now?"

"It still hurts," Crane mumbled.

Scarlett pulled the EKG machine over. She used her scrub top to wipe the sweat and grime from his chest before attaching leads to the patient's body. I listened to his heart and lungs, and Sam held a flashlight while I tried to read the EKG. Crane's rapid breathing, racing heart, and large size made it difficult to get a readable tracing.

"It's fast and irregular. It probably is atrial fib, but . . ." I paused with a pointed look at Sam. "I can't be sure if he's having a heart attack."

"He needs something for that pressure," Sam said.

Sighing with frustration, I rubbed the stubble of beard on my chin. Beta-blockers would treat high blood pressure, reduce heart rate, and could be life-saving in a heart attack, but if Crane was in heart failure, they could kill him. I hated having to make life-

and-death decisions without adequate information, but I had to wing it. There was no crackling of fluid in his lungs. His heart sounds were normal, and his legs weren't swollen. All those facts made congestive heart failure less likely. And based on the symptoms and history, the probability of a heart attack was high. I went with my gut.

"Give him fifty milligrams of Lopressor, Scarlett," I ordered.

"Over five minutes have passed," Gary said.

The Major needed another nitroglycerine. "And another nitro," I told the nurse.

"Coming right up." Scarlett slipped the pill under the man's tongue.

"We can't treat him here," I said. "He needs a hospital."

Gary looked at me incredulously. Getting Major Crane to a local emergency room through dark flooded streets seemed very risky, even impossible. But we both knew it was absolutely essential.

"I'll help you get him to the boat," Gary said as he began removing the EKG leads.

I folded the EKG tracing, put it in a plastic baggie, and stuffed it in my cargo shorts. As Gary and Sam helped Crane to his feet, I took Scarlett's flashlight.

"Sorry, Scarlett," I said. "I need it more than you do."

The trip back down the stairs and through Templeman 1 to the outside walkway was agonizing and slow. We had to pause frequently for Crane to catch his breath. Although Gary and I struggled under the man's weight, our trips to the gym stood us in good stead. Nevertheless, our patient was still sweating profusely. The ordeal had to be placing a tremendous strain on his heart.

As we struggled through the flooded walkway, the deputy's labored breathing filled our ears, but gradually I became aware of other, equally ominous sounds: inmates were shouting and banging on the tiers in Templeman 3. The noise was louder and more raucous than an hour ago. What the hell's going on over there? I wondered uneasily.

"It's going to be okay, Major," I said when we finally entered the Intake Center. As we neared the front entrance, I hid my con-

cern in an effort to keep the patient calm. "There's a boat waiting outside, and it's only a short trip to the hospital."

The boat sat where we had left it several feet from the doors.
The driver frowned as we waded toward him. The street dipped
in front of the building, and the water was waist deep when we
reached the boat.

"What's the problem?" the driver asked.

"We have to get Major Crane to a hospital," I said.

"It was hard enough getting to Albertson's when we had some
light," the driver objected. "But it's black out there now, and the
hospitals are miles away."

I motioned the driver closer and whispered, "If we don't go,
he's going to die."

He nodded grimly. "Let's get moving, then."

Before we could leave, though, we had to get Crane *into* the
boat. The inflated craft bobbed every time he leaned against it.
The major struggled with the pain, and there was no way he could
hoist his 450 pounds over the side and pull himself in. He needed
a boost.

Gary and I tightened our grips on Crane and planted our feet.
The major put his arms over the side of the boat and held on
while the driver tugged his uniform. Working together, Gary and
I tried a lift-push maneuver, hoping to get enough upward momentum to tip the patient into the boat. The scene would have
been comical—if it hadn't been a matter of life and death.

On our fourth attempt we finally got one of Crane's legs hooked
over the side. It was a warm New Orleans night, and by now we
were both sweating as much as the officer. Bracing his body to
keep him from falling out, we pushed again, and his other leg
swung up and over. Major Crane slid into the boat with a groan.

As Gary and I paused to catch *our* breath, a live rat swam by.

"I don't know which creeps me out more," Gary said. "Live
rats in the water or dead ones."

"Dead ones don't bite." I smiled and jumped into the boat.

"Oh, thanks for that." Gary followed me into the craft and
then reached back into the water to grab one of his sandals, which
had come loose. "Birkenstocks. At least they float."

"Which hospital?" the driver asked, starting the motor.

"Tulane," I answered. "It's a straight shot and the closest."

As we boated down the same street I had waded along earlier in the day, Gary looked in awe at the complete absence of light.

"You can't even tell there's a city, it's so dark," Gary said as the driver made the turn onto Tulane Avenue. "There's not a street or house light anywhere."

The driver looked at us. "Same drill as before. Keep an eye out for stuff in the water."

Nodding, I aimed my flashlight ahead of the boat.

The courthouse looked ghostly as our lights panned past its dark, deserted columns. Not a soul was in sight. The boat continued down the avenue, past small businesses and narrow houses. The motor's steady hum was the only sound in the blackness.

Then someone called out, "Help us. Get us out of here."

We didn't answer. Ignoring the cries was hard. As doctors and former military, Gary and I both had a strong sense of duty, but we were in no position to help. Silently we kept our lookout for debris.

More voices called to us from a dark apartment building.

"Over here!" A man screamed, waving a flashlight out a window. "Get us out!"

"Stop, please stop," a woman added. "We have babies and children. Please, help us."

People shouted, cried, or cursed at us from every cluster of buildings we passed. The disembodied voices were fraught with fear and despair, poignant proof of the city's utter destruction.

Gary sat stonily, his distress and compassion for the stranded people evident in his clenched jaw and somber expression. The unanswered pleas would haunt us both for a long time.

As the boat moved under the elevated interstate, we could see a glow emanating from a few buildings in the central business district. Hospitals and skyscrapers with generator power radiated hope in the heart of downtown. Even so, these streets, too, were flooded, and the driver couldn't speed up his slow pace. He cautioned us again to stay alert for submerged obstacles.

"How's the pain, Major?" I asked.

"About the same, I guess—"

Two sharp cracks split the night.

Gary's head snapped up. "That sounded like gunfire."

"Pretty sure it was," the driver said.

Until I heard the shots, I hadn't thought about the criminals who were still loose in New Orleans. During the day, I had walked through sewage and had survived encounters with fire ants, snakes, and electrical cables. The possibility of being shot had never occurred to me.

"Are those headlights?" Gary pointed ahead.

"Looks like it," the driver agreed.

The floodwaters were less deep as we moved toward the river and higher ground. Trucks and large SUVs would be able to navigate these streets. The downside of the shallow water didn't occur to me until the bottom of the boat scraped the pavement.

"Is the boat going to make it all the way?" I could see Tulane Hospital a couple of blocks ahead.

"Don't know," the driver admitted. "It's not that far, but we're really loaded down."

The scraping sounds increased as we drew closer.

"Would it help if Gary and I got out?" I asked, wincing as the boat rubbed the street hard.

"You'll probably have to," the driver answered.

Gary and I slipped into the water on opposite sides of the boat and walked alongside as it floated again. Within a few minutes, however, we had to lift and push the craft to keep it moving.

"Uh-oh." Gary stopped abruptly.

"What?" I asked. His eyes were clamped shut.

"I just stepped on a cable." Gary swallowed hard and opened his eyes.

"It's okay," I said. "There's no power."

"It's just the idea, you know?" Gary exhaled slowly. "I knew if I opened my eyes and saw darkness I was okay. If I saw a bright light, it was all over."

"No such luck. You don't get out of this mess so easily." I laughed. "Just push."

We tugged, pushed, pulled, and lifted the boat for a few more yards before it bottomed out completely. We were a block and a half from the Tulane emergency room.

Gary glanced from Crane to me.

"We have to walk the rest of the way, " I said.

Chapter 24

Forcing the patient to hike through the flood again seemed like too much to ask, but it was Major Crane's only hope of getting proper medical care.

Helping the big man out of the boat was easier than getting him in, yet as we started forward, it was obvious that his condition had worsened. Sweat dripped off Crane's face, and he exhaled in prolonged gasps.

Every few feet we stopped to rest, but the strain was wearing on Gary and me as well. Major Crane leaned on us more and more for support. He stumbled often, and I flinched every time he almost fell. Gary and I would never be able to lift the heavy man out of the thigh-high water. If he passed out, he would drown.

Charity Hospital lay just ahead, a block closer than Tulane Medical Center, but I knew the front doors were always locked at night, and no lights were visible now. The emergency room entrance was around the back, two additional blocks I did not want to walk. We pushed on toward Tulane.

"Easy does it, Major," Gary said when the patient rocked backward. We both braced to keep him upright.

The depth of the water was gradually decreasing, but it was still above our knees. However, a six-inch-high median divided the avenue.

"It'll be easier if we walk there," I said, pointing to the median. "The water won't be as deep."

Nodding, Gary tightened his grip on Crane's arm and uniform.

As we angled to the left, I spotted a flatbed tow truck in the far lane. The driver had just finished hitching up a car. While Gary and the patient paused to rest, I sprinted over to beg a ride.

"Hey!" I shouted as the truck driver opened the cab door. Dressed in wet clothes with a dark, two-day beard, I knew my scruffy appearance might be alarming, so I quickly identified myself. "I'm Dr. Inglese from the sheriff's office, and we've got a very sick . . ."

"Get out of here!" The man climbed into the cab, threw the truck into gear, and pulled away.

Stunned by the rebuff, I stood frozen for a moment, but only for a moment. Major Crane still needed an emergency room. I ran back to Gary and the patient.

Walking through ankle-deep water on the raised median had seemed like a good idea, but we hadn't thought about the cement edge being invisible under the water. Clumps of grass, ruts, and rocks covered the ground. Crane stumbled or slipped off the curb every few steps, and we all risked spraining an ankle. After a few yards, we stepped back onto the street, where the footing was safer.

Approaching Tulane Medical Center, we could see the well-lit first floor of the glass-and-concrete structure. I was filled with elation when I saw outlines of people moving inside. Perhaps Katrina had not obliterated civilization in New Orleans after all.

The floodwater was only inches deep as we trudged up the sloped sidewalk to the emergency room entrance. After seating Crane on a planter, Gary and I walked up to a security guard posted at the door.

"We need to get this man inside." I glanced back. The deputy sat hunched over, clutching his chest and breathing hard.

"Sorry," the guard said. "The hospital's closed."

"He's having a heart attack." I spoke slowly and deliberately, repeating myself as though the guard hadn't heard what I said. "We need to get him inside."

"No one's allowed in." The guard seemed oblivious to our plight. "The doors are locked."

"This is a hospital," I protested. "With power." How could a medical facility staffed with personnel be closed in the middle of this disaster?

"We're doctors at the sheriff's office." Gary pointed at Crane. "And he's a law enforcement officer . . ."

The guard blocked my way when I reached to try the doors. "The hospital's closed," he insisted with a stern tone that bordered on a threat.

I was not one to give up easily, but a confrontation with the guard wouldn't solve our problem. As I drew Gary aside to discuss our options, a gray-haired couple walked up to the door. They spoke to the guard, but he refused to let them into the building. The man had his arm around the woman, who sobbed as they walked away.

"Look at that. What's going to happen to those poor people?"

Gary looked as upset and appalled as I felt, but when he started toward the guard, fists clenched, I held his arm. There was nothing we could do.

For an instant my mind went back to my combat triage training in Korea—direct your resources for the maximum benefit. In this case that meant taking care of Crane. The couple did not appear to be in any acute distress, and they had walked here from somewhere without assistance. The deputy, on the other hand, faced a life-threatening crisis. Our obligation was clear, but it still broke our hearts.

An image of my grandmother flashed through my mind as we walked back to our patient. If that had been her, I'd want someone to help.

"I don't know how to tell you this, Major," Gary said, "but the hospital's closed. The guard won't let us in."

Crane sighed and hung his head. "What now?" He spoke softly, a mixture of fear and resignation in his voice.

"We have to get to another ER," I said with obstinate determination. There were three other hospitals within a few blocks of where we stood: Charity Hospital, University Hospital, and the VA Medical Center. Taking control and pushing on, I pulled the deputy to his feet before he could protest.

As we reached the edge of the sidewalk, a pair of headlights came into view. It was a New Orleans Police Department squad car. "Be right back," I called out as I ran onto the street toward the vehicle. Riding three blocks to an emergency room would greatly improve Crane's chances of survival.

"Stop!" I shouted and waved, but the car didn't even slow down. It sprayed me with water as it sped by.

Incensed, I stood in the middle of the road as a second car approached. The idea that the driver might run me down didn't register until the last second, when I jumped back and barely avoided being struck. In a way, I couldn't blame the guy. By now, anyone left in New Orleans must be crazed with fear, and given the gunshots we'd heard earlier, the criminals were probably out in force. My unkempt appearance made me look suspicious, and I realized that trying to get someone to stop would be futile.

I jogged back to Gary and Crane. "Sorry, Major, but we have to walk to Charity."

The deputy just nodded.

Gary and I took up our accustomed positions on either side of the man and helped him to his feet. As we started across the street, another set of headlights approached, this time from behind. A deuce-and-a-half—a 2.5-ton military transport with a canvas top—stopped beside us.

The driver wore military fatigues and peered down from the high cab. He identified his unit as National Guard and asked, "What's the problem?"

"We're doctors from the sheriff's office with a deputy in cardiac distress," I explained, putting as much information as possible in one sentence.

Another man jumped off the back of the truck. "I'm a paramedic. I can help."

"No," I explained to him. "We're doctors. None of us can do anything for him here. He needs an ER."

"Tulane wouldn't let us in," Gary said.

"Will you drive us to Charity?" I asked. Crane sagged slightly, putting more of his weight on Gary and me.

"Charity's closed, too," the paramedic said.

"Okay, then what about University?" I suggested.

When the paramedic hesitated, the truck driver answered. "University burned down."

"What?" Gary sputtered in disbelief.

"Looters set it on fire. It's closed," the driver said.

Perhaps sensing our desperation, the paramedic quickly added, "I think the VA is still open."

"Please, would you take us there?" I pleaded.

The driver thumbed toward the passenger door. "Put the patient up front. You can ride in back."

After we helped Crane into the cab, I sent Gary back to our boat to make sure the driver waited. Once the deputy was admitted to the hospital, I did not want to have to swim two miles back to the jail.

The bed of the deuce-and-a-half stood high off the ground, and we drove to the VA hospital in minutes. The emergency room entrance was at the top of a ramp, and the ground was dry. The paramedic and I got Major Crane down from the cab, and just before I entered the hospital, I asked the National Guardsmen to wait to take me back to the boat.

The electronic doors opened at our approach. The waiting room was brightly lit and completely empty. No clerks sat at the admitting desks, so I guided Crane to a chair and walked through a set of doors into the treatment area. Several medical personnel in scrubs sat behind the nursing station, talking or playing cards. Sweaty and filthy, I was struck by how well scrubbed they all were. For a moment, no one acknowledged my presence.

Finally, a nurse looked up. "Can I help you?"

"I'm a doctor from the sheriff's office," I said. "I brought in a deputy who may be having a heart attack."

"Sorry," a man said. "We're closed."

"Administration instructed us not to take any more patients," a nurse explained.

Shocked, I restated the facts. Obviously they could not have understood me. "You have to admit this man. He may be having a heart attack!"

"I'll get the physician in charge." The nurse shot me an annoyed look as she stood up and disappeared around the corner. Her colleagues resumed playing cards while I waited.

Three awkward minutes later, the woman returned with a doctor. "We're closed," he said bluntly.

Struggling to control my rising anger, I identified myself again slowly, but with an edge, "I'm Dr. Inglese with the sheriff's office." I explained that the jail's medical facilities were incapable of handling a cardiac patient.

"I understand," the physician said patiently, "but Administration won't let us admit anyone. You'll have to take him back."

I lost it.

"*Listen . . .*" I unleashed my fury on the doctor. "This man is having a heart attack. The jail has no power—no lights, no equipment, nothing. The buildings are flooded, and we have limited medications. We can't do *anything* for him there!"

The doctor glared back at me, but before he could say a word, I continued my tirade.

"You have this clean, well-lit, fully equipped emergency room, and all these doctors and nurses . . ."—I swept both arms out—"who are doing nothing but playing cards, and you're telling me to take him back?"

I had everyone's attention as I continued. "I'll *tell* you what's going to happen. You're going to treat him. I'm going to leave him here, and you're going to treat him."

"You can't leave him here." The physician in charge, obviously accustomed to being obeyed, matched my attitude and tone. He, however, had not been trudging through flooded streets all day, taking care of patients with nothing but a penlight and a prayer.

"And I'm telling you, I'm leaving, and he's staying." My eyes narrowed as I glanced at his name tag and then scanned the rest of the staff. "I want all of your names, and if you don't treat him, I'm going to give your names to the sheriff and the sheriff's lawyers, and you'll have more trouble than you ever imagined."

There was absolute silence for a moment, and then I added loudly, "I am *not* kidding."

A dark-haired nurse in her thirties suddenly got up and came toward me. She threw a disgusted look at the doctor. "I don't care what Administration says, I'm not going to let someone die in our emergency room." She paused at the door and motioned to one of her colleagues. "Come help me."

"Thank you so much," I said as the two women went past me into the waiting room.

Within a minute, they had returned with Crane, laid him on an exam table, and placed an oxygen mask over his face. As the nurses began hooking him up to bedside monitors, I took his EKG out of my pocket.

"This is the tracing we did an hour ago." I handed the paper to the nurses, explaining the patient's history. After listing the medications we had administered, I said good-bye to the deputy. He was receiving the care he needed, and I had to get back to the jail.

I stepped out of the hospital doors and looked around. The National Guard truck was gone.

Chapter 25

Traipsing the streets with Gary and Major Crane had been tough, but walking through unfamiliar terrain alone, with only one flashlight and knowing that the city was disintegrating around me, would be infinitely harder. Even more troubling, the trek would take a long time—a very long time—and I wasn't sure the boat would wait.

Another gunshot exploded in the distance, adding to my dread as I waded into the street. There were many possible explanations for the gunfire: police apprehending lawbreakers, stranded people trying to attract attention, idiots having misguided fun, or criminals looting the crippled city. Now, in addition to the hazards hidden in the flood, I had to worry about bullets.

To save time, I decided to cut through the Charity Hospital grounds. The medical facility was a collection of buildings, landscaped terraces, and walkways that spanned a city block. That decision was a big mistake. I painfully discovered that every outside area was booby trapped with submerged bushes, parking curbs, garden walls, fallen trees, and building debris. Instead of shortening the trip, the detour through the obstacle-filled maze turned what should have been a ten-minute walk into a half hour. And I was no longer out in the open.

The dark passages between buildings heightened my sense of imminent danger. I moved as fast as possible, ignoring collisions that came with increasing frequency and the cuts and scrapes on my arms and legs. I had the sensation of being followed, and every shadow had an air of menace. My mind transformed imagined threats into real terrors, like a child's primal fear of the dark.

By the time I emerged onto the street again, I was on the verge of panic. When I didn't see the boat, I plowed through the thigh-high water, yelling, "Gary! Gary!"

I couldn't hear his muffled call until I slowed down.

"Dem? Is that you?"

"Yes!" I charged forward, overjoyed to know that the boat was still there.

I relaxed once I was back aboard, and while Gary and I scanned the floodwaters for hidden dangers, I recounted what had gone on at the VA hospital.

Gary and the deputy were both furious.

"How could doctors just ignore a sick patient sitting in their waiting room?" Gary asked. "We should sue." He stared at the water. "We really are alone in this."

Communications were down; hospitals were closed; the police wouldn't stop. And medical staffs had to be threatened to help critically ill patients. What would happen to us at the jail?

Before Katrina hit, I had assumed the jail would be an evacuation priority. Now, given the devastation in the city and our inmate population, we probably weren't even on anyone's radar screen. Surrounded by water, the New Orleans jail had become a forgotten island, cut off from support. Whatever was to come, the jail staff would have to face it alone.

Gary lapsed into a depressed silence. My reaction to our circumstances was just the opposite. I thrived under pressure, especially in a crisis. During an emergency—when I worked in the intensive care unit, for example, when every second counted and every decision was crucial—I was at my best. Yes, our situation was grave, but I would deal with it.

The deputy left us on the steps of the Correctional Center. As we climbed up to the porch, the building was dark, and I realized the generators had finally failed. The lobby would have been pitch black except for deputies with flashlights.

"It's after eleven," Gary said as we headed toward Chief Hunter's office. "He's probably asleep."

"Then we'll wake him up." A film of sewage covered our skin, and I had no intention of going to bed without a shower. I was sure the chief wouldn't mind losing a little sleep to help me out.

Lucky started barking the instant we opened the door. The black, white, and brown terrier was vicious. He hated everyone but Hunter, and I was glad he was locked in his crate.

"Who's there?" Hunter grunted, waking up. He yelled at the dog to be quiet, but Lucky didn't shut up until Gary and I left with the keys to the shower.

Exhausted and emotionally drained, Gary and I just wanted to clean up and crash. We took turns in the cold shower, one of us washing while the other held a flashlight. I returned the keys to Hunter, then met Gary back in Medical Administration. He had packed some food to take upstairs to our sleeping space in Infection Control.

I wanted to talk to my parents, but my cell phone had died hours earlier. I tried my office phone. Though service was down between buildings, some outside calls were still going through.

I was thrilled when my mother picked up. Her voice quivered with relief and happiness when she heard my voice. Assured that I was fine, she handed the phone to my father, and I briefly recounted events of the day. My parents had been watching the news, and they told me that Gulfport and Biloxi had both been flattened by massive storm surges and wind. The news about Mississippi hit me hard. I had been stationed there for three years and still had friends in the area. But I was staggered when my dad said CNN was reporting that New Orleans had come through the hurricane relatively unscathed.

"They've got cameras and reporters at the Oceana Bar in the French Quarter. Part of the roof blew off the Superdome, but people are celebrating on Bourbon Street."

"New Orleans isn't okay, Dad. It's destroyed. The whole city is under water."

It took my father a moment to absorb the information. "Is it really that bad?" he asked.

"New Orleans is dead," I said, describing what I'd seen, though minimizing the danger I felt all around. I didn't want to add to his worries.

"What did your parents say?" Gary asked on our way upstairs.

"They told me the media is showing people partying on Bourbon Street."

"Well, I hope they figure out what's really going on soon," Gary added as he unlocked the door to Infection Control, "because someone has to get us out of here."

We crawled into our makeshift beds on the floor. As I closed my eyes, I drifted off to the violent sounds of inmates screaming and banging on their cells.

Tuesday, August 30, 2005

The Third Day

Chapter 26

Early morning:
CNN reports that the levee on the 17th Street Canal has
  been breached, causing extensive flooding.
Warden Gary Bordelon and Major Chuck Jones use a sledgehammer and crowbar to free inmates trapped in cells on
  the flooded first floor of Templeman 3.
Rioting in Templeman 3 has escalated, and several inmates
  have broken out of their cells.
At 5 a.m. the jail phone system goes down.

Driven by fear, Nurse Chuck Perotto struggled to keep up with
Dr. Victor Tuckler as they rushed out of Templeman 3 shortly
past midnight after treating a patient there. Wading through the
waist-high water and debris was difficult for both men, but Chuck's
prosthetic foot made the task much more cumbersome. His arti-
ficial limb had no feeling, and he relied on sight to search for
and secure solid footing. Even with a flashlight, Chuck couldn't
see beneath the water, and he stumbled every few steps. For him,
losing his visual references was the same as a blind man losing
his sense of hearing.

Stumbling again, Chuck almost fell. Hopping slightly, he managed a last-second save, then paused to catch his breath and pull
himself together. The nurse had never been so scared. The thought
of falling into the water sickened him, but that wasn't why he
was terrified. The Templeman 3 inmates were rioting.

"I think I see the door," Victor said, shining his flashlight down the corridor and quickening his pace.

A surge of angry shouts and metal banging against cell doors nearly drowned out Victor's voice. Spurred on by the noise from the inmate tiers, Chuck tried to speed up, eager to get back to the safety of the temporary infirmary.

The sounds of unrest hadn't bothered Chuck on the way into the facility, but that was before he knew inmates were loose. An unknown number of men had broken into the pipe chases—narrow crawl spaces throughout the building that housed the plumbing. Others had climbed to the roof of adjacent Templeman 4. Deputies had confined the inmates to those areas but had not yet fully secured them. Meanwhile, the hostility among the hundreds of prisoners still incarcerated on the tiers was escalating, and more could break out at any time. Some of the prisoners were trying to kick their cell doors off track, and others were setting fire to anything that would burn.

Chuck wasn't a coward, but he wasn't a fool, either. A desperate criminal wouldn't think twice about attacking anyone who stood in the way of escape. Inmates usually showed medical staff some minimal deference, but that had evaporated with the loss of electricity and the rising water. They didn't know or care that the nurses and doctors were stranded at the jail, too.

And doing everything we can to keep them healthy, Chuck thought. He and Victor had come to help an inmate with end-stage kidney failure who was having trouble breathing. The man required dialysis to keep fluid out of his lungs, but the impending storm had interfered with his hospital appointment the previous Saturday. The patient would miss today's session, too, because of the flooding.

Chuck also worried that if the patient had to evacuate through contaminated floodwater, his dialysis port—the flexible tubing that carried blood to the dialysis machine—could become infected. That was no trivial matter. Infection could rapidly spread to the bloodstream and become a life-threatening complication.

As they approached the exit, the deputy posted at the door asked, "Everything all right in medical?"

"They're doing the best they can, but some of the patients need a hospital," Victor said, "which is where I should be."

It wasn't Victor's fault he had been stranded at the jail. Chuck knew the doctor felt guilty about missing his shift at the ER and leaving the Charity Hospital staff short-handed. But nothing was going according to their disaster plans.

Glancing back down the dark corridor, Chuck thought about the nurses they had left behind in Templeman 3—all women and many of them friends. The deputies had told the staff that a massive breakout was imminent, and they should find weapons and barricade the door. Chuck and Victor had not been comfortable leaving, but they were needed back in the infirmary and had reluctantly decided to go. As the two men walked out, the frightened nurses had armed themselves with scalpels and locked the clinic door.

Another near-fall jolted Chuck back to the present and thoughts of the infirmary. The water was getting deep, and there was no communication with the outside. A timely rescue seemed unlikely. In all probability, the jail staff would have to evacuate patients without assistance.

Many inmates suffered from serious medical conditions that could easily deteriorate if exposed to sewage-tainted floodwater. One man had just undergone bypass surgery and had a fragile heart and an open wound. Another suffered from severe, debilitating anxiety. And how would Security get the 400-pound paraplegic out of the jail without infecting his bed sores or having him drown?

For that matter, Chuck realized as he scanned the chain link on both sides of the outdoor walkway, how would *anyone* get out if the water rose above the first floor? Every window was barred. They would be trapped inside the building—with 1,500 panicked inmates.

Dread gripped Chuck as he and Victor entered the claustrophobic hallway in Templeman 1. His leg muscles ached from the grueling trip. When Chief Belisle stopped them outside his flooded office, Chuck welcomed the chance to rest.

"Have you heard anything about Major Crane?" the warden asked. "Did Dr. Inglese get him to the hospital?"

"We haven't heard from Dr. Inglese since he left," Chuck answered.

"I'm sure he'll be fine," Victor said, moving on before the warden could detain them longer. The doctor paused when they reached the stairs, and he aimed his flashlight upward. "The water's higher than when we left."

And still rising, Chuck thought as he climbed above the water line. At least he could see his footing again, which made walking easier.

The temporary infirmary was quiet and dark. A few patients rested on the floor. Most of the staff had fallen asleep. One nurse sat propped in a corner, reading a paperback book with a penlight. Dr. Gore had dozed off sitting in a wheelchair.

"I'm going to make a quick pass through the room in case someone needs anything," Victor said. "Get some rest, Chuck."

"I'll try." As Chuck moved along the wall, he spotted Scarlett Maness hunched over a large, battery-powered lantern. She appeared to be writing on her arm. Curious, he walked over. "What are you doing?"

Scarlett answered with chilling bluntness. "I want to make sure they know who I am when they find my body."

Chuck's mouth fell open. The nurse had written her name, phone number, and social security number on her arm and scrub top with permanent marker. She thinks she's going to die, he realized.

Flustered, Chuck fumbled for something positive to say, but he had to settle for a half-truth. "Dr. Tuckler and I were just outside. The water's not that high. We'll be fine."

"Maybe." Scarlett began writing on her other arm.

Wet, weary, and scared, Chuck found a dry space on the floor, but he was too tense to sleep. At every rustle, snore, and groan, he snapped to attention. He welcomed the distraction when Denise Sarro came in and began rummaging through the medication bins.

"What's the problem?" he whispered to the nurse, who was staying with the female infirmary patients on the third floor.

"A hysterical inmate." Denise rolled her eyes. "She drove me crazy all night long last night, and I'm not going through that again tonight!"

"How bad is it up there?" Chuck asked.

"It's a zoo." Denise found the bottle of meds she was looking for. "There are no lights and no food. It's a million degrees, and the women haven't had much to drink all day. They're all packed in a large holding cell, and they were acting up so bad SID had to come settle them down. They threatened to grab a nurse if we came in to pass pills."

"What did you do?" Chuck asked.

"The other nurses were too afraid to pass meds," Denise answered, "but I wasn't going to let that bullshit stop *me*. I went right in there and handed out pills."

"You did not." Chuck just stared at her.

"I did too!" Denise answered defiantly. "And the whole time they were yelling, 'Give us some damn water!' Finally, I'd had enough. So I marched right up to them and said, 'I don't have no damn water my damn self! Where the hell do you think I'm going to get water! Now go to sleep.'"

Chuck laughed. He had known Denise for a long time, and she never ceased to amaze him. Despite her crusty demeanor, she really cared for her patients. Her story dispelled some of his worry, but he still couldn't sleep. He was awake when Duane Townzel returned to the infirmary at two in the morning.

Duane had spent the past several hours working with the sheriff's Search and Rescue team. He had brought his scuba gear back with him.

As Duane set the two tanks against the wall, Chuck's tension finally eased. A strong swimmer with scuba experience, Chuck knew he would be able to make it out of the building with the gear. And with Duane's help, they could get all the staff out, too.

"Are those tanks full?" Chuck asked.

"Pretty much." Duane stretched out on the floor nearby.

"Are they still rioting at Templeman 3?" Chuck asked. "They made the nurses lock themselves in the clinic around midnight."

"Security moved the nurses to the House of Detention thirty minutes ago." Duane rolled onto his side facing Chuck and propped his head on his hand. "They had an easier trip than Dr. Dileo did."

"What happened to Dr. Dileo?" Chuck asked, concerned. He was surprised when the other nurse laughed softly.

"My driver and I were in a boat near the Intake Center when Dr. Dileo came out a side door," Duane explained, "so we offered to take him to Detention. We went about twenty feet, and the motor just stopped. So Dileo had to get out of the boat and walk."

Chuck didn't understand why that was funny, but he didn't interrupt.

"Turns out there was a blanket wrapped around our propeller," Duane went on. "After we got it loose, we caught up with the doctor again in front of Intake. Dileo was just standing at the entrance, gawking through the door."

"Why?" Chuck asked.

"Well . . ." Duane paused to smother another laugh, "because Deputy Joe Keller wasn't where he was supposed to be—*behind* the information desk. He was on *top* of the information desk. It was bobbing on the water, and he was holding on for dear life. He called to Dileo to come rescue him."

"What?" Chuck gasped. "Keller must weigh five hundred pounds!"

"I know." Duane cleared his throat. "So Dr. Dileo tells the guy, 'I'm five-four, forty-nine years old, and up to my armpits in water! I can barely save myself!'"

Chuck cracked up.

"While we helped Keller, poor Dr. Dileo had to walk to Detention," Duane finished.

Chuck was still laughing when the other nurse rolled over to catch a few hours' rest. The story perfectly illustrated the absurdity of the situation at the jail. Several thousand people—deputies, civilians, and criminals—had been cast into circumstances so bizarre it was hard to believe they weren't dreaming.

But we *aren't* dreaming, Chuck thought as he tried to get comfortable. We're in a nightmare.

He fell asleep staring at the scuba gear.

Chapter 27

Chuck woke up lying in a puddle of water. His green scrubs were wet and reeked of sewage. Revolted, he scrambled to his feet.

The roof was leaking, too, Chuck realized, as he saw Duane Townzel drag a trash bag of supplies clear of a leak in the ceiling. He took the bag over to Scarlett and Lillian Ford, who were sorting supplies. Chuck started toward them as Duane grabbed another bag.

"Did they piss on this one, too?" Lillian asked. She grimaced as Duane handed her the bag.

"They pissed on everything." Scarlett raised a soggy pack of medications between her thumb and forefinger. Liquid dripped from the edges.

Stunned, Chuck stopped and looked up at the ceiling. The infirmary patients housed above them were dropping trash through an open space in the ceiling. As he watched, a stream of yellow fluid poured through.

"Why would they pee on us?" Chuck wondered with disgust. "We're here to help them."

Lillian's bawdy humor came out. "I guess they don't know they're pissing on their own drugs."

"Morning, Chuck." Duane smiled. "Sleep well?"

"Finally—but I wish I hadn't woken up to this," Chuck said, shaking his head. "Where's Dr. Gore?"

"Downstairs." Duane yanked another bag out of the target zone before one more inmate relieved himself. "After I told him what happened to me last night, he went to speak to the officers."

"Did something else happen?" Chuck pulled another bag clear.

"Yes," Duane nodded. "Before I got back and.talked to you last night, I heard this loud crash and a splash in the walkway outside."

Chuck raised an eyebrow. "What was it?"

"I couldn't see for a moment, but when I did"—Duane paused for effect—"two loose inmates were just getting to their feet. I don't know how they got free, but they were jumping from one roof to another. When they hit the walkway roof, the tin broke and they fell through."

Astounded, Chuck tried to picture two escapees crashing through the walkway roof into a cesspool of flood and sewer water. "Then what?"

"We kind of stared at each other for a minute, and then I ran like hell the other way." Duane was not apologetic. "I can handle myself, but I wasn't sure I could fight two of them in water up to my ass. So I grabbed a deputy from Templeman 3, but by the time we got back, the inmates were gone."

"They got out of the building?" Chuck asked

"I don't know. We lost them in the dark." Duane shrugged. "That's why Dr. Gore went to see the warden. He wants all the staff here when he gets back."

Chuck helped Duane lug bags while the other nurses took an inventory and repacked everything that was still useable.

By the time Sam Gore returned, the third-floor nurses were coming into the infirmary. When all fifteen staff members were present, he got right to the point.

"We've got big problems," the doctor began. "The water's still rising, and it's getting deep. There have been escapes in Templeman 3, and they've been moving inmates around Templeman 1 and 2 all night. So there might be inmates loose in here as well."

"Do you really think so?" Lillian asked.

Chuck listened intently. The doctor wasn't prone to hysteria, and he never jumped to unwarranted conclusions. If he thought there was reason to worry, there was reason to worry.

"Yeah, I ran into a group being moved," Sam explained. "The

inmates weren't handcuffed, and it would have been easy for one to slip away. All they had to do was duck under the water, under a desk, or into a side passage. No one would have seen."

"Inmates are loose in *this* building?" Pebles Jones's voice quivered. The nurse was a minister's wife and hadn't worked at the jail very long.

"For safety's sake, we have to assume so," Sam replied. "They are definitely rioting on the third floor."

"SID has been in and out all night," Denise said. "We need to get out of here."

"Except," Sam went on, "the officers have no plans to evacuate."

"What are they waiting for?" Pebles asked, scowling.

"I don't know. That's why I'm making the call." Sam slowly scanned the worried faces watching him. "We're going to swim to the Correctional Center." The building was a couple of blocks away.

"I can't," Tracy Nichols gasped, her eyes wide with panic. The tiny nurse's outburst shocked everyone. She was always one the rest of the staff could rely on to pick up the slack. Nothing ever seemed too hard for her to tackle.

Chuck had never seen her look so terrified.

"There's nothing to discuss, Tracy," Sam said evenly. "We've done a lot for the infirmary inmates, but we're not going to die for them. We're leaving—now."

Tracy started shaking. "But I can't swim."

"Neither can I," said Vera Brumfield, another nurse. "Not very well."

"That's not a problem," Duane quickly interjected. "I rescue people who can't swim all the time. We'll get you all out safely. Promise."

"Definitely," Chuck said. "I'm a good swimmer, too."

"So am I," Denise added.

Nodding, Tracy folded her arms across her chest. She wasn't happy, but she trusted Duane.

"What about the patients?" Denise pointed upstairs. "Some of those guys can't even walk. There's no way they're swimming out of here."

"And what about the families upstairs?" Eddie Williams, one of the male nurses, chimed in.

"I'm sure the deputies will look after their families," Sam said. "I don't want you worrying about *anything* except getting out." Dr. Gore's tone was stern. "I'll swim over to the Correctional Center ahead of you and tell the sheriff what's going on. I'll let him know the building needs to be evacuated—infirmary patients first."

"Should we take some of this stuff with us?" Lillian motioned toward the trash bags full of medications and supplies.

"No." Sam shook his head. "You'll need your hands free to swim and to help the people who can't. Getting yourselves out is your *only* priority. Understood?"

"Works for me," Scarlett said.

Several pairs of eyes flicked to the writing on Scarlett's arms and clothes, but no one mentioned it.

Sam smiled tightly. "Then I'll see you at the Correctional Center."

As the physician turned to leave, Pebles Jones said, "We need to pray."

No one objected. Linking hands, Dr. Gore, Dr. Tuckler, and the nurses bowed their heads.

Pebles spoke in a clear, steady voice. "Thank you, Lord, for watching over us. Guide our steps and keep us safe. Amen."

Moving away from the group, Sam pulled out his cell phone and dialed. Chuck noticed the doctor's surprised expression when the call went through.

"Lisa, it's me." Sam paused briefly. "I just wanted you to know I'm all right. Everything's flooded, but we're going to swim to the Correctional Center. We'll be fine. I love you. Tell the kids I love them, and I'll see them soon. . . . Lisa?"

Sighing when he lost the connection, Sam snapped the phone closed. He hesitated, then opened it again and pulled up a picture of his children. He stared at them for a moment and blinked back tears before closing the cell phone and putting it in his pocket.

The scene shook Chuck's composure. The unflappable doctor rarely showed emotion. His distress emphasized the seriousness of their circumstances.

Lillian walked up and put her arms around Sam. "Everything's going to be fine, Dr. Gore. You'll see. You just get to the Correctional Center and let them know what's happening over here."

Sam returned the hug and left. Denise and the third-floor nurses headed out the door behind him.

"Where are you going?" Duane stepped into the hall with his scuba tank and gear already strapped to his back.

"To get our things upstairs," Denise snapped.

"Dr. Gore said no things!" Duane protested.

Denise stopped and turned around. "We have to get some stuff, Duane. We'll need ID and ATM cards—money—when we're evacuated. We'll be right back."

When the nurses hadn't returned in five minutes, Duane turned to Chuck. "The longer Tracy has to think about this, the harder it's going to be. Let's get this group out, and I'll come back for the others."

"Good idea." Chuck glanced at Tracy. The frightened nurse was shaking and breathing in short, quick gasps, but she pushed herself past Chuck and into the hall to join Duane, who waited with half a dozen other nurses.

Victor Tuckler ran across the room and picked up his red backpack. Pebles grabbed her black one and slipped it over her small shoulders as she raced out.

Anxious to get going, Duane waved the group to follow him down the stairs.

Chuck called to Scarlett. "Let's go, Scarlett!"

"In a minute." The nurse was going through her things, apparently in no hurry to leave.

"Scarlett, c'mon!" Annoyed, Chuck watched Duane and the group move down the stairs and out of sight. The glow of their flashlights dimmed, then disappeared.

"Go on," Scarlett said. "I'll stay here and wait for the others until Duane comes back."

"Okay." Lifting the second scuba tank, Chuck switched on his flashlight and walked out of the temporary infirmary.

It was 6:30 a.m.

Chapter 28

Chuck caught up with the group before they reached the outside door. The water was almost up to Tracy's chin, and they were moving very slowly.

"What's that?" Tracy's voice cracked with fear at the sight of some large object in the water. It was still pitch-black inside the building. The beam of her flashlight panned wildly back and forth.

"It's just a laundry bin," Duane said. "I have an idea. Tracy, you get to ride." He clamped on to the top edge of the floating cart and pulled it closer.

Tracy stretched to peer inside. "I can't get in there."

"It's the only way," Duane said softly. "The water gets deeper outside, and you won't be able to walk much farther." Before she could protest, he picked her up and set her inside. The cart wobbled precariously.

Squealing, Tracy grabbed on to the sides.

"Sit!" Duane ordered.

Petrified, Tracy slowly sat down and wrapped her arms around her knees. The early morning air was warm and muggy, but she shivered uncontrollably.

Slinging the air tank over one shoulder, Chuck grabbed the end of the cart to keep it from tipping over. He held it steady while Duane and Lillian helped Vera, the other non-swimmer, inside. She sat behind Tracy, cradling the smaller woman between her legs.

The dread that had dogged the group through the darkness didn't abate when they moved into the gray light of sunrise. The stench of diesel fuel leaking from storage tanks and the rancid smell of rotting food was nauseating. One of the women gagged. Someone else grumbled, but no one hung back. Holding his backpack high in the air, Victor tried to calm Tracy as he and Chuck pulled the laundry cart through the flooded walkway.

Suddenly Chuck stumbled, and the motion caused the cart to rock. Startled, Tracy screamed and jerked, which made the rocking worse. Behind her, Vera did her best to calm the other woman.

"You have to stay calm, Tracy," Victor said gently.

"I can't swim," Tracy retorted through strangled cries.

At the junction of the T-shaped walkway, Duane turned left toward the Intake Center. The building faced the jail's kitchen and warehouse, which were directly behind the Correctional Center.

As they moved past the halfway mark, Lillian pointed toward a gate on the left. "Can we get out there?"

"That gate's locked," Duane said. "Just keep going. We're almost there."

A moment later, Pebles glanced up. "Look at that! The storm tore a big hole in the roof."

Chuck caught Duane's eye. Neither explained that escaping inmates had fallen through there the night before.

When the group entered the Intake Center, Chuck saw the information desk adrift in the large room, but Deputy Keller was no longer on top of it. A mass of plastic soda bottles, papers, and floating foam chairs filled the water's surface. Chuck grabbed one of the seats to ferry his scuba tank. Lillian reached for a second chair to use as her own flotation device.

Duane made a quick inspection of the room. Satisfied that no inmates were lurking under the water, he announced, "I'm going to get the others. You'll be okay here till I get back."

"Don't be long, honey," Lillian cooed, joking to relieve the tension.

All eyes followed Duane to the door. His strength and rescue expertise had given everyone a sense of security, and the nurses were visibly unnerved when he moved out of sight.

For the first few minutes, the group waited patiently. Lillian rested on her foam-chair life preserver. Pebles discovered that her waterproof backpack floated. Victor leaned against the wall holding his pack clear of the flood. Chuck steadied the cart with Tracy and Vera inside.

After a nerve-racking twenty minutes, Pebles asked, "What's taking Duane so long?"

"Maybe we should go on ahead," Victor suggested.

Chuck agreed. Getting restless, too, he waded to the entrance and pushed on the door, but it wouldn't open against the pressure of the water. Grunting, Chuck pushed again, then again. Victor added his weight, but the door wouldn't budge.

"We'll have to go through the booking area and out the garage," Chuck said.

Floating the air tank in front of him, Chuck moved to a door across the room. It led to the large room where new arrestees were booked in to jail. From there he thought they could eventually make their way out of the building.

Chuck punched the buttons to unlock the door, but nothing happened. He tried a second and a third time with no success. In frustration, he ran a hand over his sweaty, shaved head. "We've got a problem."

Tracy looked stricken.

"There's got to be a way out," Lillian insisted.

"There is," Chuck said reluctantly. "We have to go through Templeman 3." He knew the inmates had been rioting in the building for hours, but there didn't seem to be any other option.

"If that's what we have to do to get out of here, fine," Pebles said, convinced.

"Let's go," Lillian said, throwing an arm around her foam chair and dragging it with her.

No one spoke as the group retraced its steps to the junction of the T-shaped walkway. When they turned left toward Templeman 3, Sam Gore's words echoed in Chuck's mind like a dire prediction: "All they had to do was duck under the water, under a desk, or into a side passage. No one would have seen."

At the entrance, Chuck pounded on the door to get the guard's attention. "Let us in," he yelled.

"You can't come through here," the deputy yelled back. "They're rioting."

"But we can't get out through Intake," Chuck insisted. "The doors are locked."

"I've got my orders." The deputy was sympathetic, but unyielding. "There're inmates loose, and it's too dangerous. Nobody comes in, and nobody gets out."

Sagging, Chuck waved the group to move back down the outside walkway. Even if the deputy relented, they'd be foolish to risk a confrontation with desperate escapees.

"We're trapped, aren't we?" Lillian asked. Nothing had flustered her all morning, but she looked terrified now.

Chapter 29

Chuck Perotto shared Lillian Ford's fear. The water was still rising around the Templeman complex, and there were no more exits. Chuck was shaking, but he had to keep the others calm. "Let's go back toward the infirmary and find Duane," he said. "He'll know what to do."

The vote was unanimous. Even Tracy preferred moving to standing still and doing nothing. However, she screamed every time the cart lurched.

There was no sign of Duane and the second group of nurses as they approached Templeman 1. Instead they saw Chief Rudy Belisle in the walkway, wading slowly toward them, neck deep in water. Suddenly the warden turned to the right. A wide roll-up gate in the chain-link fence was open.

"That wasn't unlocked before." Lillian glared at the opening.

"I didn't see it," Pebles said, "but it was kind of dark."

"Doesn't matter," Victor Tuckler said. "It's open now."

"You okay, Chief?" Lillian eyed the aging warden with concern as the group followed him through the gate.

"I'm fine," Belisle mumbled.

"Which way?" Victor asked.

A twenty-foot cement wall surrounded the entire Templeman complex. The flooded alley between the buildings and the wall resembled the moat around a medieval castle.

"Left," Chuck said. The most direct route was to circle around

Templeman 4 and Templeman 3 until they reached an exit gate onto the street. He led the way, pushing the foam chair that held his air tank.

Tracy started to shriek again as the laundry cart bobbed in the floodwater, and her panicked movement made it rock even harder. Victor grabbed the cart's edge to hold it steady.

"Just shut up and close your eyes and pray," Lillian snapped at the younger woman. "You know the Lord. Now just shut up and pray."

"Amen," Pebles added.

As they moved behind Templeman 4, Chuck nervously glanced up. He couldn't see any inmates on the roof, but the next five minutes seemed five times that long. No sooner had they cleared that building and rounded the far corner of Templeman 3 than the water took on an oily orange hue.

"What is this?" Pebles asked, wrinkling her nose.

"Diesel fuel." Chuck's nostrils flared with the sharp smell. Two storage tanks were leaking fuel, and an orange film covered the water. The diesel clung to their clothes and stung fresh scratches and cuts.

Suddenly, Lillian shrieked in fear.

"What's the matter?" Pebles stopped dead.

"Snake!" Lillian pointed with a shaky hand.

Pebles started moving backward. "Is it poisonous?"

Victor stopped abruptly, causing the laundry cart with the two nurses to dip violently to one side. Both Tracy and Vera shrieked as the doctor struggled to keep them from tipping over. Lillian grabbed the other side to help.

"Make it go away! I hate snakes." Tracy jiggled nervously, on the verge of tears.

"What are you worried about, Tracy?" Pebles held her arms close to her chest, her eyes never leaving the seven-inch snake sliding slowly through the water. "You're riding in that plastic thing!"

"If somebody doesn't catch that snake, we're going to *really* freak out," Lillian said, positioning the foam chair between her body and the reptile.

"I'll get it." Chuck snatched a plastic bottle floating nearby, then grabbed the small snake and dropped it inside. He set the bottle adrift. "Harmless."

"It is now," Lillian said.

"Forget the snake," Victor said. "The gates are closed."

Everyone turned to look down the wide drive. The massive gates at the exit to the street were closed. Chuck frowned. Closed gates meant locked gates.

"We're trapped—aren't we?" Pebles asked softly.

"No, the garage is open." Chuck pointed toward a wide open door ahead and to the left. The covered garage was attached to the Intake Center and also opened to the street. It was the same garage they had tried to reach from the inside.

Chuck plowed through the oily water, still pushing the foam chair and air tank. The garage entrance was blocked by a traffic jam of partially submerged cars and trucks.

"We'll have to climb over these cars to get through"—Chuck paused—"but the laundry cart won't fit."

Tracy glanced around frantically. "I'm not getting out of this cart."

"You are if you're going with us," Lillian said. "And there's no point putting it off."

Chuck wedged the foam chairs and scuba tank between two cars to keep them from floating away. Then he waded to the laundry cart and helped Lillian pull the plastic bin with the two women over to the first patrol car.

Tracy huddled in the bottom of the cart, shivering and sobbing, while Chuck helped Vera climb out and onto the hood of the vehicle, which was a couple of inches below the water. He stayed with her as she moved to the next car in line. She waited on the roof of an SUV while Chuck went back for Tracy.

"Okay, Tracy." Chuck braced himself for a panic attack. "Your turn."

Eyes wide, Tracy vigorously shook her head and started to scream. The high-pitched bursts made it impossible to hear anyone else talk.

"Stop all that damn screaming!" Lillian's eyes flashed. "The good Lord didn't get you this far to let you die now."

"I'm scared." Tracy cringed into a corner of the cart. "I can't do it."

Chuck realized that, unless the woman was faced with something worse, they'd never get her out of the cart. "Then stay here, Tracy. C'mon, Lillian."

"You're just going to leave me?" Tracy gasped.

"Not if you get out of that damn cart." Lillian was done coddling her, and Tracy knew it. The frightened woman held out her hands.

Chuck and Lillian lifted Tracy onto the patrol car. While Chuck coaxed Tracy and Vera across the line of cars, Lillian helped Pebles get started.

As the nurses crawled on hands and knees or inched along on their stomachs, Chuck picked up the laundry cart and threw it over the cars as far as he could. Scrambling after it, he heaved it clear of the blockade. When Tracy and Vera reached the end, he helped them back into the plastic bin while Pebles steadied it, and then Chuck scooted back across the cars for Lillian and Belisle.

"You and Chief Rudy ready?" Chuck asked after he heaved the two foam chairs over the cars as well. When Lillian nodded, he set the air tank on the patrol car and climbed up. He took hold of the warden's arm, and Lillian helped the elderly man up from behind.

While Chuck guided the warden onto the next car in line, Lillian climbed up and waited for Victor, who was bringing up the rear.

Holding his backpack over his head, the doctor slipped on the oily metal and almost fell into the water. He yelped as he caught himself and safely climbed onto the hood, still holding his pack.

"What are you protecting in that bag?" Lillian asked him.

Chuck was curious, too. Victor seemed as terrified of getting his backpack wet as Tracy was of drowning.

"I've got the pictures of Lily's birth and her first few months," the doctor explained, referring to his baby daughter. "They're the only things I took from my house."

Chuck smiled. Victor and his wife had tried for a very long time to have a child. They had just about given up hope when they found out they were expecting. Lily was their miracle. No wonder Victor treated the backpack like gold.

The stragglers helped each other crawl from one car to the next. When everyone had made it through and gathered at the garage exit, Chuck thought the worst was over. He could see the kitchen 200 feet down the driveway and across the street. They would be able to walk through that building to the back porch of the Correctional Center.

Lillian held on to one side of the laundry cart and Victor grasped the other as they all started toward the street. When Tracy started crying out again, Lillian rolled her eyes. "Chicken in a bucket," she declared. The other nurses chuckled.

The water deepened, and halfway down the sloping drive, Chuck tightened his hold on the foam chair and air tank. The street was a river of swift currents and churning rapids.

"Don't try it!" A deputy called over to them from the kitchen loading dock. "It's too deep!"

"We can't stay here!" Chuck shouted back, wondering where Duane and the rest of the nurses were.

"The road dips so much the water's over *my* head!" The deputy was six feet tall.

Turning away, Chuck set his jaw and gave Victor a pointed look. The water was too deep and the current too strong to risk using the unstable laundry cart. "Tracy first," he said. "We'll float her over on a chair."

"Here," Lillian said. "Use mine."

"Me? On that thing?" Tracy lost it. "No, no—I can't. Please, I . . ." She screamed, a full-throated cry of terror as Chuck pulled her out of the cart.

The water on the driveway was only waist deep. Chuck set Tracy on her feet and held on to the panicked woman as he spoke with a firm voice of authority. "You're going, Tracy, and you have to calm down. That's it. No discussion. Got it?"

"That's enough!" Lillian's annoyed "mother" voice penetrated the younger woman's fear. Tracy got quiet.

Gasping for air, Tracy let Chuck position her, stomach down, on the chair. She closed her eyes, and her fingers clamped the front edge.

"Paddle your feet, Tracy," Lillian instructed.

Chuck shoved off, holding on to Tracy and the chair. As they neared the point, the deputy by the kitchen jumped into the water and intercepted them. Chuck turned back while the young man finished ferrying Tracy across. The deputy left the nurse on the loading dock and swam back to help Chuck with the others. In the process, however, he lost his grip on the foam chair, and it was swept away in the current.

Chuck snagged a plastic garbage can lid from the water to use as a boogie board and turned to Vera. Flanked by Chuck and the deputy, she held on to the lid with her hands and kicked. When they reached the kitchen, the two men took a couple of minutes to recharge.

"My turn." Pebles shrugged off her backpack. Her hands were slick with diesel fuel, and the surging current tore the bag out of her grasp. She lunged for it, snatching the end of a strap and saving it from being carried away.

"I'm right behind you," Victor called as Pebles struck out, holding on to her backpack and kicking.

A strong swimmer, Pebles made steady progress. However, she couldn't fight the current. The deputy jumped back in to help before the rushing water took her too far. Victor held his backpack of pictures high over his head. At six feet tall, he could almost walk across, taking occasional bounces to get a breath.

When Chuck swam back to get Lillian and Chief Belisle, the nurse pointed out that he had to take Duane's scuba tank across first. They would both need their hands free to help the warden swim, and there was no safe place to leave the scuba gear.

"I'll wait here with Chief Rudy till you come back," Lillian said.

Chuck pulled the scuba tank and foam chair against his chest and kicked off across the street one more time. Exhausted, he was instantly pushed downstream, powerless to compensate for the current. The deputy appeared out of nowhere and pulled him back to the dock.

"Thanks," Chuck said, breathless. His legs shook from the exertion, and he needed a moment to recover. Doubled over with his hands on his knees, he looked up at the sound of a motor.

Two deputies in a boat pulled up to Lillian and the warden. One of the deputies hauled the old man into the boat, then they drove off—leaving a dumbfounded Lillian staring after them.

"What the hell was that?" Victor asked, astounded.

Chuck was just as amazed, but Lillian waited.

"Take a break, Chuck," the deputy said. "I'll get her."

With the tall deputy tugging on her scrubs, Lillian swam across the street. Chuck did not relax until the infirmary head nurse was safely on the dock.

"That wasn't so bad," Lillian said, smiling.

"I don't want to do it again!" Tracy laughed.

"You won't have to." Hoisting the air tank, Chuck looked at the loading dock doors. "The Correctional Center is right on the other side of the kitchen."

"And the water's only up to our knees!" Pebles exclaimed. She took a flashlight out of her backpack and turned it on to light their way through the dark building.

As the group filed inside, Lillian started singing. "Wade in the water . . . wade in the water, children. . ."

Roused by the old spiritual, everyone joined hands and sang as they walked to safety.

My friends and I in front of the Intake Center one year after the storm: doctors Gary French, me, Sam Gore, and Mike Higgins. (Lillian Ford)

The Correctional Center prior to evacuation; civilians and staff crowd the porch as a boat docks at the front steps. (Jim Beach)

A front view of the flooded Correctional Center after the evacuation was completed. (William Devlin)

The flooded street in front of the Correctional Center two days after Katrina hit. Debris and diesel fuel float on the water; the DA's office and flooded parking lot are visible in the distance. (Sam Gore)

The DA's lot after the water receded; water lines are visible on the abandoned vehicles. (John Netto)

The back porch of the Correctional Center. Families and staff camped on blankets under the overhang for five days. The area became crowded with local residents and deputies from other buildings. (Sam Gore)

Food and water were stored and rationed from an area on the back porch.
(William Devlin)

Some of the medical staff: (*top row*) doctors Victor Tuckler and Sam Gore; (*bottom row*) nurses Chuck Perotto, Lillian Ford, and Kentrisha Davis.

Nurses Scarlatt Maness, Jan Ricca, and Denise Sarro.

The sallyport entrance into the basement of the Correctional Center; the driveway slopes down below street level.

The sallyport during the flood. (William Devlin)

The information desk in the front lobby of the Correctional Center. The open door to the fire escape stairwell on the left was where deputies and medical staff took position to stop rioting inmates.

The inmates broke through cinderblock walls to escape from tiers in the Correctional Center. (Jim Beach)

Security glass failed stop the inmates' advance. (John Netto)

As they escaped from the tiers, inmates demolished security control modules and ripped ductwork from the ceiling. Small inmates attempted to escape through the air ducts. (Jim Beach)

Correctional Center inmates tore through reinforced concrete to reach the fire escape stairwell. (Jim Beach)

When rioting inmates reached the roof, they painted messages on windows to signal for help: "Man Dead Help! Help Help." (Jim Beach)

Inmates painted messages on the roof to signal helicopters flying overhead: "Help! 4 Days Need Food."

Tulane Avenue during the hurricane. (David Skeins)

Tulane Avenue after the storm; the patrol car on on the right is completely submerged. (David Skeins)

The courthouse on Tulane Avenue after the waters receded; here, too, water lines have been left on the vehicles. (John Netto)

Maximum security inmates from Old Parish Prison seated on the court-house steps awaiting evacuation, wearing red wrist bands and plastic flex cuffs. (David Skeins)

Sheriff's deputies and state correctional officers dock at the courthouse steps to evacuate Old Prison inmates; a sub-merged truck can be seen in the background.
(David Skeins)

Numerous state agencies sent airboats to assist with the evacuation; this one passes over a submerged automobile.
(David Skeins)

The Intake-Templeman complex: The Intake Center (*lower left*) is connected to Templeman 1, 2, 3, and 4 by a fenced walkway (white roof). Templeman 1 and 2 are visible (*far right*). (Sam Gore)

A close-up of the walkway with its chain-linked sides.

Nurse Duane Townzel, inside the walkway after the flood, points to the water level mark.

The front of the Intake Center (*upper left*) during the flood; the garbage truck is parked at the kitchen loading dock (*lower right*). (Sam Gore)

The garage entrance to Intake after the flood receded, with water lines on the front wall. Inmates housed in the Templeman complex were evacuated from this garage. (John Netto)

Inside of the Intake Center several weeks after the storm. Most of the water was gone, but the flood had destroyed arrest records stored in the building. (John Netto)

The flooded visitors' entrance to the Intake Center. Deputies from the Templeman buildings stood on the half-wall for hours, awaiting evacuation. (William Devlin)

The visitors' entrance once the water had gone; this type of debris was common in and under the floodwater. (John Netto)

The upper stories of Templeman 3, with smoke residue surrounding several windows. Inmates hung burning sheets and blankets from the windows to attract attention. (John Netto)

Old Prison inmates signaled for help, hanging signs from the windows. (Jim Beach)

Correctional Center inmates hung sheets from windows to signal for help. Templeman inmates used ropes made from sheets to climb out of upper-story windows in an attempt to escape. (Jim Beach)

Templeman 3 inmates knocked a hole in the building's concrete wall to get out. (John Netto)

Interior shot of Templeman 3, weeks after the storm. During the flood, the debris floated on the water, impeding movement through the building's hallways. (John Netto)

Inmates used fire to burn through reinforced Plexiglas they couldn't break. (John Netto)

A typical inmate tier in Templeman 3. Weeks after the storm, the flood-water had receded. (John Netto)

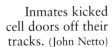

Inmates kicked cell doors off their tracks. (John Netto)

The Broad Street overpass rising out of the flood; the overpass served as the evacuation point for the jail. (Davis Skeins)

Jail inmates and deputies on the overpass during the evacuation. (LA Department of Corrections)

Dr. Marcus Dileo flanked by nurses Yolanda Dent and Lakesha Favis.

The scaffold built from Interstate 10 to the top of the Broad Street overpass. Inmates and staff had to climb down the structure to reach buses for evacuation. (Sam Gore)

Sam Gore (blue shirt) and I just after our arrival in Baton Rouge. We survived! (Sam Gore)

Brady Richard in the stairwell of the Correctional Center. Inmates broke through safety glass in the security door.
(Sam Gore)

Mike Higgins, Georgie, and Mobie safely at home.
(Patrick Drennan and Mike Higgins)

Following the storm, military personnel performed sweeps of all residences, looking for survivors and pets. Unfortunately, markings like "1-Dead Attic" were all too common in New Orleans. Many Sheriff's Office staff lost family members to the storm.
(John Netto)

Chapter 30

Back in the second-floor gym, Denise Sarro was pacing, wishing Duane would hurry up. The other three nurses had just arrived from the third floor, and she and Scarlett were ready to go. She glanced at Carol Evans. The usually calm, motherly black nurse looked upset.

"It's going to be all right, Carol," Denise said. "Duane will be back soon, and we'll all be out of here."

Another nurse—a young, thin LPN named Kentrisha Davis—drew Denise aside. "Miss Evans isn't worried about leaving," she said.

"Then why is she crying?" Denise asked.

"I answered the phone when her husband called yesterday afternoon," Kentrisha explained. "Carol was out passing meds, and he said, 'Can you please find my wife because this is probably gonna be the last time I talk to her.'"

For the first time in ages, Denise was speechless.

"So I ran out to the tiers and told her to come quick," Kentrisha said quietly. "He said the water had broken down the back door of their house and was up to the second floor. He couldn't swim and didn't know what to do."

"Damn." Denise looked back at Carol.

"Miss Evans told him to go to the attic and try to get out on the roof. Then the phone went dead." Kentrisha paused. "She hasn't heard from him since."

As Kentrisha went back to Carol, Duane walked in. He was

still wearing his scuba tank and diving gear, but the upper half of his shirt was dry. The first group did not have to swim under-water.

"I left the others at the Intake Center to come back for you," Duane said. "We need to get going."

Denise hurried toward the door with the four other nurses close on her heels. Duane led the way down the stairs, but only three had flashlights, and the going was slow.

Kentrisha balked when the water rose above her knees. "I didn't know it was this high."

"This is nothing," Duane warned her. "It's a lot deeper on the street, maybe over your heads."

"How are we going to do this?" Denise asked.

"I've already thought about that." Duane stopped at the bot-tom of the stairs and began to unroll the fire hose attached to the wall outside the first-floor infirmary.

Scarlett sniffed the air, then inhaled sharply. "Is the building on fire?"

"The inmates have been cutting up all night," Denise said. "I'm not surprised they're setting fires."

"Fire's not the problem," Duane said. "The flood's so deep and the building's so dark I don't want anyone getting lost." He cut the hose with a large diving knife and held up the severed end. "Who wants to be first in line?"

Scarlett raised her hand. "Denise and I are both good swim-mers."

"So am I," Kentrisha added.

"But I'm tall, a plus-size lady, and I float." Scarlett smiled down at the smaller woman. "So I can keep the rest of you afloat."

"I'll anchor the back," Denise said, "and we'll put Kentrisha in the middle."

Townzel wrapped the hose once around Scarlett's waist and handed her the cut end. "Hold tight to that." Then he coiled the hose around the other nurses. When all the women were linked, they started out.

Scarlett looked back. "I feel guilty about leaving the inmates behind. What are they going to do?"

"Dr. Gore's taking care of that, Scarlett," Denise reminded her. "Just worry about us getting out of here."

Their flashlight beams created eerie shadows as they made their way through Templeman 1's long black hallway. When they finally reached the outdoor walkway, sunlight revealed the horrors that contaminated the flood, including a grotesque head of a Barbie doll floating in the water. Denise tried not to think about wading through the filth, but the sickening stench of sewage and diesel fuel was inescapable.

The sight of the four bedraggled women in front of her, tethered by the fire hose, suddenly struck Denise as funny. We're like a waterlogged chain gang, she thought, and nearly made a joke. She stopped herself. The other nurses were clearly terrified.

The usually boisterous group moved in stone silence. The only noise was the shouts of inmates through the windows above them.

The fire hose was heavy, but Denise didn't complain. Water covered everything as far as she could make out beyond the chain-link fence, but nothing was visible below the murky surface. No one would be able to see a person who went under. It was safer to be tied together.

Treading slowly and carefully at first, the nurses picked up the pace when they turned at the T junction. They were almost to the Intake Center when Carol looked up.

"There's a hole in the . . ." The nurse's words were choked off when she tripped over something in the water. With a cry of surprise, she stumbled forward. She didn't go down, but her momentum yanked Kentrisha hard.

Pulled off balance by the heavy hose dragging on her thin frame, Kentrisha collapsed, barely managing to keep her head above the fetid water. She was obviously shaken as she stood up.

"Are you okay?" Carol's voice shook. "I am so sorry."

Smiling tightly, Kentrisha nodded. "I'm fine." Slowing down again, they arrived in the Intake Center without another mishap.

The lobby was empty. The other nurses had gone.

"They probably got tired of waiting and went on ahead," Denise said.

"I sure hope so." Plastic bottles and papers bobbed in Duane's wake as he hurried to the exit. He hit the glass door hard, but it didn't budge. Bracing himself, the muscular nurse threw his whole weight against it, and the door slowly swung outward. "C'mon, ladies."

Scarlett shielded her eyes as they crossed a narrow patio to the sidewalk. "I still don't see them." The writing on her arms and clothing was clearly visible.

"They're probably already at the Correctional Center," Carol said.

Taking the lead, Duane glanced back. "How's everyone doing?"

"How do you think we're doing, tied with a fire hose and soaked in sewer slime?" Denise joked loudly and sarcastically. She could see the warehouse ahead, but several cars parked by the loading dock were barely visible in the water. The flood was getting too deep to walk.

Kentrisha stopped moving. "I'm on tippy-toe, and the water's up to my chin!"

Standing five-seven, Scarlett hadn't noticed that the shorter woman had to tilt her head back to keep the water out of her mouth. "Then you better start swimming, Kentrisha."

Kentrisha's eyes widened. "You're out of your head if you think I'm going to swim over there all tied up." Before anyone could stop her, she loosened the hose and stepped out.

Astonished, Denise blurted, "You undid the hose?"

"I'm not going." Calm and quiet, Kentrisha didn't look panicked, but tears streamed down her cheeks. "I'm not going, not tied up to everyone. It's too deep, and the water's moving too fast."

"You can't stay here," Duane insisted.

"Yes, I can." Kentrisha turned back.

Duane, who was accustomed to handling frightened people in rescue situations, was supportive without giving in or adding to the nurse's pressure. "Wait by the wall until I come back for you, Kentrisha."

No one moved until the young woman climbed onto a half-wall outside the entrance of Intake.

After slipping on his fins, Duane adjusted the fire hose to take up the slack. Picking up the front end, he glanced down the line of expectant faces. "You all set?"

"No, but . . ." Scarlett waved him to move. "Just go."

A powerful swimmer, Duane pulled while the four women kicked and paddled across the surging water in the street. Scarlett was tall enough to push off from the bottom, but the shorter women had to swim the whole way. Once they were on the warehouse loading dock, Duane swam back for Kentrisha.

Tired, wet, smelly, and out of breath, the nurses watched Duane and Kentrisha with crossed fingers and mumbled prayers. The brawny nurse waved his arms and pointed toward the dock. Kentrisha just shook her head.

"C'mon, Kentrisha. You can do it," Denise muttered again and again, as though her mantra could somehow prod the panicked nurse into action.

"What's wrong with her?" Carol asked, beside herself with fear for her friend.

Denise shrugged, puzzled when Duane went back into the Intake Center. He returned a few minutes later carrying the wooden bench that usually stood outside the restrooms. He dropped it in the water. The bench floated.

After a little more coaxing, Duane convinced Kentrisha to lie on the bench on her stomach. Holding on to the end, the small nurse stared straight ahead while Duane pushed the bench through the water and across the street. As Kentrisha climbed onto the dock, the nurses met her with whoops of joy, group hugs, and laughter.

Denise exhaled as she opened the doors into the warehouse. They looked like a band of refugees and smelled worse, but nothing in her memory made her feel as jubilant as wading through the dark building on the way to the Correctional Center.

Chapter 31

Noon:
On a windless, cloudless day the temperature in
 New Orleans is ninety-five degrees.
Fires flare around the city as looting continues.
Infirmary patients are the first to be evacuated to the
 Broad Street overpass.
The few Correctional Center deputies with guns arm
 themselves.

Brady and I sat under the overhang on the back porch of the
Correctional Center while we ate. Lunch consisted of an odd selection of items the deputies had salvaged before the kitchen flooded
on Monday, mostly sandwiches, cold Vienna sausages, fruit cocktail, and Meals-Ready-to-Eat. The supply of food and drinks was
noticeably smaller than yesterday, a disconcerting fact that didn't
seem to trouble the civilians eating MREs for the first time. The
families were too busy checking out the various combinations and
trading items to consider the dwindling provisions. I, however,
was concerned.

Although we had personal food stashes in Medical Administration, the situation could become dire if we were stranded at
the jail for a long time.

Brady took a bite and made a face. "The bread in this sandwich is soggy."

"Too much humidity and no refrigeration," I said. "Be happy you've got food."

The same can't be said for people in the other buildings, I thought. By now, some of the inmates and staff must be really hungry. Verret had told me they hadn't eaten since Monday morning. If Jail Administration had taken the advice of Major Beach, food and water would have been distributed to all the buildings before the hurricane hit. Now the extensive flooding had ruined much of the food supply, and it was impossible to deliver what little remained.

Across the way I could see a hole in the kitchen roof, where the huge venting system had been ripped off in the storm. Beyond, the upper floors of Templeman 3 were also visible. The temperature inside the dark building was surely over a hundred degrees. Hot, hungry, and scared, the inmates had kicked out windows and were screaming or waving sheets and burning blankets through the openings. Some held up crude "help" signs to attract attention, apparently unaware that evacuation of the tiers was already under way.

Brady followed my gaze. "Good thing they got the doctors and nurses out of there last night."

Several hours after I sent Marcus Dileo to the House of Detention, the rest of the staff had moved there as well. The medical clinic in Detention was on the second floor, well above the flooding. We had heard some minor commotion from the building, but nothing to indicate that inmates were trying to break out. Which is a good thing, I thought. In the Psychiatric Unit, on the tenth floor, some of the patients were dangerously psychotic.

An outburst of yelling and banging erupted above us. The inmates in the Correctional Center had been relatively quiet until this morning. Now the disruptions came and went in waves, starting on one tier then moving to another and another until they gradually subsided. The disturbances were unnerving, but Captain Verret's deputies had the inmates secured.

In any case the noise probably didn't bother the medical staff from Templeman 1 too much, I thought. Not after what they had gone through this morning.

I had been shocked to find Sam Gore, Victor Tuckler, and the infirmary nurses at the Correctional Center when I came downstairs at eight in the morning. The details of their harrowing evacuations were astounding. They all felt lucky to be alive, but once the initial survival euphoria had worn off, they just wanted to get clean. The nurses had spent the past few hours sparingly using bottled water, rubbing alcohol, and wet-wipes to scrub off the filth. They had left most of their belongings, including spare clothes, behind, but Verret had scrounged some orange inmate scrubs for the nurses to wear. Many had written "staff" in black marker on the front and back, and Scarlett had cut her pants into bright orange shorts. The nurses were a comical sight, but they were safe.

"Hey, Mike!" Brady grinned as Mike Higgins came over with Georgie and Moby. He rubbed the bearded collie behind the ears. "How you doing, Georgie?"

I glumly stared at Moby.

Mike smiled as he tugged the leashes, drawing his dogs back. "I know you like them even if you won't admit it."

"The only thing I want now is peace, quiet, and this sandwich." I wasn't kidding.

Gary and I had been busy all morning treating "walk-by" patients. Wherever we were, deputies and family members approached us for care with minor problems that were mostly stress related or the result of chronic illnesses—diabetes, asthma, or high blood pressure. A few people had more serious conditions, which had been exacerbated by the extreme heat.

Brady went with Mike to walk the dogs along the porch. I finished my sandwich and then went inside to use the restroom. When I got within a few feet of the public bathroom, the odor of urine and feces overpowered me. Too many people had been using very few toilets. I passed it up and instead went upstairs to use the small bathroom in Medical Administration.

Paul was listening to a battery-operated radio in his office.

"Any news?" I asked.

"Yeah, and it's all bad." Paul leaned back in his chair. "The pumping stations still aren't working, and three levees broke."

"Three?" That stopped me cold. "Which ones?"

"The Industrial Canal, the 17th Street Levee, and the London Avenue Canal." Paul glanced at the radio. "There hasn't been any official word yet, but all of the Ninth Ward and New Orleans East is lost."

"Oh, God. A lot of our people live in those areas," I said. Gary's house was in Lakeview near the 17th Street Levee, and many of the nurses lived in New Orleans East.

Paul nodded, distressed. "Nurse Mazant is pretty sure her house is gone; Audrella is really upset. Her husband refused to evacuate, and she doesn't know if he got out."

"Where is she?" I asked.

"In the clinic," Paul said. "She's getting meds ready to pass out."

"Any idea when we might get rescued?"

Paul shook his head. "I heard the mayor and the Jefferson Parish president blasting the Feds about not getting help here fast enough, but no one has any answers. The National Guard is picking people off rooftops, but there's a lot more people needing rescue than anyone was ready for."

I used the bathroom and left. The humidity inside the building was so high that my shirt was damp with sweat, but there was no point changing. It was nearly as hot and humid outside.

The foyer outside Medical Administration and the corridor to the stairwell were littered with trash, but deserted. The families who had been staying there had moved their belongings and prison mattresses downstairs to escape the heat and the dark. Even in the daytime, the windowless hallways were dim, and flashlights and batteries were in short supply. And increasing noise from the inmate tiers added to the abysmal atmosphere.

Downstairs, with the front doors of the Correctional Center open again, the lobby was cooler, but the smell from the restrooms was intolerable. Most people had chosen to camp outside on the wide porch. After sundown, at least, the night air would offer some relief.

Captain Verret was standing by the information desk. His olive green work shirt was streaked with sweat and dirt, and he held a small yellow walkie-talkie.

Curious, I paused to ask, "Does that radio work?"

"Only in the building," Verret said, "but that's all I need to stay in touch with the deputies on the tiers. Good thing Paul had extras. All the phones are out."

As I started to leave, Verret called me back.

"Just so you know, I had to stop Nurse Mazant from passing out meds. The inmates are so riled up it's not safe."

"They should be okay," I said. "The inmates with serious conditions already have meds for several days. The others should be fine. When things calm down, we can check on them."

"Don't count on things calming down any time soon, Doc," Verret said bluntly. "It's dark and hot on the tiers. The inmates haven't eaten since yesterday morning, and they may not get fed again before they're out of here. It's crazy up there—getting way too risky."

Trying to ignore the muffled sounds of banging and yelling above, I changed the subject. "All my people are out of the Templeman buildings and the Intake Center, but I haven't heard from the clinics at the House of Detention, Conchetta, or the Old Prison. Do you have any news?"

"No, but you can catch John Lacour." Verret motioned down the hall, where he said the Old Prison warden was talking to the sheriff. As Verret moved away to take an incoming call on the radio, I was struck again by how calm and collected he was.

When Warden Lacour emerged from the sheriff's office, he told me that flooding had forced the Old Prison nurses to the second floor. They had taken some medications and supplies with them, but most of the records and drugs had been left behind. I quickly wrote a note to Jan Ricca, telling her to be sure to send the medications and whatever records she had with the inmates when they were evacuated. I handed the message to the warden and headed back outside.

The wide front porch had transformed into a refugee camp packed with people, blankets, mattresses, and suitcases. Most dogs were on leashes, but cats were kept in carriers, and I saw a couple of caged rabbits. The evacuees napped, read books, played games, or sat in groups talking and watching the flood, which was still rising. Everyone had picked something to use as a depth gauge. I glanced at the blue van belonging to one of the medical assistants. It was now almost completely underwater.

A boat pulled up to the steps and dropped off a couple of people. The drivers were in the process of evacuating inmates to a nearby interstate overpass, and they had become a grapevine for news throughout the jail, carrying messages and oral reports.

They told us that Templeman 1 and 2 had started moving prisoners that morning, beginning with the infirmary patients. The sheriff's office only had five boats, and most of those were small, holding no more than five passengers. The process, however, sped up dramatically after the unexpected arrival of large airboats from St. James Parish. The off-duty deputy drivers who had volunteered to assist with the evacuation effort. The extra help bolstered morale, and the additional boats allowed for the movement of significantly larger numbers of inmates.

The overpass where the inmates were being held was surrounded by water, forming a small island where security was easily maintained. From there inmates could be taken to a nearby highway. The sheriff had requested buses from other government agencies to transport the inmates to correctional facilities in Baton Rouge and western Louisiana.

For a self-indulgent moment I wondered how my own house had weathered the hurricane. The basement had probably flooded, I thought, though any other damage depended on whether the roof had survived. I quickly realized that dwelling on the possibilities would make me frantic. Besides, I was lucky compared to the residents of the neighborhoods near the jail.

I could hear people shouting for help from the upper floors of nearby apartment buildings as they waited for rescue that seemed far too long in coming. Evacuees were beginning to stream in to the Correctional Center any way they could—wading, swimming, or paddling on doors and air mattresses. The scene was sobering but also comical.

A group of Latino men had mounted their own rescue effort using the side of a house as a raft. They had lashed tires to the sides and corners to keep it afloat. Pushing and kicking, they ferried people from the neighborhood to our facility, then turned back to find more. I had already watched as they saved several families, and their undaunted perseverance inspired us all.

A middle-aged black man swam slowly down the street. He had been going back and forth between the jail and nearby houses all day. People had tried to coax him onto the porch, but he had refused, insisting that he was helping people. He would only pause on the steps for a few minutes of conversation or a quick snack before venturing back into the flood. As far as I knew, he was always alone and hadn't saved anyone. He was a popular topic of discussion, and everyone thought he was crazy.

The unexpected sight and sound of a Red Cross helicopter passing overhead drew every eye and prompted a round of cheers.

"Wonder when they'll be back," Gary said, watching the receding helicopter as he dropped down beside me.

"Hard to say. They'll probably help people stranded on roofs before they worry about us."

"Yeah," Gary scoffed. "We're just stranded at a jail with a few thousand rioting inmates."

"They're being evacuated," I reminded him.

Gary rested his arms on his knees. If he was relieved that the inmates were being moved, he didn't show it. His thoughts were on his home. "If the hurricane didn't take the new roof off my house, I bet some of those tall pines fell on it. And Lakeview's flooded. I don't know what I'm going to do."

"Your house may be fine, Gary, but even if the worst happened, your roommate and your dogs are safe. And you have insurance. Right?"

He shrugged half-heartedly. "Yeah."

"Right. You've got savings, a great family, and you're a doctor. No matter what happens, you can find a job." I motioned at a man carrying a child piggyback as he and his wife waded toward the Correctional Center. They had nothing but the wet clothes they wore. "A lot of people have lost everything—our nurses, too. Some of them don't even know if their families are okay."

"Dr. French?" A woman walked up, holding a toddler. She looked frantic. "Her fever's up again."

"Let's take a look." Standing up, Gary took the woman into the shade of the overhang. No matter how worried he was about his own life, with Gary everyone else came first.

"Hot enough for you?" Brady walked up, wiping sweat off his forehead with the back of his arm.

"It's worse upstairs." It would take more than hot weather to get me down.

"Be glad you're not at Templeman 3," Brady said. "Things are really heating up over there, and I don't mean the temperature."

"What happened?" I asked, frowning.

Brady uncapped a bottle of water and took a long swallow. "One of the boat drivers told me a couple of guys broke through the bars and jumped out a window."

I looked up when a sheriff's boat pulled close to the porch steps. Sam Gore walked over to talk to the two deputies as they secured the craft to the railing.

"How's it going on the overpass?" Sam asked.

"It's insane over there," the driver said. "There's over a thousand inmates, none of them handcuffed, and, except for a couple of SID guys, we don't have guns."

"There's only ten of us." The other deputy pointed to himself and the driver. "Maybe twelve."

"Not enough, that's for damn sure." The driver took off his baseball cap, smoothed his hair back, and put it back on. "It's hot, there's no water, and everyone's getting restless. You know how they say something is a disaster waiting to happen? Well, this is it."

As the two men walked into the Correctional Center lobby, the second deputy paused to look back. "Almost forgot. Nurse Hartzog wants us to bring some supplies and medications."

The deputies' news took me by surprise. Hedy Hartzog was the head nurse of Templeman 4, which housed female inmates.

"What's she doing on the overpass?" I asked.

"She was evacuated with the women earlier this morning," the

deputy explained. "But she's worried about the guys from the infirmary. Some of them are in bad shape."

"The infirmary patients are still there?" Sam looked shocked.
"Why weren't they bused out?"

Sam asked the questions going through my mind.

"That's why we came to pick up food and water," the deputy
said. "The buses didn't come. They might not get here until tomorrow."

Chapter 32

Mid-afternoon:
Evacuation of Templeman 1 and 2 is nearly complete.
Inmates in the Correctional Center receive their first meal in
  twenty-eight hours.
Deputies distribute food by boat to other jail facilities.
Incidents of violence increase between deputies and inmates
  on the overpass.

Sam, Brady, and I watched the two men until they vanished through
the front doors. "They can't possibly carry enough food and water
for everyone," he said.

That was a problem, but it wasn't *my* priority. We had a sudden, unexpected medical crisis on our hands. I looked at Sam.
"We can send Nurse Hartzog a responder bag, but I don't think
we should send medications."

"I agree," Sam said. "There's no way to know what she'll need.
Most of the infirmary patients already have several days' worth
of meds—if they remembered to take the drugs with them."

We had to assume, though, that some inmates had forgotten
or lost their medications in the rush of evacuation. And some drugs,
such as insulin, couldn't be dispensed in advance. In any case, a
number of Sam's patients were too sick or unreliable to manage
their own meds.

"If anyone has a serious medical problem," I continued, "the deputies should bring them here. We have shelter, beds, and equipment."

"And water," Brady said. "Do you want me to get a responder bag?"

"Yeah, and any other first aid supplies you think Nurse Hartzog can use." I glanced at the boat, which the deputies were now filling with food and water. There was no guarantee they would remember to wait for medical supplies. "Don't take too long."

Sam turned to me as Brady hurried inside. "I have some really unstable patients on that overpass, Dem."

I knew what he was thinking. Some of the infirmary patients were so sick, they might not survive the wait on the overpass. Patients with open wounds or compromised immune systems had already been evacuated through sewage, increasing their risk of infection. And, although everyone stranded on the overpass would suffer from dehydration and heat exposure, the ordeal could well prove fatal to some of the sicker inmates.

"We need a staff meeting, Sam," I said. "Round up everyone you can find and have them meet back here as soon as possible."

I passed the word to several nurses gathered on the front corner of the porch, while Sam went to find the others. Within a few minutes, fifteen nurses were settled around the steps, and Sam came back out with Gary, Mike, Paul, and Victor. Brady dropped the responder bag and other supplies in the boat and leaned on the railing.

"Did you call me here to accept my resignation?" Scarlett joked.

"It looks like the DA's office is sinking," Chuck said, gesturing across the street as he eased down onto the concrete steps.

"The water's still getting higher," Brady said. "Cheryl's blue van drowned."

Everyone laughed, and I marveled at the tenacity of my staff. They had weathered a hurricane, swum to safety through sewage, and spent the last few hours tending to the medical needs of inmates, employees, and family members. Hearing them joke lessened the tension and worry that threatened to drag me down.

"I am *so* glad my family evacuated before all hell broke loose." Denise looked relieved.

"Wish I'd evacuated before the storm," Scarlett added sarcastically. "Then I wouldn't look like this." She pushed tangles of matted hair behind her ears and struck a sexy pose.

"Scarlett, you'll always look beautiful to me," I teased.

"Have you seen my leopard underwear?" Scarlett pulled the waistband of her orange scrubs down to reveal the top of her spotted underwear.

I laughed and called everyone's attention back to business. "I just heard that the infirmary patients are still on the overpass. They could be there all night, maybe longer. No one knows when the buses will arrive." I went on, "What if it takes another day? Then, after the buses do get here, the patients will be on them several *more* hours before they get where they're going."

"Probably Hunt or Angola," Sam interjected, referring to the state prisons.

"The point is," I continued, "the medical departments at the state facilities will be processing hundreds of inmates at once. It'll take a while to identify the really sick ones."

State prison facilities, where convicted criminals were sent to serve out their sentences, were only used to processing 100 inmates a week. The medical departments of the prisons would be completely unprepared to treat 7,000 inmates, many of them gravely ill.

"The receiving nurses and doctors won't have charts or med records," I said. "And most of our inmates don't know the names or doses of their medications."

"Some don't even know the names of their illnesses," Sam pointed out.

"And I doubt that the facilities will have enough drugs on hand to treat everyone," I added. "By the time the doctors sort it all out, some of the infirmary patients are going to die."

"What a mess." Gary sighed, rubbing his face. "A lot of my HIV guys are on seven or eight different meds."

The group's initial levity evaporated as the enormity of the crisis sank in.

"If we send records and medications, we can speed up the process at the prison facilities," I said.

"Except the infirmary charts are under water," Scarlett countered.

"And they pissed all over the meds." Lillian's eyes flashed.

"But the med records are on the second floor, right?" I asked. The nurses kept a single-page medication record for each patient that listed the patient's name, diagnoses, and all prescribed drugs.

"We moved the med records upstairs when we set up the temporary infirmary last night," Denise said sharply. "And not all the meds are ruined."

"If we get those, we can save the medical staffs at Hunt and Angola a lot of time and trouble." I shifted my gaze from Sam to Gary. "And maybe save a few lives, too."

"There's just one problem," Chuck said. "When we left Templeman 1 this morning, the ground floor was filling up with water. I'm not sure you can get to the second floor."

"First you have to get *to* Templeman 1," Scarlett pointed out. "Take my word for it, you do not want to go swimming in that shit!"

I had realized we'd have to wade through Templeman 1 to reach the infirmary, but swimming *to* the building was not part of my plan. We needed a boat. However, before I dealt with that, there was another issue I wanted to discuss.

"I think a doctor and a couple of nurses should go with the patients to Hunt and Angola."

"That's what I've been thinking all morning," Sam said. "That would take even more pressure off the receiving medical personnel. We *know* these patients."

Sam wouldn't abandon his patients, but no one else jumped at the idea.

"So do we draw straws to see who goes?" Scarlett asked.

"Do we have straws?" Chuck laughed.

The reluctance I sensed was understandable. Everyone had endured a lot over the past few days. Oddly enough, that was the key to getting volunteers.

"We could be stuck here another week," I said, "covered in sewage, with food and water running low, and prisoners trying to escape. Anyone who goes with the patients will have air-conditioning, food, and hot showers tomorrow."

Suddenly, none of the infirmary nurses could pass up my offer.

The boat moored to the porch railing gave me another idea. "I need someone to go to the overpass now, with the supplies."

The nurses just stared at me. But I wanted to get some help to Hedy Hartzog. With 200 infirmary patients plus deputies and hundreds of other inmates, she couldn't possibly handle every medical problem that came up. I picked someone.

"Think about this, Kentrisha," I said. "The first people to the overpass will be the first ones off. Air-conditioning, hot water . . ."

The young nurse looked surprised to be singled out, but she was competent and reliable, and she agreed to go.

"We'll send the records and meds over as soon as we can," I told her, "along with the rest of the nurses."

"Maybe a boat could drop me off at Charity Hospital on the way," Victor said. "I'm two days late for my shift."

I promised Victor I'd look into it and motioned for Kentrisha to follow me as I started toward the doors. We intercepted the boat deputies coming out of the Correctional Center again, and they agreed to ferry the nurse to the overpass.

"If anyone gets really sick, don't try to treat them," I instructed Kentrisha. "Send them back here."

I wished her luck and went to the sheriff's office to find the officer who was coordinating inmate evacuation. I explained my need for a boat, emphasizing that it would take only ninety minutes, maybe less, to transport a few volunteers to Templeman 1 to collect the necessary items.

The answer was definitive: "No, I'm sorry. I don't have a boat to give you."

I couldn't argue with his reasoning. With few boats, rising water, and thousands of inmates still to evacuate, no boats could be spared. There were hundreds of employees and family members waiting to leave, as well. From Administration's perspective, getting people out of the buildings before the rioting escalated or exit routes were blocked was a higher priority than retrieving drugs and medication records.

But my responsibility was the welfare of the patients. Their chances for survival would be greatly improved if we had the records and meds. I had to accept the decision, but I didn't have to give up. The rebuff just made me more determined.

The staff was waiting on the steps where I had left them. The decision to get the records excited everyone; it was something useful we could do in the face of natural forces we couldn't control. But when I announced that we couldn't have a boat, spirits plummeted.

My stubborn streak had kicked in. "We still have to get the records."

"How can we do that without a boat?" Gary asked.

"We'll have to swim over and carry the stuff out," I said, jump-starting the discussion again.

"What?" Scarlett looked aghast. "We barely got out of there alive this morning."

"She's not kidding, Dr. Inglese." Chuck looked me in the eye. "You have no idea how hard it was."

"I *know* you don't think we're going back in that water." Lillian challenged me with a hint of condescension. "It was nasty when we swam over this morning, and it's worse now."

"Swimming through all that diesel probably isn't safe," Brady said.

It was a valid point. A red film of diesel fuel coated the surface of the water and clung to anything that floated.

"It isn't just a matter of 'Let's go get the meds.'" Paul had been silent until now. "Or dealing with deep water and sewage. Inmates are loose. They're desperate, rioting, and setting fires. Going back in there is a really stupid thing to do."

I took a moment to consider his words. I'd known Paul for several years and trusted his judgment. For one thing, he wasn't as impulsive as I was. Paul made decisions after carefully weighing all the options. In this instance, his objections were correct. The first tenet of emergency response was: do not put yourself in danger. But I wouldn't let go of the idea.

"Some patients are going to die if we don't get those records and meds," I said stubbornly. "I might swim over there, find out it's not safe, and swim right back. But I have to try. If I don't, I think I'll always regret it."

I try to be eloquent when speaking to a group, but I got a little sappy when I was begging friends to put their lives on the

line. "I won't ask any of you to come with me. It's too dangerous. You have to decide for yourselves."

When I stopped talking, everyone was quiet. The possibility
that no one would follow me was more unnerving than actually
going through with the plan.

Chapter 33

I looked to Sam for support. We'd been friends for so long I was sure he'd back me up. Instead, Sam rolled his eyes. I took that to mean he didn't want to go and tried to give him an out. "You need to think about your wife and kids, Sam."

"Oh, I'm going." Sam laughed. "I'm just not thrilled about swimming through that stuff again."

"You guys are crazy," a nearby deputy chimed in. "I just left Templeman. They're moving hundreds of inmates, and you'll have to push through them in the dark building. A lot of them are really pissed off. I wouldn't do it."

"I thought they finished evacuating Templeman 1," I said.

"The walkways are still packed with inmates waiting for boats." The deputy's tone and expression were deadly serious. "And they haven't done a sweep yet. Inmates could be hiding anywhere."

"That's one of the reasons we left this morning," Chuck added. "It was just too dangerous to stay."

"I have to do this." My resolve hardened as the debate intensified. The arguments were good, but with patients' lives at stake, none of that mattered to me.

I gave everyone a moment to consider. As they broke off into groups, I realized I had put them all in an extremely awkward position, exactly what I wanted to avoid. There was no guarantee the mission would succeed and no need for more than five or six of us to take the risk. Sam had already volunteered, but I wanted to give the others an opportunity to opt out without embarrassment.

Walking over to Mike, Gary, and Brady, I joked with the psychiatrist. "What do you think, Mike? Am I crazy?"

"Yes," Mike replied, smiling, "but we've known that for a long time. If you're going, I'm going."

I turned to Gary. "How about you?"

"I have to think about it some more."

Brady volunteered enthusiastically. "I'm with you."

Relieved that I wouldn't be setting out alone, I left so the others could decide without pressure. Ten minutes later, I called the staff back together.

As Gary passed me, he said, "I'm in."

I smiled. His initial reservations aside, I never doubted that Gary would be at my side.

When everyone returned, we discussed the logistics of the operation. Since wet meds and records would be worthless, I sent Brady to get trash bags from Medical Supply.

"I'd like to go with you," Denise said.

Surprised, I stared at the five-foot-two nurse. "That wouldn't be wise."

"Why not?" Denise asked, her voice shrill with indignation.

I chose my words carefully. "It'll be tough going, Denise. We have to carry a lot of stuff through deep water, and there're loose inmates everywhere. I don't think a woman should come."

Spotting a few nurses frowning, I added, "You know I'm not a chauvinist, but we have to be realistic."

Denise fell silent.

Sam stared past me, deep in thought. "As long as we're over there, we might as well get the records and meds from the third-floor clinic, too."

"That's a lot to carry and keep dry," Gary said.

Lillian threw up her hands. "If we could get two nurses over in a laundry cart, you can get a bunch of trash bags out the same way."

"And you can float things on those foam chairs," Chuck reminded us.

"I'm coming," Denise announced insistently.

My head snapped around. "I told you I don't think that's a good idea."

The determined nurse grabbed my arm. "I helped move the infirmary. Do you know where we put the diabetic records?"

"No," I replied.

"Where we put the HIV meds?" Denise held my gaze without flinching. "Or where the keys to the med carts are?"

"No," I admitted.

"Then I'm coming," Denise stated firmly. "I'm a strong swimmer, and you need someone who knows where everything is."

Beaten by her logic, I gave up. "Then I guess you're coming with us."

She smiled.

A few minutes later, Brady returned with trash bags and two extra flashlights.

"Are we ready?" Brady asked. He and Denise were gung-ho. Sam, Gary, and Mike were less eager but resigned.

"Let's just get this over with," Gary said.

Based on their experience that morning, Denise and Sam agreed that going through the kitchen was the easiest route. Anxious to get started, we maneuvered through clusters of adults, children, and pets to the back porch. Pausing at the top of the rear steps, we braced ourselves for the plunge back into the disgusting water.

"Dr. Inglese!" The sheriff called from the far corner of the Correctional Center porch. "Could I see you for a minute?"

"Yes, sir." I hurried over, wondering what had distracted him from the evacuation effort.

"I just had a report of two inmates down, maybe dead, in Templeman 3—on D-side," the sheriff said, referring to one of the tiers. "But no one can confirm it. Go over and see if you can help."

Chapter 34

I hurried back to the medical staff and filled them in on the new emergency. Since I'd need help, I asked Sam to accompany me. Mike, Gary, Brady, and Denise would wait thirty minutes before crossing to Templeman 1. Sam and I would meet them there.

As the two of us started down the steps, the thought of wading through the filthy sludge made me nauseous. But backing out wasn't an option. If the sheriff's information was correct, two men could be dead or dying.

"I can't believe I'm doing this again." Sam grimaced as we crossed the courtyard between the Correctional Center and the kitchen.

The chest-deep water was cold, a marked contrast to the ninety-plus air temperature, and the sharp odor of diesel fuel overpowered the earthy smell of silt. I was wearing shorts and flip-flops again, and the oily red fuel covered my clothes and burned my exposed skin.

When we climbed up to the kitchen, the water inside reached only to our thighs. There were no windows inside the building, and the shift from bright sunlight to darkness was startling. Even with flashlights, minutes passed before our eyes adjusted.

Prior to the storm, the workers prepared breakfast, lunch, and dinner for 6,400 inmates in this massive facility. The amount of soggy bread and spoiled sandwich meat adrift in the flood showed how abruptly meal preparations had been abandoned.

"Do you remember the way?" I asked Sam. I rarely visited the kitchen and was completely lost.

"I think so," he said, panning the area with his flashlight.

While Sam got his bearings, I was struck by the unsettling absence of sound. The walls and water isolated us from the noise of motorized boats and human activity outside. However, when we moved forward, the silence was broken by the *whack* of plastic food warmers and trays slamming into each other. Foam furniture, bread wrappers, soggy bread, MRE packets, trash, and rotting lunch meat covered every square inch of the water's surface. We couldn't take a step without pushing debris out of our way, but that was less hazardous than what lurked beneath.

Tabletops were visible, but a mass of litter floated between them, and we continually cracked our shins and feet on submerged pots, toppled chairs, and machinery. Flip-flops offered my toes no protection from unseen utensils and appliances, and there was no escape from the acrid odor. My physician's mind imagined infections starting in every scratch and cut the sewage water touched.

I lost track of time as I followed Sam through the maze of counters, stoves, and cooking vats. When we passed through the doors into the warehouse, the black darkness changed into shadowed gloom. My heart literally leaped with relief when I saw a sliver of sunlight through the loading dock doors.

"We're almost out of here," Sam said, picking up the pace.

The warehouse was easier to navigate, and we were temporarily blinded again when we emerged into the glare of the hot, New Orleans sun.

Standing on the loading dock, Sam gestured toward the Intake Center across the street. "The water's deeper here, but the currents don't look as bad as this morning."

There was barely a ripple on the surface of the water, but there was a prominent orange hue. The layer of diesel was much thicker here, and the water would be over our heads where the street dipped.

"No point putting this off." I lowered myself into the water and started to swim. With each stroke, the oil slick splashed into my face, burning my mouth and eyes. My clothes and hands were covered with fuel, and I had no way to wipe my eyes clean. Frustration made the irritating sting and bitter taste worse.

Then I slammed into something under the water, cracking my shin hard.

"What?" I gasped, puzzled.

"A truck," Sam said with a chagrinned smile. "I found it on the way over this morning."

"Thanks for the warning," I shot back sarcastically.

"Sorry, I forgot." Sam chuckled. "If you pull yourself up, you can walk on the bed."

Taking his advice, I swung my legs over the edge of the pickup and stood up. The water in the bed was just above my knees. I was coated from head to toe in an oily, red sheen, and my eyes and nostrils still burned.

Three steps later I was back in the water. Three strokes after that I cracked my leg again.

Sam laughed. "Oh, and there's a car under there, too. You can see the antenna sticking up."

"Uh-huh," I said, less than amused. "I see it—*now*." I walked across the roof of the vehicle and slipped back into the fetid water. At least we were clear of the parking lot.

Assured there were no other sunken vehicles in the roadway, I swam with more confidence. The shock of running into something a third time stopped me dead in the water.

"Now what?" I complained. "I'm on the sidewalk."

"Remember that cement trash can in front of the Intake Center?"

"Not really." I eyed Sam narrowly. "Are there any more surprises you'd care to share with me *before* I go on?"

"No, I think you've pretty much hit them all."

This time when Sam laughed, I laughed with him. It took the edge off our precarious position and kept me from worrying about what waited for us in Templeman 3.

Chapter 35

The flood in front of the Intake Processing Center was only four feet deep, and we stopped to catch our breath. A dozen Templeman 1 deputies were standing outside on a patio and half wall. The building overhang offered some protection from the sun, but the water was chest-deep. Sam recognized those who had been assigned to the infirmary.

"How long have you been here?" Sam called out.

"Hours!" A man called back. "Since right after the nurses left this morning."

It was now nearly three in the afternoon. The deputies had been standing in the water for the past eight hours, first guarding inmates being transferred to the overpass, then waiting for a boat to pick them up. They were tired and wet but not in danger. Considering their predicament, they were in particularly good spirits.

"Have a nice swim, Doc!" Another deputy quipped as we continued on our way.

We could see a chain-link gate open in the walkway, guarded by three deputies in a boat. Two were armed with guns, and after Sam and I identified ourselves, they let us in.

The walkway was packed with inmates on their way to the evacuation staging area. They stood in the water with hands on their heads, and many had their shoes tied together and draped around their necks. The line was almost at a standstill. Sam and

I both noticed the scarcity of deputies within the corridor, but neither of us considered turning back.

We waded against the flow of traffic, squeezing between the tightly packed bodies and yelling, "Let us through. Let us through!" only when the crush made it necessary.

Most of the inmates moved to let us pass, but a few muttered threats and pushed back when they realized we were jail staff. We ignored the intimidating words and looks—until two men blocked our path. Paul's warning about the dangers ran though my mind again. These were hardened criminals who wouldn't hesitate to harm us for the smallest reason.

"Some people are hurt," I said, trying to push between the men. "We're doctors, and we need to get through."

"Deputies or inmates?" one asked, looking me in the eye.

I stared back, instantly aware of just how vulnerable Sam and I were. The deputies were spaced far apart. If we were assaulted, it would take them too long to reach us. Sam looked just as scared as I felt.

"Inmates," he and I answered in unison.

After the men eased back to let us pass, we tried to keep our heads down and our mouths shut. We did not want to give anyone an excuse to act up.

The line of inmates ended at the T junction. Turning toward Templeman 3, we sped up as much as possible in the waist-high water, but the sense of imminent danger remained sharp when we entered the building. The building's halls were dark and oppressive, even with our flashlights turned on. The water felt cooler, and there was no noise. Even with no inmates in sight, I was still plagued by thoughts of stray prisoners crouched in the darkness.

Neither Sam nor I knew how to find the D-side tiers and the inmates in trouble. We headed toward the sound of voices, hoping to find a deputy to give us directions. We called out the minute we saw flashlight beams emerge from around a corner: "It's Dr. Inglese and Dr. Gore." Surprising tired deputies in the dark would not be a good idea.

Two SID deputies, wearing body armor and holding shotguns, shined lights in our faces. Sam and I didn't move until they recognized us. Finally they lowered their weapons, and I explained why we were there.

"I haven't seen anyone hurt or dead," the shorter deputy said, "but a bunch of inmates are stuck upstairs. They kicked the doors off the tracks, and we can't get them open," he explained. "They're not going anywhere soon."

The deputies agreed to take us up to D-side to look around. As Sam and I followed the armed men deeper into the building, my tension began to ease. Relaxing, however, proved premature.

The reinforced doors leading to the second floor were closed and locked. Neither deputy had the key.

"We can't get up this way," the deputy said, "but you can reach the stairs from the other side through the Intake Center."

Exasperated, Sam and I turned around and began the long process of retracing our steps. The walkway was still packed wall-to-wall with inmates, and the line was still not moving. When we reached the gate in the chain-link fence, I yelled to the deputies in the boat. "Let us out!" They quickly opened the gate, and we swam through.

Bored and waterlogged, the deputies on the patio jeered and laughed at us. Sam and I just smiled and waved as we waded by.

"I can't believe they're still waiting," Sam muttered when we were out of earshot.

I realized several more hours might pass before a boat came to get them.

The water rose above our heads as we paddled down the street toward the garage. Garbage drifted around us, and I pressed my lips closed to avoid getting water in my mouth, but I had become oblivious to the diesel-sewage smell.

The roar of an engine coming up fast from behind caught me off guard. I turned, expecting to see a small boat. Instead, Major Beach was speeding toward us on a bright blue jet ski.

Tall and husky with thinning hair and dark sunglasses, his shirt and shorts flapping wildly, the director of Food Services looked absurdly out of place in the disaster zone. Like a cartoon clip, I thought with a grin. My good humor ended, though, when the jet ski roared by, dousing me with water.

Sputtering, I waved and shouted, "Jim! Come back!"

"He can't hear you!" Sam peeled a wet piece of paper off his neck.

"Hey! Jim!" I yelled again, louder. I didn't want to swim if I could hitch a ride. Alerted to our presence, Beach slowed and circled back.

"What's up, Doc?" Beach asked as he throttled down. "Need some help?"

"How about towing us to the Intake Center garage?" I said.

"You got it. Grab on."

Sam and I found handholds on opposite sides of the machine. Clutching a piece of fiberglass, I clamped my mouth and eyes shut as we took off. Sam lost his grip and slipped off into the wake, set adrift and left behind. Somehow I hung on all the way to the garage.

Chapter 36

Treading water by the garage, I waited for Sam to catch up. The flood extended all the way up the sloping entrance ramp. Half-submerged cars lay everywhere. I could hardly believe that the nurses had made it through here that morning.

Now the structure was filled with dozens of inmates standing waist deep in water with their hands on their heads. Fewer than fifteen deputies stood guard. Only three had firearms, but the inmates were amazingly well behaved.

The garage was being used as the Templeman evacuation point. A stalled pickup truck was parked on the ramp with the back end facing the street. The bed, barely above the water, served as a loading dock. Inmates climbed into the back, and from there, they stepped off the tailgate into rescue boats. Once a boat was full, it pulled out and turned toward the overpass. Then another boat took its place.

When Sam reached me, he took a minute to catch his breath before we waded into the garage. Chief Bordelon, the warden, stood near the door, directing the flow of inmates and shouting instructions with an authoritative voice that belied his babyish face. Gentle appearance aside, the warden was all business, fair, and respected by everyone. He brought order to the chaos around him.

"Hey, Doc." Bordelon gave us a quick nod as we walked up. Then he looked back at the inmates filing out of the Intake Center.

"Looks like you've got your hands full," I said. Through the glass wall behind him, I could see hundreds of men crowded together inside. "How long have you been at it?"

"Eighteen hours, more or less." The warden watched the inmates as he spoke. "It's slow going, but we're making progress."

"I'm surprised they're so calm." I looked down the line of men between the door and the pickup truck, wondering how many had been banging and yelling on the tiers last night.

"They act up until they see what things are like out here," Bordelon said. "A couple of them told me, 'Man, if we knew it was this bad, we wouldn't have done all that stuff.'"

"Sam and I were just in Templeman 3. A deputy told us there are still inmates stuck in cells." Recalling that the warden and Chuck Jones, his second in command, had been preparing to force cells open last night, I quickly added, "Couldn't you get them all out?"

"You have no idea how hard we tried." Bordelon exhaled in frustration. "We got most of them, but it wasn't easy." Equipped with a crowbar and sledgehammer, the warden and his deputies had tackled the flooded cells on the ground floor before freeing inmates trapped on the upper tiers.

Many of the doors had to be pried open using the crowbar on the bottom edge. In those instances, Bordelon or Jones ducked under the water to position the crowbar correctly. While the deputies outside the cell pried and pulled, the inmates inside pushed. Once the gap between the floor and the door was wide enough, the trapped men swam out. Some doors opened from the side, allowing the inmates to squeeze through.

"We started at ten o'clock last night and didn't finish until four thirty this morning," Bordelon said. "But we opened every door that could be opened."

"What about the guys who are still trapped?" I asked.

"We'll have to cut them out," Bordelon said. "Maintenance is trying to find a blowtorch that isn't under water."

I explained our reasons for being there, but the warden had not heard about any down inmates.

"But I haven't talked to the sheriff since yesterday. Our radios aren't working." A shoving match started between two inmates, and Bordelon cut off our conversation to go break it up.

Sam and I walked into the Intake Processing Center. Although I had been in and out of other buildings since the hurricane, they had all been dark. The utter devastation here was lit by sunlight streaming in through the windows. Desks and tables were overturned, computers were submerged, and arrest records floated on the water. The room was packed with restless inmates, pushing and shoving to reach the garage outside.

I didn't know how long it had been since we left the Correctional Center, but more than thirty minutes had certainly passed. Mike, Gary, Brady, and Denise were probably on their way to Templeman 1 or were already there collecting the records and meds. I hoped they were having an easier time than we were. Sam and I were still a long way from the third floor of Templeman 3.

Our progress through the mass of inmates was slow. I noticed more deputies than we had seen before, and many with weapons. But they looked exhausted as they herded the inmates toward the exit.

I saw a man suddenly slip under the water. An observant deputy prodded the inmate back to the surface, but I couldn't help wonder how many others had tried the same ploy and succeeded. If an inmate escaped detection, he could easily move clear of the prisoner line and hide behind the furniture.

Nervous sweat dotted my face, but I maintained a stony expression as we moved through the press of inmates. Some of the men cursed us, and a couple made threatening gestures. The all-too-familiar knot in my stomach tightened when a deputy barked, "Hey, you two! Get back here!"

The deputies all wore uniforms. In our wet T-shirts, Sam and I resembled inmates going the wrong way. We quickly explained who we were and our purpose.

After a moment of scrutiny, the deputy scowled. "You sure you want to be walking around Templeman 3 alone?"

"The sheriff sent us," I said.

"Then be careful." The deputy motioned toward the ceiling. "It's really hot up there, and those men haven't had any food or water today. They're mad as hell and taking it out on anything they can get hold of."

"Are any loose?" I asked intently.

"Probably, and they won't care if you're doctors," the man said as he moved on.

Intent on the emergency, I had lost sight of the danger.

"This is not good." Sam stopped and looked at me. "A lot of these guys are addicts, and they hate me 'cause I won't give them drugs."

Sam and I had often talked about the problem. Drug addiction was rampant at the jail, and inmates were cut off from their sources. Many faked medical problems and tried to convince the jail doctors to prescribe controlled medications.

I shared Sam's concern, but he had been stabbed last year while treating an inmate in the infirmary. His fear of being attacked was worse than mine. In addition, Templeman 3 was dark, and we didn't know our way around the building. We needed an escort.

"Sloan!" I shouted, spotting a deputy I knew.

An ex-airborne infantry veteran, David Sloan was eager to help when Sam and I explained our mission. He moved us rapidly through the mob, parting a path through the inmates with, "Make a hole! Make a hole!" The pistol he brandished served to emphasize his commands, and none of the inmates hesitated to move aside.

We left the inmates behind and entered the room where arrestees were normally "dressed out" into jail scrubs. Their personal effects were collected and stored in the property room a short distance ahead. We could see walls of hanging clothes several racks high.

Suddenly, two inmates popped out of a doorway. They had separated from the pack, and they bolted when they saw us.

"Get over here!" Sloan raced away to apprehend them.

Alone again, Sam and I continued on. The last rays of light faded when we crossed the Templeman 3 threshold, and we were enveloped by an ominous blackness. The cacophony of voices and movement was suddenly gone, too.

The lack of light and sound shifted our senses into overdrive.

The caustic smell of fuel and smoke stung my nostrils, and a taste like copper pennies filled my mouth. The only noise besides our breathing was the slosh of water against the walls as we shoved debris from our path. Cinderblock walls, steel doors, putrid water, and the ever-present threat of an enemy lying in wait brought scenes from the movie *Aliens* to mind.

The smell of smoke and burning plastic grew stronger. Acutely aware of the diesel clinging to my skin, I nudged Sam. "They're setting fires again, and we're covered in fuel. We're gonna go up like Roman candles."

Sam was not amused. The foul air and water were disgusting, but they wouldn't kill us. Fire and escaped inmates could.

Ahead of us, flashlights suddenly pierced the dark.

"We're doctors!" Both of us yelled. "Don't shoot!"

Chapter 37

Two more SID deputies appeared, both heavily armed. We identified ourselves and asked about the two inmates in trouble. The deputies had been sweeping the building, looking for escapees, but had not heard about any injured men. When I asked them to take us to D-side, they told us that would be impossible.

"Can't do it," one of the men replied. "The deputy with the keys swam off. He smelled the fuel and said, 'This is asking too much. The hell with it.' Then he left."

"He left?" Sam gasped. "And the doors are locked?"

"Afraid so." The deputy led us to the doors to prove it. They were locked.

I exhaled with exasperation and looked at Sam. "If we can't get upstairs, there's nothing more we can do here."

"No one knows about any injured inmates anyway," Sam muttered as we started back. "We went through all this for nothing."

Angry and frustrated, I knew complaining wouldn't change anything. "We might as well help the others get the meds."

The deputies returned to their patrol, leaving Sam and me to find our own way out. We didn't encounter anyone else until we passed the property room. Five or six prisoners were looting the inmates' valuables stored inside.

"Hey, you guys!" I shouted, rushing forward. "Get out of there!"

"Are you crazy?" Sam grabbed my arm, pulling me back.

I was so exhausted I had reacted to the vandalism without thinking. Sam's words instantly alerted me to my mistake. We were unarmed, outnumbered, and the enemy. Five or six inmates could easily overpower us.

Without another word, we hurried toward the intake area and the safety of armed deputies. Sloan was back at his post.

"A bunch of inmates are looting the personal property, Sloan," I informed him.

"I'm on it." The deputy turned and slogged through the water.

When Sam and I re-entered the garage, Chief Bordelon and Major Jones were still loading inmates onto boats.

More than an hour after we had left the back steps of the Correctional Center, our mission had reached a futile end. Sam and I set off to find our colleagues in Templeman 1.

Chapter 38

Evening:
Eighty percent of New Orleans is flooded.
Approximately 100,000 people are stranded in the city,
25,000 at the Superdome.
The Ernest N. Morial Convention Center is opened for
evacuees.
The Correctional Center loses running water.

We'd been back from the Templeman complex for an hour. The dinner line stretched down the side of the Correctional Center, but it was moving quickly. The selection of food and drink available on the back porch had shrunk drastically, and people didn't need time to make up their minds. Almost everyone skipped the leftover sandwiches—barely edible after sitting unrefrigerated for a day—and chose an MRE.

Standing next to me in line, Gary rubbed a red scratch on his arm. "I thought a shower would help, but that diesel still burns."

"My skin and eyes are irritated, too." I was sore where the diesel had saturated my T-shirt. Even after vigorous scrubbing, an oily residue like suntan lotion remained. Everyone who had been in contact with the contaminated water was feeling the effects of the caustic fuel. The raw sewage might also be a problem, but hopefully, soap and clean water had averted any serious infections.

"At least we still had showers in this building," Gary added. "We owe Chief Hunter another one, that's for sure."

Fortunately Hunter and I were good friends. This was the fourth time in two days he had let me use the sheriff's shower. Everyone who had gone back to Templeman 1 had finished showering just before the Correctional Center lost running water. Now we were in the same boat as the other buildings in the jail.

I glanced at Brady, Mike, Sam, and Denise, who were sitting with Paul under the front edge of the overhang. They had looked like shipwrecked refugees when we finally made it back with the records and meds. Washed and wearing fresh clothes, they looked relaxed and actually cheerful.

"Why can't I have a soda?" the man in front of me bellowed at the kitchen worker. "That guy over there has one!"

"He didn't get it from us," the deputy said from behind the food table. "We ran out of soda before lunch."

"You're lying." The man leaned across the table to intimidate the deputy. "You've got them stashed somewhere."

"I'm telling you, I've got water or Gatorade." The worker looked annoyed, but he didn't lose his temper.

"I *want* a soda!"

I didn't know if the heavyset man was a rescued civilian, a deputy out of uniform, or a female deputy's husband, but his behavior was way out of line.

"Okay, look . . ." I stepped up, snapping the man's attention away from the deputy. "The kitchen's low on everything, and these people are working day and night to feed us. So why don't you just lay off?"

"Piss off." The man sneered at me, grabbed a bottle of water, and walked away.

Gary pulled me back as I started after him. "Just let it go. Not worth it."

I stared at the man's back, fuming. Sure, people were tired, scared, and worried. They didn't know what had happened to their homes or, in some cases, their families. Still, nothing justified abusing the kitchen staff. Those guys were just doing their jobs and doing them well.

Gary and I stepped up and chose MREs. When Gary took a bottle of water, I turned to the worker. "I want a soda."

The deputy laughed at my joke. "Thanks for that, man. They've been giving us hell all day long."

No one knew when any of us would be leaving. The inmate evacuation was going painfully slow. Roughly 4,000 inmates remained, and that didn't count employees, their families, or people rescued from the nearby neighborhoods. The Templeman complex still wasn't finished, and they hadn't even started moving inmates from the Old Prison, Conchetta, the House of Detention, or the juvenile facility, let alone the Correctional Center, where the commotion seemed to be worsening every hour.

Although the kitchen's provisions were running low, my colleagues and I could last two weeks on the personal supplies we had in Medical Administration. Red Cross helicopters had also dropped several boxes of MREs earlier in the day, though with just twelve meals to a box, the few boxes that landed on the Correctional Center roof had not significantly added to the food supply. The boxes that hit the water in the street had been lost. The meals were sealed in waterproof packets, but no one wanted to wade out to get them. Most people in the building had no way of cleaning up.

The loss of running water meant no more showers for us either, and the poor inmates had probably had their last drink.

"What did you get?" Gary peered at my dinner when I opened the packet.

"Spaghetti and meatballs." I knew from experience that it was one of the better choices.

"Lucky," Brady said. "The beef stew is terrible."

Gary nudged my elbow. "I'll take that dessert cookie, if you don't want it."

"Forget it, Gary." Mike's eyes lit up with a mischievous gleam. "He's eating everything that comes near him, whether it's good for him or not."

"I'm in military mode," I said. "Storing all the fat I can for later."

Mike poked me in the stomach. "It's working. You'll be the only one here who gains weight during Katrina."

"You'll wish you hadn't been so picky when the food runs out," I countered.

MREs were designed to be high in protein and calories; that meant high in fat. Mike hated eating them. In survival training, they had also told us that MREs were low in fiber to keep soldiers in combat from having bowel movements. At the time, I thought that was trivial. Now, given the state of the bathrooms at the Correctional Center, I considered it a definite plus.

"You know, I still can't believe what you guys went through at Templeman 3," Paul said, suddenly serious. "Loose inmates, fires. I knew it would be dangerous. Weren't you afraid?"

"It was scary, but I had Sam to protect me," I said, laughing.

"You're laughing, but it was a really brave thing all of you guys did today." Paul set his empty MRE package aside. "Getting those records and meds is going to save some lives. But you never did tell me how you did it."

Sam began. "Well, after we left Templeman 3, we swam over to Templeman 1." He shot me a sidelong glance, smirked, and made an arcing motion with his arm. "Then Dem tripped and ruined one of the few flashlights we have left. So we were stumbling in the dark with one flashlight when we ran into the others coming down from the third-floor medical clinic."

Denise picked up the story. "The gymnasium door was locked, and we didn't have the key. But I wasn't coming back empty-handed after getting that crap all over me again. So we got everything we could from the clinic."

"Five trash bags full," Brady said.

"Anyhow," Sam continued, "we still had to get the records for the infirmary patients, which is why we went in the first place. So Gary, Brady, Mike, and Denise waited, while Dem and I went back to the Intake Center and got a key from a deputy."

"Then we went back to Templeman 1," I went on, "but it was the wrong key!"

Paul's jaw dropped. "You've got to be kidding."

"No," I said. "Sam and I were so exhausted we would have quit right then if it wasn't a life-or-death situation."

"What'd you do?" Paul's head jerked around when glass fell

from a window overhead and broke on the tiled floor several feet away.

A slight smile curled the corner of Gary's mouth. "So they swam *all* the way back to the Correctional Center . . ."

"I knew Chief Belisle was here," Sam explained. "We thought he might have the keys, but he didn't. At that point I had enough, but Dem swam back to tell the others."

"By the time I made it to the Intake Center, they were already there with all the records and meds."

"From the infirmary, too?" Paul asked.

Mike nodded. "While we were waiting for Sam and Dem, we decided to salvage what we could from the flooded infirmary on the first floor. Believe it or not, Denise found the key to the second floor."

"It was just sitting on a shelf," Denise shrieked.

"So we put everything in trash bags," Mike went on, "and hauled them out in a couple of laundry carts."

"But we didn't have to swim the stuff back," Gary said. "Just as Dem reached us, we flagged down a boat and they brought us all back here."

Paul looked at Sam and me. "You guys must have been in that water for hours."

"Yeah, God knows what we're going to catch," Sam remarked, reminding me of the diesel oil burns on my chest.

"Be glad you didn't run into a poisonous snake," Paul said. "The boat drivers are seeing a lot of moccasins."

"I heard there was an alligator at the Old Prison," Mike said.

"That doesn't surprise me," Brady said. "With this much water, gators are bound to get into the city."

"Wish someone had told me that before I swam all over hell and gone today," Denise said, looking startled when a roll of toilet paper sailed down and landed a few feet from where she was sitting. "They're really getting out of hand up there."

"Hey! We need some water!" A voice called from above, and the end of a sheet dropped into view. "C'mon, somebody!"

Brady looked out from under the overhang. "They tied a bunch of sheets together and hung them out a window."

"We could try sending up some water," Gary said.

Gary, Brady, and I walked over to the serving area the kitchen workers had set up. Bottled water, Gatorade, MREs, and commercial-size cans of fruit cocktail and assorted vegetables were stacked against the wall. We asked the deputy for some water for the inmates. He cast a worried glance at the few cases remaining, but he gave us nine bottles.

"Lower the sheet some more!" Brady yelled to the inmate above. The prisoner wasn't visible through the narrow window, but the sheet dropped several more feet and a hand waved through the opening. We tied three bottles of water in the end of the sheet. "Okay! Haul it up!"

The bundle rose slowly toward the open window. Whistles and a whoop of triumph sounded when the inmates pulled the water inside. Then the sheet dropped again. We repeated the maneuver twice more, until all the bottles were gone.

"Send some more!" The inmates shouted. "We need more!"

"I'm sorry, but that's all there is." Gary obviously felt bad that he couldn't do more.

Suddenly, two rolls of toilet paper on fire rocketed downward.

"Look out!" I yelled, once more very conscious of the oily residue on my skin.

"Holy shit!" Denise jumped back.

Gary and Brady kicked and stomped the smoldering rolls to smother the flames.

"Don't kick them into the water!" I warned them. "The diesel fuel!"

"Unbelievable." Mike shook his head in disgust. "We give them water, and they try to set us on fire."

"Not to mention that we spent all day swimming in the sewer for them," Denise said. "What a bunch of ingrates."

"Well, look at it from their side," Gary said. "It's hot. They don't have water. It's dark up there, and they don't know what's happening. They must be scared to death."

"The deputies are going to have big trouble tonight," Paul stuffed his uneaten food packets in his pockets. "I hope they can handle it."

"I hope they stick it out," I said. "I still can't believe that Templeman 3 deputy took off with the keys."

"He's not the only one," Paul said. "The boat drivers said a lot of deputies are tossing their uniforms and leaving."

Rumors about desertions were flying around the Correctional Center, but all the deputies I had seen were working incredibly hard. "We saw deputies standing in water for hours getting the inmates out," I said. "Most of them haven't slept or eaten since yesterday. I can't believe they're still on their feet."

Denise focused on the deserters. "Where do they think they're going in this flood?"

"The overpass or home. Some are scared, but some are probably just worried about their families." Paul expressed more compassion than I was feeling at the moment.

"We're all worried about something," Gary muttered, "but we're not running."

"Things are bad in Mississippi, too," Paul said. "Between the wind and the storm surge, Gulfport and Biloxi were flattened."

"Have you heard any news about St. Tammany?" I asked.

Paul shook his head. "No, but I'll keep an ear open."

It had only been two days since I had spoken to my staff at the smaller jail, but it seemed much longer. I was worried about how they had fared during the hurricane. With cell phones offline and the jail telephone system down, I had no way of finding out. We were cut off from the world.

Chapter 39

The Correctional Center lobby had become Medical Central on a whoever-grabs-the-doctor-first basis. Gary, Mike, Sam, Victor, and I were all ambushed after dinner as we walked back through the building. After a long, rigorous day, we just wanted to relax on the front porch and catch up on the latest news trickling in from the boat drivers. But every time we finished handling one patient's medical problem, another person latched on to us.

I assured a young woman that she probably wouldn't get sick from the contaminated water. Rescued from a second-story balcony by boat, she had only been knee deep in the flood for a short time. With no cuts or scratches on her skin, infection seemed unlikely. However, I told her to come back if she developed any problems.

Gary finished bandaging a deputy's hand and walked over as my patient left and another civilian tugged my arm.

"Doctor?" The elderly black man looked frantic. "I need my pressure medicine. I didn't bring it with me."

"Try to calm down," I suggested gently. The man's trousers and short-sleeve shirt were still damp. Another evacuee who had made it to the jail with nothing but the clothes on his back, I thought. "We'll get you what you need."

"Do you know what medicine you're taking?" Gary asked.

"It's a little white pill." The patient held up his thumb and forefinger to indicate the size.

Gary and I looked at each other. His response was not unusual. Most people trusted their physician's judgment. They took whatever the doctor prescribed without bothering to remember the drug's name or dosage.

"Hey, Doc!" A deputy limped in the front doors and caught my eye. "Got a minute?"

"Go ahead," Gary told me. "I'll take care of this gentleman." He smiled at the anxious patient. "First we need to get a blood pressure reading."

Gary led the elderly man toward the supplies we had piled in a corner of the front lobby. We had brought down stethoscopes, blood pressure cuffs, bandages, skin lotions, alcohol, and over-the-counter medications from the second-floor clinic and Medical Supply.

It had become impractical to run upstairs every time a patient needed medicine or first aid supplies—impractical and consider-ably more difficult. The inmate unrest had escalated, and since noon the fire escape doors had been locked as a precaution. Every time we made a trip upstairs, we had to ask Sergeant Ross to un-lock the first-floor door and give us the keys to the security doors on the second and eighth floors.

"What's the problem, Deputy?" I motioned the limping man to one of the chairs we had reserved for medical use.

"I've been standing in water since yesterday, and my feet hurt like hell." The man winced.

"You'll need to take those boots off." Although I knew ex-posure to the filthy water was a health risk, I was still stunned by the condition of the deputy's swollen feet.

The skin he still had was white and wrinkled, like fingers left in water too long, but ten times worse. The macerated skin was peeling off in strips, exposing beefy red tissue beneath. I had read articles about trench foot among the troops during World War I, but I had never seen an actual case. I was pretty sure I had one now.

"How bad is it?" the deputy asked.

I was honest. "It's pretty bad, but we can fix this if you stay out of the water."

"I can't do that, Doc," the man responded. "We're short of deputies, and they need me out there."

"No matter what I do, this is going to get worse if you don't keep your feet warm and dry," I explained. "They may already be infected."

"Doc, I *have* to go back," the man insisted. "Just fix me up for now, and I promise I'll come back as soon as I can."

His dedication was laudable but a really bad idea from a medical perspective. However, his set jaw and steely eyes left no margin for discussion. He was going back out regardless of what I said or did.

"Okay, but first let me take care of those sores," I said. I found a towel and handed it to the deputy. "Dry your feet and sit here with your shoes off. I have to get some antibiotics and cream from the clinic upstairs, so it might be a while."

As I started toward the stairwell door, I saw Victor grab a mop bucket to catch a young boy's vomit. The medical problems we had been treating were getting worse: fever, rashes, diarrhea, cuts, and skin irritations. Anyone with a significant exposure to flood water—deputies and evacuees—needed antibiotics and tetanus shots. The influx of evacuees was also increasing, and many of them had lost or forgotten meds for serious conditions such as diabetes, heart failure, and emphysema. Most of the employees and family members had brought medications, but only for a day or two. Now their pills were running out.

We can't keep going upstairs each time we see a patient, I thought. It made more sense to bring *everything* we needed downstairs and set up an emergency clinic on the first floor. I glanced around for Sam. He was standing alone with a stethoscope draped around his neck. I hurried over and pulled him aside before another patient demanded his attention.

"Makes sense," Sam agreed after I explained my idea. "It would sure be easier than running up all those steps in the dark. But where should we set up? We'll need a triage area and a space for all the drugs and supplies—a *locked* space, or you know stuff will walk off."

That was a problem. Major Beach had to post guards on the back porch to keep people from stealing food and water.

Sam turned slowly, surveying the first floor. He pointed through the metal detector by the information desk to the computer room, on the far side of the lobby near the restrooms.

"What about putting everything in the computer room?" Sam asked. "There's only one way in, and the door locks."

"That would work, and we could section off an area right outside for patient care. I'll see if I can get the keys."

Chapter 40

I headed toward the sheriff's administrative offices in the Correctional Center, while Sam turned his attention to a panicked deputy with an elderly parent. Along the hallway I passed the room where we had stashed the bags of records and meds from Templeman 1 for safekeeping. Denise had volunteered to sort them, and Chuck and Scarlett were assisting her. They seemed to have everything under control.

Gerald Hammack, the director of Technical Services, was in his office. A tall, jovial man, he listened attentively while I detailed my request. He agreed to let us have the computer room and gave me the keys, on the condition that the room would be manned or locked at all times to protect the equipment. I assured him that the medical staff wouldn't leave our things unattended, either.

Rushing back to the lobby, I called the staff together. Doctor Shantha's son, Vinnie, who was hanging out with Mike, joined the group.

"Whatever you want doesn't involve swimming, does it?" Lillian asked with a sly smile.

"No," I said quickly. "No more swimming." Everyone laughed, and after I explained, they enthusiastically supported bringing supplies down to the first floor. "We can probably get everything we need in two or three trips."

With the nurses crowded behind me, I led the way to the stairwell door. Captain Verret intercepted me and asked what I was doing. When I told him, he looked stricken.

"No one else goes up," Verret said. "It's too dangerous, especially for this many people."

"We've been running up to Medical Supply and the clinic all day," I said. "This way, we go up, grab what we need, and we won't have to go back again."

"You don't understand." Verret lowered his voice so my curious staff couldn't overhear. "The inmates are close to breaking out on the tiers. We fed them at noon, but that's probably the last food or water they're going to get."

Verret had stationed two deputies on every inmate floor. Each pair was equipped with a single flashlight, a walkie-talkie, and—if they were lucky—a firearm. To conserve batteries, the deputies were standing in the dark listening to the activity on the tiers. They could hear cinderblocks cracking, pipes banging, and ductwork being torn from the ceiling as the inmates tried to break free. Periodically, the deputies turned on their flashlights, unlocked the outer door to the tiers, and looked around. They left quickly after inspecting for damage, but their brief presence helped maintain control.

My frown deepened as he talked. I didn't know the rioting in the building had gotten so bad. "Are any inmates loose?"

"We don't think so, but it's hard to know for sure." Verret sounded worried. "Some of the deputies are too afraid to go upstairs, and it's getting too risky for the teams up there to go into the tiers and look. Danny Boersma and I have been going from floor to floor to reassure them, but it's not helping much. There's no way I can let your staff go up."

Somehow, I had to change his mind. It might be days before help arrived, and medical supplies would be critical.

"Verret, people are getting sick—civilians, deputies, *and* inmates. They're going to need meds. If the inmates are close to breaking out, we *have* to go. It might be our last chance."

Verret wasn't easy to convince. "They're pulling pipes out of the showers and using them to break windows and chip away at the cinderblock," he said.

The windows on the tiers were Plexiglas reinforced with wire, but desperate inmates with enough time could eventually break through. Hell, I thought, we just sent water up through a broken window.

"It's dark," Verret went on. "They're yelling and lighting fires . . ."

"I just saw a deputy downstairs with trench foot," I said. "The skin is just peeling off the muscle. If I don't get him antibiotics, he could lose his feet."

Verret hesitated.

"We're facing a medical crisis here," I pressed on. "Just give me two deputies with guns. We'll be done in no time."

The acting warden finally agreed.

I related the dangers to the staff, but no one backed out. Guns in hand, Verret and Deputy Skyles covered us as we headed up the pitch-black stairs.

As we climbed past the inmate floors, we could hear the sounds of destruction on the far side of the locked security doors. The clang of metal against metal and crunching of glass rose above the steady drum of pounding on concrete. I thought of the deputy teams standing alone in the dark and wondered if I had the courage to do their job. Inmates who broke out wouldn't hesitate to jump or kill them.

Halfway up, Paul fell behind. "Go on. I'll catch up."

"Don't worry about it, Paul." I knew he had severe arthritis in his knees, and I didn't want him to climb if it was too painful. "We'll be back down in a few minutes."

Verret unlocked the fire door outside of Medical Supply, which was not on an inmate floor, and stood back to let everyone pass. Then Brady used his keys to open the supply room. Once everyone was inside the large space, I started calling out the most critical items. As I listed, Brady pointed the staff in the right direction.

"Chuck—get IV fluids, tubing, and catheters. Gary—bandages, alcohol, peroxide, and skin creams." The doctors and nurses grabbed cartons off the shelves as I went on. "Mike, Vinnie—Imodium, over-the-counter pain killers, insulin, and antibiotics."

"Bring the medication carts over here," Sam said. "I'll go through them to make sure we haven't forgotten anything."

"Do it quickly. I don't want to be up here any longer than necessary." Verret waited by the door, tense and concerned.

"We'll need all the tetanus serum you have in stock, Brady," I said. "Needles and syringes, too."

"Some vitamins wouldn't hurt," Gary suggested. "And a few scalpels."

"Sutures," Sam added.

"I'm on it." Lillian grabbed an empty box and headed in the direction Brady indicated.

I raised my voice so everyone could hear. "If you see anything on the shelves I didn't think of, grab it!"

When the boxes started to pile up by the door, Brady and I began handing them to nurses to carry downstairs.

"Did we get gauze?" Gary asked me. "And alcohol wipes. We need those."

"We need a bucket brigade," Lillian said as I handed a box to Scarlett.

"How much longer, Doc?" Verret checked his watch.

"A few more minutes," I said. Verret was as single-minded about security as I was about medical.

"We *need* a bucket brigade," Lillian repeated.

"What?" I glanced at her annoyed, then looked away when Gary called my name again.

"Think this is enough?" Gary held up a box full of gauze and bandages.

"Let's wind this up, okay?" Verret asked.

"We're almost done," I said, catching myself before I snapped at him. The extra pressure wasn't speeding up the process; it just grated on my nerves.

Lillian grabbed my arm. "This would go a lot faster if we set up a bucket brigade."

"What are you talking about?" I was being verbally assaulted on all sides, and I was out of patience.

"A bucket brigade!" Lillian threw up her arms. "You know, like firemen did in the old days. They'd get buckets of water from the well and pass them down a line of people. That way they didn't have people running back and forth. They just handed it to the next person in line."

I stared at her. I was desperately trying to think of all the things we might need. Verret was on my case to hurry things up, and Lillian was babbling on about buckets. Just as I started to put her off, I realized—the idea was brilliant!

"We have to do a bucket brigade!" I shouted.

"Oh, do you think?" Lillian said sarcastically. "Yes, indeed, what a good idea."

There was no time to give her credit; I was too busy assigning people to positions down several flights of stairs, but I'd apologize later.

The first nurses going down tried carrying boxes, but it was too awkward and dangerous to hold a flashlight and lug a box at the same time. The stairwells were dark and wet, and the cement steps were slippery. I chose a few nurses to hold flashlights on the landings.

Once the box brigade was in place and moving, the system worked quickly and smoothly. The nurses only had to go down a few stairs to hand the cartons off to the next person in line. When Gary started down with the final box, the nurses stationed along the route went down with him. Verret, Brady, and I were the last to leave.

The instant Brady locked the doors to Medical Supply, Verret pushed us into the stairwell and locked the security door behind us. "C'mon, people, move!" the captain shouted as we rushed downward. He wasn't happy when I halted on the second-floor landing and called Gary back.

"We have to get a few more things from the clinic," I said. "It will only take a second, I promise."

Verret looked down at the lobby exit just one flight below, then unlocked the door. "I'll help you carry."

We sprinted down the hall to the medical clinic. I found a trash bag and began pulling medications off the nurses' carts. Verret, Brady, and Gary gathered more meds, first aid kits, and other supplies. After two or three minutes, Verret hustled us out and down the stairs. As soon as we were through the security door into the lobby, he locked it.

"That's it," Verret said. "No one's going back up."

Mike stood by the information desk talking to Deputy Ross

as we approached. His head snapped around. "I am," he whispered to me. "My dogs are still up there."

"And I'm not leaving all my food," Gary said, matching Mike's conviction.

We'd have to deal with that problem later, I thought to myself. The deputy's case of trench foot came first.

Chapter 41

"Do you need anything else, Mike?" I asked. We had scrounged three flashlights, which dimly lit the computer room. Vinnie held another one so Mike could read the labels on the medication bottles.

Mike waved off the question. "Not right now. As soon as Paul and Brady finish clearing the desks and moving the computers, we'll get this mess organized."

I smiled as I stepped over and around boxes on my way to the door. The three men—four counting nineteen-year-old Vinnie—were completely focused on transforming the high-tech center into a functioning pharmacy and nursing station.

"Where should we put the emergency clinic?" Gary asked Sam as I joined them outside in the lobby.

"Why not right here?" Sam swept his arm across the space between the information desk and the computer room. "Then all the supplies would just be a few steps away."

I liked the idea, but there were a few drawbacks. The floor was awash in filthy water, some tracked in from the flood, some from the overflowing toilets. Hundreds of people were using the restrooms on the back wall, and the facilities reeked. Only a few courteous people took the time or trouble to flush with floodwater.

"It's not as hygienic as I'd like, but we can mop the floor." I moved away from the wall to survey the whole area. A line of chairs to my left partitioned the computer room corner from the remainder of the lobby. They were permanently anchored to the floor and provided a barrier on one side. The rear lobby wall would serve as the other side of the clinic. Despite the smell, this was the best place to set up for triage.

Several families were camped outside the computer room, but they would have to move. The space was packed with green prison mattresses, and pillows, suitcases, and other personal belongings were scattered around. Having no other options, we began to clear the area in front of the door. Aware that we were handling people's possessions, we carefully moved the items elsewhere in the main lobby.

"What the hell are you doing?" An angry woman yelled in my face. "That's our stuff."

I tried to be reasonable. "Look, we have to set up a medical clinic, and we need this space. We're just moving you over a little to make room."

"No way." She glared at me.

"Yeah, forget it," a man said. "We were here first."

"You'll move, or we'll have you forcibly removed." I'd had a really hard day and was in no mood to argue. In a crisis, medical necessity trumped squatters' rights.

For a moment, it looked like the couple would press the issue. However, they gave up and grudgingly collected their things, muttering curses under their breath.

Once the floor was clear, we had to establish the site as medical territory. Sam and Gary pulled the metal detector by the information desk over to the row of chairs. They placed the side of the detector against the chairs, about ten feet from the wall. Using a roll of bandage tape, I ran three lines of tape from the other side of the metal detector to the back wall, like police tape around a crime scene. Once I finished, we had cordoned off an area the size of a small bedroom.

We immediately moved into the clean-up phase. I volunteered to mop. I wanted Sam and Gary to find a prison mattress and two of the collapsible cots the deputies were using as beds.

"Where are we supposed to get those?" Gary asked. "Nobody will give them up just because we ask."

Exhausted, frustrated, and running on adrenaline, I was quick to snap. "Dammit, Gary! Just take any mattress or cot that's unguarded. Patients come first. If anyone gives you a hard time, call Verret and have them shot."

Gary blinked, then gave me a sheepish nod as he and Sam walked off.

By the time I found a mop and finished cleaning the floor, they were back with a mattress and two cots. I didn't ask where or from whom they had gotten them. We positioned the beds in the cordoned-off space. Pleased with the results, I checked in with the computer room crew. Mike and Paul were almost done setting up the pharmacy, with medications arranged by type. Vinnie and Brady had placed treatment supplies and equipment on the cleared desks and stacked boxes holding the excess nearby. At ten o'clock, for all practical purposes, the emergency clinic was ready to go.

Leaving Gary and Sam to begin seeing patients, I went back to check on the status of the records and meds we'd brought from Templeman 1. We had to get them to the overpass before the buses arrived in the morning and the inmates were sent to prisons around the state.

"We're almost done," Chuck said as I entered the large office. He opened a trash bag that was full of records.

Denise, Chuck, and Scarlett had organized them and sorted the drugs, repacking the medications in smaller trash bags and labeling them accordingly.

"This stuff is ready to go," Denise announced. "When are they sending a boat?"

"I'll go find out," I said, leaving them to finish up.

When I walked onto the front porch, I was immediately reminded of the dangers surrounding us. The flash of fire was visible from windows in the upper stories of the Old Prison two blocks away, and the smell of smoke drifted down from the inmate floors in the Correctional Center. People huddled in groups, watching the water, listening to news on radios, and speaking in low, ominous tones. Every thought, word, and nervous laugh was laced with fear and despair as the day ended and all hope of imminent rescue waned. Even my usual optimism was gone.

I had asked for a boat hours before, hoping to send the records and meds straight to the overpass and perhaps get Victor to his ER. My request had been denied. Inmate evacuation was the sole priority, and every boat was needed while there was still daylight.

Now, when I finally found the officer in charge and asked again, no boats were available. The volunteers from St. James Parish had left at dark, and one of the jail's boats had broken down. Only four small sheriff's boats were still transporting inmates. They were planning to work through the night, and I was told—bluntly—that no boats could be spared.

Denise didn't take the news well. "You mean we did this for nothing!"

"No, not at all." I was fuming, too, but I didn't have the authority to commandeer a boat. "The inmates won't be moving off the overpass until tomorrow morning at the earliest. As soon as help returns, we should be able to get a boat."

Chuck set the last bag of drugs aside. "If not, these extra meds will still come in handy."

Very handy, I thought, as the four of us walked toward the clinic. With hundreds of potential patients, the first-floor emergency clinic could use the additional stock.

Late as it was, business was booming at the new clinic. Sam and Gary had piled boxes and chairs by the flimsy tape to discourage people from ducking underneath. I had to laugh when I saw a sign proclaiming "Medical Clinic" written in blue marker and hung on the metal detector. Scarlett went into the computer room to inspect the new pharmacy. Denise and Chuck immediately began a standard triage routine.

Gary and Sam enlisted my help with the new wave of patients as they lined up. Several people who had spent considerable time in the water were waiting for antibiotics. Everyone we saw received a tetanus shot.

Gary, who had become adept at handling worried parents and sick children, was taking care of a baby with a fever of 102. Sam calmed a civilian having a panic attack, Victor was seeing to an asthmatic woman, and I treated another deputy with trench foot.

By 11:30 we had seen everyone who needed help. The nurses volunteered to man the clinic in shifts overnight, both to safeguard the supplies and help anyone who required assistance.

Sam and Victor chose to sleep on the porch with the infirmary crew, but Gary, Brady, Mike, Vinnie, Paul, and I wanted to spend the night in the privacy of Medical Administration with our food and water. Although Captain Verret had cut off access to the second floor, I was determined to change his mind again. Besides, nothing would keep Mike away from his dogs.

Chapter 42

I found Verret in the Control Room behind the information desk. The monitors, where deputies usually tracked all activity inside the building, were dark, but the location had become the acting warden's command post. He turned down my request to sleep upstairs before I even finished my sentence.

"I pulled all the deputies back to the first floor right after we got your supplies, Doc. The teams on the upper floors would have been completely cut off if inmates below them had broken out."

There were more than 300 inmates per floor. Two deputies with a single gun couldn't have fought off a rampaging mob.

"A group of us have been doing random checks," Verret continued. "Boersma, Skyles, Brunet, and a few others have really come through. We go up every so often to see if anyone's loose."

"Are they?" I asked.

"Some have breached their tiers, but they haven't gotten into the stairwell. One inmate did get into the ductwork on the seventh floor," Verret continued. "You can hear him crawling around in there, but he won't answer when we call."

Verret seemed adamant, but I tried one more time. "Where are your guys sleeping?"

"We're still sleeping in shifts on the second floor," Verret said.

"Listen," I began, "all of our stuff is up there in Medical Administration down the hall from where you are. Mike's dogs are there, too, and we really need some sleep. You can lock us on the second floor tonight and get us down in the morning. If the inmates get into the stairwell, they're not going to waste time breaking *onto* the second floor—there's no way out. And your guys will be sleeping between us and the door."

Verret relented, probably more out of friendship or fatigue than the strength of my argument. There was some risk, but I didn't care. I just wanted to eat and sleep.

Verret and Skyles escorted us upstairs. Steel and concrete muted the sounds of yelling and banging on the floors high above. Before they left us in the foyer outside Medical Administration, Verret gave us a chance to change our minds.

"You sure you want to stay here, Doc?"

"We'll be fine," I assured him.

Nodding, Verret and Skyles backtracked down the hall.

We were all too hyper to go right to sleep. Mike and Vinnie took Moby and Georgie into the foyer to relieve themselves. Mike was meticulous about cleaning up after them. Thanks to Paul's precautions, water from the trash cans could be used to flush their business. In fact, we all used Paul's trash can water to flush, and I was sorry we had laughed at him for storing it.

We met in the hallway for a midnight snack.

"If the wind blows the roof off your house or a tree smashes it and everything gets ruined from the rain," Gary mused, "does the insurance company call that flood or wind damage?"

"Don't you have flood insurance?" Mike asked.

"Yeah, but this disaster is going to cost the insurance companies billions." Gary frowned. "They'll figure out a way not to pay."

Similar questions had occurred to me, but I tried not to think about them.

"I'm a little worried about how I'm going to get these guys out of here," Mike said, scratching the bulldog behind the ears. "Moby can't swim."

Paul sat slightly back from the group, unusually pensive and quiet. He just shook his head when Mike offered him a low-fat bagel chip. The large container was almost empty.

"I'm a little worried about how *we're* going to get out of here." I was only half-joking.

"Have you heard the people stuck in their houses," Brady

asked. "Yesterday when I took supplies to the House of Detention and the Old Prison, they were screaming for help and the boat driver wouldn't stop. I can't get the voices out of my head." His eyes welled up with tears, and his voice cracked.

"Don't think about that, Brady," I said evenly, trying to keep him from losing control. "There's nothing you can do."

"The same thing happened to us when we took Major Crane to the ER last night," Gary interjected. "They were yelling, 'Help us, help us! We have children here.'"

Brady broke down. "It's so horrible."

"Stop it! Both of you," I said sternly. "We've got a job to do, and we can't afford to fall apart. When this is over, we can all go drinking and lose it then. But while we're here, just suck it up." I paused to look at every face. "I mean it."

I hated being so hard on my friends. The situation was affecting me, too, but we had to keep it together.

Paul deliberately changed the subject. "What do you think about those deputies who swam off?"

"I wonder how many have deserted," Mike said.

"Or how many are just sitting around doing nothing," I added. "I've seen a diabetic deputy twice since yesterday. Both times his vitals and sugar were normal, but he complained that he's too weak to work. Either he can't handle the stress or he's lazy, because there's nothing wrong with him."

Everyone had a story about someone behaving badly, even Vinnie. He thought the people who had harassed the kitchen staff were "ungrateful jerks."

Finally Mike, Vinnie, Paul, and Brady bedded down in the Medical Administration offices. To escape the smell of dogs, Gary and I went down the hall to the clinic. The two examination rooms were stiflingly hot, so we pried open the windows and stretched out on the exam tables.

I had too many things on my mind to doze off quickly.

It was unbearably warm, but at least we had water and an open window. Conditions had to be hellish for the inmates. Despite the danger they presented, I felt bad for them—and a little guilty because I wasn't hungry.

Still, there was no telling how long before food became a

problem. Everything stashed upstairs was probably out of reach for the duration. At least our clothes and toiletries were still in Medical Administration.

I closed my eyes, still troubled by how harshly I had just treated my friends, though I knew it had been necessary. In Korea, I had learned to take charge and manage personnel in crisis situations. There we had to function independently with minimal resources. Circumstances at the jail now required similar skills and decisions.

I had also grown up with a strong work ethic, encouraged to put the needs of others first and believing I could accomplish anything if I worked hard enough.

Confronted with the daunting task of keeping the Medical Department running, I had attacked the problem—not with pessimism—but with an entrenched belief that my staff and I could do whatever had to be done.

I drifted off worrying about the doctors and nurses in the other buildings, wondering if they had enough food, water, and supplies, wishing I could do more to help.

Wednesday, August 31, 2005

The Fourth Day

Chapter 43

Early morning

Outside the House of Detention medical clinic Dr. Marcus Dileo turned onto his side, trying to get comfortable as he lay on the hall floor. He hadn't had much rest, food, or water in the past thirty hours, and he couldn't sleep. He didn't have a mattress, blanket, or pillow, and even at three in the morning there was noise from the civilians camped out nearby.

A flashlight beam sliced the darkness in the clinic behind him, and a parent scolded a child who wouldn't settle down. Twenty nurses and their families were crammed into the nursing station and exam room. Marcus had chosen the hallway to escape the crowded conditions and commotion. If the kids weren't running, screaming, or throwing trash on the floor, they were crying or complaining.

They have a lot to cry and complain about, he thought, shifting onto his back and linking his hands under his head. Supplies were low, and the heat was nearly intolerable.

Marcus had been in the House of Detention since late Monday night, when Dem Inglese had sent him to cover the clinic. He had readily agreed, though he might have had second thoughts if he'd known in advance that his trek to the building would take him through filthy sewer water deep enough in places to cover his head. He had managed a sink bath for his head, arms, and chest, but he was still wearing the same blue scrubs he had on when he left Templeman 3 more than thirty hours ago. Slow to dry in the humidity, the damp cloth clung to his sweaty skin. His stomach growled, reminding him that he'd only had a boiled egg and a hotdog—no bun—since Monday evening. All his provisions had been left behind.

Sighing, Marcus rolled onto his side again. He could not recall when he had been more miserable. He had been crazy to volunteer. That thought generated a pang of remorse. He was a doctor, and the clinic at Detention needed him desperately. They had seen patients nearly nonstop since his arrival—deputies, inmates, and family members. No one was immune to the infections, rashes, fevers, and other problems caused by the lack of food and water and the unsanitary environment.

The first patient he had seen at the House of Detention was a diabetic deputy with an infected ingrown toenail. Marcus had surgically drained the abscess, started the patient on antibiotics, and provided regular wound care, but the man might still lose his toe.

As Marcus began to fall asleep, a nurse shouted his name.

"Dr. Dileo! Dr. Dileo!" Yolanda Dent ran into the hallway from the nearby stairwell. "An inmate upstairs is having a really bad asthma attack," exclaimed the tall outgoing nurse.

A burst of adrenaline immediately roused the doctor to full consciousness. Reaching for the stethoscope beside him, Marcus followed the nurse into the clinic. They grabbed asthma medications and a responder bag and then went upstairs. Neither of them had a flashlight so they used the banister to guide them through the dark stairwell.

As they neared the fifth-floor landing, they began to hear chanting and banging on the tiers, large communal rooms with small, four-man cells along the sides. When Marcus and Yolanda entered the hallway, they could make out loud gasps and wheezes—the sounds of the asthmatic patient—above the inmate noise. The hall was stiflingly hot, and Marcus wasn't surprised someone had suffered an asthma attack.

Two deputies stood in front of the tier, one with a flashlight and the other holding a lighter. Another nurse, Lakesha—Kesha—Favis, knelt on the floor outside the bars, shining a penlight on an inmate inside. The man was sitting up, struggling for every breath. Some of the other thirty inmates on the tier yelled, banged, or threw burning trash through the bars. A few were bent over the stricken man, talking to him.

"Can you bring him out here?" Marcus asked a deputy.

"Can't do it," the deputy answered. "They're rioting too bad."

Squatting down, Marcus studied the patient. The man's respiratory noises lessened—a bad sign indicating that he was barely moving air. Putting his hand on the man's head, Dileo tried to reassure him. "We brought some medications for you."

"Help me," the man pleaded in a barely audible voice, just before he slumped over.

The doctor called to him, but the inmate didn't respond. Reaching through the bars, Marcus touched the man's chest. The patient was not breathing, and the urgency of the situation hit the doctor hard. He didn't have a nebulizer to deliver asthma medicine, and there was no electricity to run one anyway. Metal bars separated him from the patient, and he saw no way to save him.

Moving closer, Marcus checked for breath coming out of the man's mouth. Suddenly, an inmate thrust his arms through the bars, grabbed the doctor's head, and slammed it against the metal. The doctor was caught completely off guard. Stunned by searing pain, he saw stars explode and fell onto his back.

"Dr. Dileo!" Kesha leaned over him, yelling. "Are you okay? Are you hurt?"

Marcus blinked hard for several seconds before he could respond. He mumbled, "I think I'm all right," and then slowly sat back up. A few more seconds passed before he could focus. Then another surge of adrenaline jolted his system, and he snapped back.

Glaring into the tier, Dileo pointed to the inmate who had assaulted him. "Get him away so I can help this man."

Two inmates pulled the assailant to the back of the tier as he screamed curses at the doctor. "They don't care about us," he ranted. "Why should we care about them?"

Several other inmates knelt by their unconscious cellmate and asked how they could help.

"Put him on his side and push him as close to the bars as possible," Marcus instructed. As he examined the man, he could feel slight air movement from his lips, but the inmates were yelling

and banging too loudly to hear breath sounds with his stethoscope.

A deputy shouted at the inmates to be quiet, and the noise
abated somewhat.

Marcus listened closely to the man's lungs with his stethoscope.
Hearing faint respirations, he asked Kesha for the pulse ox, to
measure the amount of oxygen in the patient's blood.

"You gotta help him. He's dying," one of the inmates said.
"He's dying."

The pulse ox read 78 percent, a dangerously low level. Knowing the man would die in minutes if he didn't do something, Marcus looked at the deputy. "Are you certain we can't get him out
of the tier?"

"If we open the door, all the inmates will rush out," the deputy
said. "Whatever you're going to do, you'll have to do it through
the bars."

Frantic, Marcus searched for a solution. His head throbbed,
but he forced himself to concentrate. The patient was unconscious
and couldn't use an asthma inhaler. In the dark they couldn't in-
sert an IV through the bars. However . . .

Marcus looked at Yolanda. "Get me an epi-pen, fast." The concentrated epinephrine solution was used to treat life-threatening
allergic reactions. "And some oxygen."

Taking the penlight, the nurse raced back to the second-floor
clinic. She returned in what seemed like seconds with an epi-pen,
an oxygen tank, and a face mask.

The inmates rolled the unconscious man flush against the bars.
He still had no visible respirations. Following the doctor's orders,
Kesha reached into the tier and raised the patient's right arm.

Marcus could barely see in the faint light. He took the cap
off the epi-pen and jammed the spring-loaded injector into the inmate's upper arm as hard as he could.

A sharp pain in his thumb stopped the breath in the doctor's
throat. He had made a terrible mistake. Unable to see clearly, he
had grabbed the pen upside down and injected the full dose of
epinephrine into the fleshy base of his own thumb. The inch-and-
a-half long needle was buried to the hilt.

Chapter 44

Marcus Dileo quickly pulled the epi-pen needle out of his hand, but it was too late. Within seconds, the concentrated adrenaline solution reached his heart, which began to race. The doctor's face flushed, his throat tightened, and his chest started to ache. Light-headed and short of breath, he fell backward, striking his head again. With a vice-like pressure constricting his chest, he struggled to breathe.

The nurses responded immediately.

"Are you all right, doctor?" Yolanda Dent crouched over him.

Marcus heard their conversation from a hazed distance and tried to answer as Kesha Favis placed the pulse ox on his finger. Along with the amount of oxygen in his blood, the machine registered a heart rate of 180 beats per minute.

"Are you going to be okay?" Yolanda asked again. She and Kesha slapped his face and called his name.

"My heart's racing," Marcus gasped. "Palpitations."

As he slowly regained full consciousness, the doctor wiped sweat from his eyes. He tried to sit up, but his right arm wouldn't respond. Something was seriously wrong, he realized as the nurses helped him. His hand was numb and wouldn't move. A peculiar, icy feeling gradually spread up his arm, and within seconds, the limb hung at his side—paralyzed. His mind, however, was clear, and despite his chest pain and labored breathing, he quickly assessed his own medical situation. He had a heart condition and might be in big trouble, but he wasn't dying. The inmate was.

"I need another epi-pen—fast," Marcus said to Kesha. As the nurse grabbed the penlight and bolted for the stairs, he ordered Yolanda to put an oxygen mask on the inmate. Then he had her recheck the inmate's pulse ox.

When the nurse said the reading was 58 percent, Marcus shuddered. The value was critically low. He's going to die right here, the doctor thought. What will we do with his body? If he dies, the inmates will riot for sure.

This time it seemed like an eternity before Kesha returned. She was winded when she emerged from the stairwell carrying several boxes of medications.

Crouching down, the nurse handed Marcus an epi-pen. "I brought a couple—just in case."

He fumbled with the syringe as he tried to remove the cap with his good, left hand. The doctor focused on remaining calm as the pain in his chest intensified. Taking hold of the inmate's arm, he double-checked the direction of the injector and slammed the needle into the man's skin. As soon as he finished, he called for another pen. Marcus jammed the second syringe into the man's buttock, then sat back and waited.

He didn't have to wait long. A few minutes later, he could hear the patient breathing. After another few minutes, the inmate began to stir, and Marcus asked the other inmates to sit the man up. When the deputy had again quieted the tier, the doctor listened to the patient's lungs. He heard wheezes, a good sign. The man was moving air again.

Kesha recorded another pulse ox—95 percent.

When the inmate opened his eyes and muttered a few sentence fragments, Marcus relaxed. The crisis had passed. He waited several more minutes until the patient was alert enough to take instructions about an asthma inhaler. The aerosolized medication would keep his airways dilated. After several puffs, the inmate's breathing improved even more. Then Marcus turned his attention to his own problems.

"I can't move my arm. It's numb," he said to the nurses, trying to hide his panic. The consequences of the accidental injection could be dire. He might lose his arm or could well be having a heart attack.

Yolanda helped him to his feet, but when Marcus stood up, he nearly fell over with dizziness. He had trouble breathing and leaned on the nurse as she guided him down the hall. After resting on a table for a short while, he allowed Yolanda to help him down the stairs.

When they were back on the second floor, Yolanda brought the doctor a blanket from the clinic. Marcus lay down in the hallway again and gratefully accepted a bottle of water and the wet washrag the nurse placed on his head.

"Are you okay?" she kept asking.

Marcus nodded, paradoxically calm, given the fact that he knew he really could die. He had a history of blood pressure problems, and after the adrenaline shot, his blood pressure had to be dangerously high. He didn't check it. He didn't want to know.

The chest pain had diminished but still felt intense, and his arm hung at his side, useless. He asked the nurse for a nitroglycerine tablet from the clinic meds. Then, closing his eyes, Marcus tried to slow his breathing as he sank into a depressed resignation.

Assuming he came through this medical crisis, other horrible realities loomed. He was certain that Katrina had destroyed his house in Lakeview. He could actually see his car totally submerged in floodwater from the windows in the House of Detention. Even worse, he had no idea what had become of his children, who lived in nearby Metairie. And his brother had refused to evacuate. Exhausted, famished, in pain, and emotionally spent, Marcus Dileo mercifully fell asleep.

Chapter 45

Midmorning:
Correctional Center deputies cannot distribute food and
water because of increased rioting.

Dr. Dileo awoke to stifling heat and the stench of sweaty bodies.
Groggy with fatigue, he glanced at his watch. Several hours had
passed. His chest pain was gone, and his breathing had returned
to normal. He still couldn't move his right arm, but he *could* wig-
gle the tips of his fingers—a promising sign. The sleep had helped.
He felt better physically, and things didn't seem quite as hope-
less.

Over the next several hours, Marcus relaxed and drank as
much water as he could find. There wasn't any food. Gradually
he found he could move his fingers, and he sat in the hall, watching people come and go from the medical clinic. The nurses could
handle the patients while he continued to recover. Sunlight filtered in through three broken windows. The light lifted his spirits, but not enough to offset the heat and humidity of the late
summer Louisiana day.

Last night, without warning, deputies had shot out several windows to let cooler air into the building. Terrified by the sudden
sound of gunfire, the clinic staff had panicked, assuming the
inmates were trying to shoot their way out of the House of Detention. After things eventually calmed down again, they appreciated the breeze, but now there was glass everywhere.

"Dr. Dileo!" Yolanda Dent burst through the clinic door. The usually calm nurse had her arms around a young woman, a medical assistant named Keri Marsalis, who was new to the jail. "We need your help."

As they approached, Marcus saw that their scrubs were covered in blood. Blood also streamed down the nurse's arms.

"Keri cut herself. It's spurting blood," Yolanda said. Keri's finger was wrapped in gauze, and the nurse held it tightly against her own body.

"What happened?" Marcus asked.

The nurse explained that some inmates still in Templeman 3 across the street were jumping out windows. Trying to get a better look, Keri had leaned on the window ledge and cut her hand on the shattered glass.

Within seconds Kesha Favis arrived with water, alcohol, gloves, and more gauze. The hall was much lighter than the windowless clinic, and Marcus sat Keri down where he could see. He pulled her hand free of Yolanda's firm grip and removed the gauze. Blood began to pump out of the wound.

"We've got a bleeder here," Marcus said, referring to the laceration. He immediately clamped his good hand around the finger to stop the bleeding and ordered Kesha to get sutures, a surgical kit, and some lidocaine.

She returned with the supplies in a plastic washbasin and sat down to assist him. Marcus had Kesha tightly squeeze the base of Keri's finger while he examined the wound. It was deep—to the bone. The tendon and artery had both been severed. Even with pressure applied, blood flowed profusely.

Marcus cursed under his breath. He was an internist, not a surgeon. In the best of circumstances, he wasn't qualified to repair such an extensive laceration. Today, he had poor lighting and only his left hand. But if he didn't act, Keri would lose the finger.

Marcus managed to draw lidocaine into a syringe with his good hand.

"I feel sick," Keri said. She looked queasy and ready to pass out. "I'm going to throw up."

A second later she vomited into the washbasin the nurse held in front of her.

"Close your eyes and don't look," Marcus told Keri as he swabbed her finger and injected it several times.

Keri kept her eyes shut and her jaw clenched.

As the doctor worked, another nurse stepped out of the clinic. "There's an emergency upstairs."

"You and Yolanda will have to handle it," Marcus said evenly. "I'm busy, and I need Kesha here." He shook his head. Could things possibly get any worse?

Working clumsily with his left hand, Marcus sutured the wound. He had partial use of his right fingers, which helped, but the process was extraordinarily cumbersome and the pace agonizingly slow. Kesha comforted the patient as Marcus painstakingly closed the severed artery and then repaired the tendon. Finally he closed the deep and superficial layers of skin and sat back, astonished. He had just accomplished the nearly impossible.

Keri had said very little during the procedure, and she sighed with relief when Marcus finished. While he bandaged Keri's finger, the other two nurses returned from upstairs. The emergency had involved another inmate with asthma. The man was fine now, but clearly heat and stress were taking a toll on everyone, inmates and staff alike.

When the nurses took Keri back into the clinic to give her antibiotics and painkillers, Marcus sat alone in the hallway and wondered how much longer they'd be stranded. He had no idea what was going on outside. No one at the House of Detention had news from the other buildings, and he hadn't been in contact with Dr. Inglese since Monday night. Marcus just hoped that the other clinics were having an easier time.

Chapter 46

"The water stopped rising," I said, leaning on the porch railing of the Correctional Center. "The flood level on Cheryl's van is the same as last night."

Sam and I took advantage of the lull in patients by relaxing on the front porch. The early morning hours had passed without incident. Captain Verret had escorted us down from the second floor at seven, and since then events on the first floor had been routine. Victor and Gary would call us if the caseload became more than they could handle.

"Yeah, I think it has." Sam agreed. He looked over at several plumes of smoke visible in the distance. "I wonder if that's from the blast we heard this morning. It woke all of us on the porch."

There were reports of fires and explosions all over the city. The news that the sheriff's mechanic shop had blown up was the second biggest topic of conversation at breakfast. The *main* thing on everyone's mind was the scarcity of food.

I jumped at the sound of gunshots.

"That sounded close." Sam's head snapped toward the interstate.

"Too close," I said. Stories about looters and shootings were also flying along the grapevine. The idea that criminals had taken random potshots at people was chilling. "I heard someone shot at John Daniel's Blackhawk helicopter when he tried to land at the Superdome this morning," I said. The director of purchasing for the sheriff's office had been flying back from a staging area in Gonzales, Louisiana, where law enforcement agencies were co-ordinating rescue efforts.

Sam's eyes widened. "Is he all right?"

"Yeah, but they couldn't land. They had to go back."

Sam shook his head and sighed. "I can't wait to get out of here."

Rescue couldn't come soon enough for me either, though I knew we wouldn't be going anywhere for a while. Even though the State Department of Corrections had shown up with more airboats, so far they were only moving inmates. The Templeman buildings were almost clear.

"Look at that!" Sam laughed and pointed.

I turned toward the street, where four people were paddling up to the Correctional Center steps in a hot tub. They climbed out, wet and exhausted—just like all the neighborhood people who had found their way to the jail. The Latino men with the side-of-a-house raft still returned every few hours to drop off more evacuees.

My gaze shifted upward as another helicopter flew over. Military and Red Cross copters were a constant presence in the sky now. I watched as one dropped another load of MREs. As usual, many of the boxes hit the water and were lost.

Sam abruptly shifted gears from intrigued onlooker to concerned physician. "Do the officers know if the buses have gotten to the overpass yet? I'm really worried about the infirmary patients. They've been there over twenty-four hours, and yesterday was really hot."

"I am, too," I said. "I'll see what I can find out."

On my way back to the emergency clinic, I detoured into the sheriff's office to make my case for a boat one more time. We still needed to take the records and meds to the overpass.

Chapter 47

At his makeshift command post behind the information desk, Captain Verret listened to his deputies' report with mounting concern. The men had just returned to the lobby from patrolling the upper floors.

"We didn't go onto nine," Deputy Skyles explained. "I'm not sure, but it sounds like the inmates have breached the tiers."

"Are they in the stairwell?" Verret asked for clarification.

"Not yet, but they will be," Captain Boersma said. "It's just a matter of time."

Verret warily eyed the closed stairwell door, then counted heads to make sure all his people were accounted for. "No one's left upstairs, right?"

"Captain?" Sergeant Patrice Ross interrupted. "One of the deputies took Nurse Mazant up to the second floor an hour ago."

"What?" Verret's mind raced. He thought he had made it clear: no one was to go up.

"She insisted on getting meds for the diabetic inmates," Ross continued. "She said they couldn't wait."

"Are they still up there?" Verret asked.

"Nurse Mazant is," Ross explained. "But the deputy came back down a half hour ago."

Skyles frowned. "If those guys get into the stairwell, she'll be trapped."

"It'll be worse than that if they get onto the second floor and find her alone." Verret drew his gun. "Let's go."

None of the deputies needed detailed instructions to know what Verret intended. Guns in hand, they ascended the flight of steps with all senses alert.

Judging by the echoing voices above, Verret was certain that inmates were indeed in the stairwell. He swore under his breath. The nurse was a small, thin woman, and her medical status wouldn't protect her.

When the men reached the second-floor landing, Verret and Boersma positioned themselves with weapons raised to stop anyone coming down. They could hear the inmates above, but no one was in sight. Skyles unlocked the door and held it open. Deputy James Brunet halted just inside the door, while his colleague Lance Wade ran to the medical clinic directly ahead.

Shifting his gaze between the stairs and the hallway, Verret was attuned to every sound. He tracked the beam of Wade's flashlight as the deputy moved down the dark corridor.

Audrella Mazant smiled when the stocky, normally jolly deputy pulled the clinic door open. "Hi, Wade." Her cheerful voice made it clear she was unaware of the danger. She carried a plastic box. "What are . . ."

"C'mon!" Wade shouted and grabbed her arm.

"Let go, Wade," Audrella cried. "You're hurting me."

"I'm trying to save you," he insisted, pulling her.

The startled nurse dropped the box, scattering pills across the floor. She looked terrified as Wade yanked her toward the stairwell.

"Wade, let her go!" Skyles yelled.

"I'm just trying to get her out," Wade yelled back.

"The inmates are loose, Ms. Mazant!" Brunet explained.

Seconds later, the nurse and the deputy were out on the landing and on their way down the stairs. Skyles locked the door behind them, while Verret and Boersma provided cover until everyone was safely in the lobby and the first-floor security door again shut tight.

Chapter 48

I was walking out of the sheriff's office, fuming about the latest turndown of my request for a boat and still trying to figure out a way to get the meds and records to the overpass, when I saw Captain Verret speaking to Nurse Mazant. Audrella seemed shaken as she walked out to the front porch, and I intercepted the acting warden to find out what had happened. He briefed me on the nurse's recent rescue from the second-floor clinic.

"I know she just wanted to get meds to the inmates," Verret explained, "but they wouldn't give a damn what she was doing."

I stood there in awe. Audrella's house had been lost in the flood, and she didn't know if her husband had survived. Yet, instead of dwelling on her own problems, she was trying to care for her patients.

"We've got inmates loose on nine, Doc," Verret said. "Nobody goes upstairs again—for anything. I don't want anyone getting hurt—inmates or personnel."

Neither do I, I thought, heading toward the clinic, though I knew we'd have to find a way to get to Mike's dogs.

I saw Victor examining a baby, and I didn't want to interrupt him. Instead I waved Sam into the pharmacy, where Gary, Mike, Brady, and Scarlett were packaging antibiotics into three-day packets. Denise searched for additional vials of tetanus immunization serum. When I told them my request for a boat had been denied yet again, their reactions ranged from dismay to fury.

"Are you serious?" Denise barked. "No boat?"

"All the boats are needed for the evacuation." I repeated what I'd been told.

"We only need *one* boat for *one* trip." Sam's eyes clouded with anger. "Someone is going to die!"

"I have half a mind to swim the damn records and meds to the overpass myself." Denise's nostrils flared, and she rubbed a large patch of reddened skin on her arm. Everyone who had swum through the diesel-laden water yesterday had reddened skin and itchy rashes. My chest stung much worse today.

"What about the buses?" Sam asked. "Have they started moving people?"

"Nobody here knows," I said.

Muttering, Sam left to take care of a woman who had slipped and pulled a muscle.

"What's wrong with the baby?" I asked when Chuck came in to get Tylenol liquid for Victor's small patient.

"Fever's a hundred-and-three," Chuck said. "A lot of kids are coming in with high temps and rashes. I hope the antibiotics hold out."

I didn't remind him that we had an additional supply in the sheriff's office. I still hoped we could get those medications to the overpass. I set those thoughts aside and went to treat another deputy with an infection. Dispensing antibiotics and giving tetanus inoculations had been the primary order of business all morning.

"Dr. Inglese—"

I looked up as Gloria Scott, a medical assistant at the jail, entered the clinic. I was in no mood for another debate about the health of her husband, who had suffered a mild heart attack a year ago.

"Gordon has a bad heart, Dr. Inglese. We have to get him to a hospital."

"We checked Gordon last night. He was fine," I said. He had no chest pain, and his vital signs were normal. I suspected his wife was using his condition to get the two of them evacuated as soon as possible. But if Administration wouldn't spare a boat to carry meds for 200 seriously ill inmates, I wasn't going to request transportation for someone who wasn't really sick.

"I'm worried about him," Gloria persisted.

"Then bring him here, and I'll check him again." My words were clipped and my tone sharp, but I held my tongue. When I saw Gerald Hammack, the director of Technical Services, burst out of the stairwell door with a gun in his hand and a deputy on his heels, I excused myself and hurried over.

"Are you okay?" I asked, noting Hammack's rapid breathing.

"Yeah, Danny just saved my ass." He nodded at Captain Boersma and holstered his gun. "And I just ran down three flights of stairs."

"Why were you upstairs?" I knew Verret had prohibited access.

"The sheriff sent me up to the switch room to see if I could get a phone working," Hammack explained. "We have circuits that run on batteries, and he wanted me to make some calls—to let someone know that our situation here is serious and we need more help."

"Did you get anyone?" I raised an eyebrow.

"A few people." Hammack shrugged. "Then the batteries quit. I couldn't do anything else so I went to leave, but the stairwell door was locked."

"You were up there alone?" I glanced at Boersma. If the loose inmates breached the stairwell, no place in the building would be safe.

"No one told us he went up there," Boersma said. "I found the door open during a sweep and locked it."

Hammack continued, his words tumbling out in a rush. "So I'm thinking, 'Oh, shit. This is going to be ugly. No one knows I'm here!' I was sure I'd be left behind. I had one of those big bottles of water, but no food."

His fear was justified. Once the jail was evacuated, it might be weeks before anyone came back.

"So I started banging on the door and yelling. 'I'm stuck! Get me out of here!'" Hammack grinned. "Boersma was doing a sweep and heard me. He unlocked the door, and we both got the hell out of there."

"It's a good thing we got Gerald and Nurse Mazant out," Boersma said. "Inmates from the ninth floor got into the stairwell."

"Where are they now?" I asked.

"We herded them onto the roof." Boersma's demeanor was matter of fact. "They're locked there—they can't go anywhere. But it won't be long before more break out from other tiers."

Hammack looked at his watch. "I could use some lunch. How about you, Doc?"

"After I check with the clinic." I needed a moment to adjust to the new reality: inmates had breached the stairwell. Sooner or later, they'd overrun the building.

Chapter 49

Afternoon:
Deputies in the House of Detention fire shotguns on the tiers
to quell rioters.

For most of the people stranded at the Correctional Center, food
took precedence over medical attention for minor ailments. Victor volunteered to man the clinic during the noon slowdown while
Sam, Gary, Mike, and I ate. I was grateful we still had MREs, but
the pre-packaged military meals went down better with company
and conversation. Soon after we sat down, it became apparent
that my colleagues' spirits were waning. I wasn't surprised, considering the latest news reports and the state of our surroundings.

"I'm sick of spaghetti." Sam poked at his food.

"I'm sick of being here," Gary complained. He leaned to the
side, shielding his food packets as two boys ran by. They had
been wrestling and chasing each other since we arrived. "Stop
horsing around!"

The boys ran off, laughing.

Kids of all ages—from toddlers to teens—congregated on the
wide back porch. Many were running amuck, barefoot with dirt-
streaked faces and clothes.

"My dogs are cleaner than those kids," Mike observed. "Why
are their parents letting them play in that water?"

"It's no wonder so many kids are getting sick." Gary opened
a package of crackers and jam.

All heads turned when Paul came over. "They just shut down the rescue effort at the Superdome. People are shooting at the helicopters."

"Really?" Gary was aghast.

Paul shrugged. "That's what they said on the radio."

"What the hell's wrong with people?" Mike snapped, incensed. "Why would anyone shoot a rescue helicopter?"

I was incredulous. "They must be crazy."

"Some probably are," Sam said soberly. "A lot of addicts are out there roaming the streets, and their sources are gone."

"Any idea how long before they get us out of here, Paul?" Mike asked.

Paul stared at the tiled floor for a moment before answering. "Hard to say. Word has it that they've stopped evacuating inmates because someone shot at boats from the Department of Corrections."

Everyone stared at him, momentarily speechless.

"Isn't *anything* going to go right around here?" Mike asked in annoyance.

I was frustrated, too, but at least we had food and dry shelter, and knew what was happening. The rioting inmates had no idea if or when rescue would come.

High on the Templeman 3 building we could see a sheet stretched between two windows. "Help us!" was printed in large letters. And here in the Correctional Center the inmates on the tiers cried out constantly for water and shrieked for help every time a helicopter flew overhead. They pounded so hard on the walls and pipes that we could feel the vibrations in the building's wall.

Paul frowned as charred pieces of a burned sheet fluttered down. "I heard that some inmates broke out of the tiers upstairs."

The tension around me suddenly escalated. "Verret rounded them up," I quickly interjected. "They're locked on the roof."

"They still got out," Mike said.

Paul nodded. "Scarlett wrote her name and social security number on her clothes again. She really thinks she might die."

A spat between two civilians erupted by the back doors just as Brady came out to join us. He talked the two men down before one of them threw a punch. The number of arguments and shoving matches had increased steadily over the past twenty-four hours. The confrontations were mostly about ridiculous things, such as cutting into the food line or intruding on personal space. Raw nerves, stress, and uncertainty fueled tempers everywhere.

By the food tables, a large woman stood arguing with a kitchen deputy. Everyone was tired and scared, and too many people were taking their anxiety out on the food servers. Major Beach's workers continued to handle the abuse with commendable patience.

"Makes you wonder if these people are jerks in real life, too," Mike said.

"I bet they are," I said. "People's true colors come out in stressful situations."

I looked toward the courtyard in front of the kitchen and noticed several deputies wading through the chest-high water carrying boxes of salvaged food supplies. Brady left to lend a hand, and I followed him.

Where the back porch steps met the water, the orange film of diesel fuel stopped me for a moment. The burning sensation on my chest was getting worse, and I dreaded going back into the foul liquid. However, I ended up not having to take another plunge. Before Brady and I were ankle-deep in water, the two deputies handed us the boxes. We made several trips to the tables with cartons of Ensure, MREs, and commercial-size cans of corn, turnip greens, fruit cocktail, and tuna. The items were not particularly appetizing, but hungry people would eat whatever was available.

"Makes your mouth water for my jambalaya, doesn't it?" Brady asked with a grin.

"No." I wasn't *that* hungry.

Both of us halted abruptly at the sight of movement on the wall of Templeman 3. A door on the third floor—the entrance to a pipe chase—flew open, and inmates lowered a rope made from bed sheets tied together. One man began climbing down the side of the building.

"Look at that guy!" Brady exclaimed when the inmate dropped into the water. "Unbelievable!"

Gunshots rang out as another man started down. He slid downward faster, followed by a few others who jumped from the third-floor opening.

Trying to locate the source of the shots, I scanned from Templeman 3 to the House of Detention and finally made out an SID deputy there, squatting on the second-story porch roof aiming a sniper rifle. He fired again to stop more men from jumping out. The inmates in his sights froze for a second, then pulled the door closed.

"Were those live rounds?" I asked.

"Riot police use rubber bullets," Paul said as he, Mike, and Gary came up behind us.

The surreal scene continued as the SID deputy fired every time the door opened—until finally the inmates gave up.

"I bet deputies are already fishing them out of the water," Brady said. "They won't get away."

I didn't think the inmates had jumped to escape. The evacuation was proceeding so slowly, they probably thought they were jumping to save their lives.

With lunch and the sideshow over, we turned to head back inside. Suddenly, two plastic bottles dropped from a window above and broke on impact.

Gary walked over to take a closer look. "It's urine," he said, his face wrinkled with disgust.

"Oh, that's just wonderful," Mike said, appalled. "Those are probably the same bottles we sent up yesterday."

Chapter 50

My friends and I were quiet as we walked to the clinic. Being bombed with urine was revolting, and it was hard to maintain empathy for the inmates when their actions were so vile. As Captain Verret had pointed out earlier, the incarcerated men didn't care that the medical staff was there to help them. Anyone not behind bars was the enemy.

I vowed not to forget that again.

As we entered the lobby, I spotted Verret and his deputies by the stairwell door. Captain Hammack had joined the squad, and they all held flashlights and guns. They looked poised for a sweep, and I walked over to get an update on the situation. If the inmates resisted the deputies' efforts to contain them, there could be serious injuries and the medical staff would have to be prepared.

The noise filtering through the security door was much louder than before.

"Going up again?" I asked Verret.

"Have to. They're making a hell of a racket, and we need to know what's going on." Verret looked past me. "Gerald, stay here and guard the door."

"Will do." Hammack's hand flexed on his Beretta 92F when Verret motioned Sergeant Ross to unlock the door.

Shouts and banging reverberated off the cinderblock walls. I stepped back to let Verret and the men enter the stairwell. Hammack, the jail's normally affable technology wizard, took up a position inside the open doorway, gun drawn and all business. If inmates came down the stairs instead of Verret, he would be ready.

Intrigued and tense, I watched from one side, wondering how Verret and four deputies could manage 800 rioting inmates.

"Coming through!" A frantic voice diverted my attention.

Two deputies rushed in through the front doors, supporting Captain William Devlin, and I dashed across the lobby to meet them. "What's the problem?"

"He's been driving a boat," one of the deputies explained, "and he hasn't slept in thirty hours."

"He hasn't eaten or had much to drink, either," the second man added.

"Doc, I need help," Devlin said. Six-two and 320 pounds, the big man looked dazed and confused.

I pointed the deputies toward the clinic. "Let's get him to a bed."

Devlin was bright red, sweating, and slightly incoherent—all signs of heat exhaustion. It had been brutally hot for two days, and we had already treated several cases.

The deputies laid Devlin on the prison mattress, and I took his vital signs. He had a pulse of one-thirty, and his blood pressure was one-twenty over seventy. The treatment was simple: fluids to rehydrate and glucose for energy.

Devlin was so dehydrated, his veins had collapsed, and I needed an experienced nurse to place an intravenous line. I called Chuck Perotto over. "Start an IV and hang a liter of D5-half-normal saline wide open."

"What's going on?" Devlin asked as Chuck tied a tourniquet and swabbed his arm.

"It's just heat exhaustion," I assured him. "Don't worry. I have an RN here to help you."

"I don't want an orange," Devlin protested. "I had one earlier."

At first, I was puzzled, then I laughed. "Not an *orange*, Devlin. An RN."

Devlin closed his eyes and passed out before Chuck finished inserting the IV.

When the line was in place, Chuck attached the bag of saline, then hesitated, perplexed.

"What's wrong?" I asked.

"We don't have an IV pole. There's no place to hang the bag."

I grabbed a roll of bandage tape from a pile of supplies and taped the bag to the top of the metal detector. Then I made sure the fluid was flowing.

"Works for me." Chuck grinned.

Leaving Devlin in Chuck's care, I went out to the front porch, where Paul and Brady were trying to get news from the overpass. As I walked out, a Department of Corrections boat arrived carrying two civilians, a middle-aged man and a boy in his late teens.

Paul recognized them. "That's Jan Ricca's husband, Harry, and her son, Morgan."

After Paul introduced us, Harry asked about his wife. Jan was fine, I explained, but the nurse was still stranded at the Old Prison. They wouldn't be able to join her, but we could try to let her know that they were safe.

"How'd you get here from uptown?" Brady asked.

"We swam a mile through the flood to I-10," Harry said. "I thought the interstate would be dry. But when we got there, we could see a gang of thugs robbing everyone who tried to go up the on-ramp. They had guns and baseball bats so we waded farther down before we climbed up to the road. They chased us for a while but finally gave up. Then we walked three miles to the Superdome."

"From what I hear, that's not any safer." Paul frowned. "The radio said people are getting robbed, beaten, and raped."

"We didn't stay," the teenager said.

"A National Guardsman told us it was like a war zone inside." Harry glanced at Morgan. "I wasn't taking him in there, so when we saw a boat tied up, we decided to come here. I felt bad about taking it, but I didn't know what else to do."

"What happened to the boat?" I asked, curious.

Morgan sighed. "We gave a couple of guys a ride, and halfway here they stole it."

"They had a gun," Harry said. "I wasn't going to argue. Right after they left us, the Corrections boat picked us up."

"Do you have any food?" Morgan asked. "I'm starved."

Paul and Brady took the two of them to the back porch. Before they had gone a few steps, a deputy with a radio walked up to me. "You're Dr. Inglese, right?" he asked. "They need you. They're evacuating Conchetta, and an inmate's having a baby."

Chapter 51

It took me a moment to absorb the deputy's news. It wasn't unusual for female inmates to be pregnant, but we always sent them to Charity Hospital when it was time to deliver. We were not prepared for a birth under normal circumstances—and this was anything but normal.

"Is she just having contractions or is the baby actually coming out?" I asked, alarmed.

The deputy repeated the question into his radio, which apparently still functioned.

"She's standing here telling me it's coming soon," the voice at the other end said.

Ordinarily, I would have gone to the patient, but the Conchetta medical clinic was on the first floor and clearly underwater. It would be too difficult to deliver a baby there. "Tell them to bring her here."

"It might take a while," the deputy explained. "The first floor's flooded to the ceiling, and they're taking the women out through a hole in the wall. This morning Devlin cut a window out with a blowtorch."

"They need to move her as fast as possible." As the deputy relayed my order to Conchetta, my attention was drawn to the water. One of the sheriff's boats had just pulled up.

Sam jogged down the steps as Matthew Mills, a young deputy he knew, jumped out of the boat. Short and boyish looking, he wore black fatigue pants and a black vest with no shirt. He and the boat driver were badly sunburned, and both were armed with shotguns.

"Have you been to the overpass?" Sam asked anxiously as I arrived. "Are they busing people out yet?"

"They started around noon," Mills said. "None too soon, either. It's bad over there."

"How bad?" I asked, worried about my two nurses, Hedy and Kentrisha.

"Like hell, only worse." The deputy wiped sweat off his face with the back of his hand. "There's no place to get out of the sun. The inmates are crazed, and a bunch of deputies quit."

"Quit?" Sam scowled.

"A couple swam off," Mills went on, "but others are just refusing to help. Some took off their uniforms and are sitting there pretending to be civilians."

"There are civilians?" I was aghast. Conditions on the overpass were much worse than I had imagined.

"Mostly families of jail staff and locals who swam there, but the civilians aren't the problem. The deputies who are sitting around hogging all the food and water are the problem." Mills paused, obviously furious. "We came to get supplies for the guys that are working. They're starting to pass out. We need some water."

"Have you gotten any sleep?" I asked. Mills wasn't in as bad shape as Devlin had been, but he looked haggard.

"We can't sleep, Doc," the deputy said. "If we take a break, no one steps up to relieve us, and there's not enough of us to cover a couple thousand inmates as it is. We've almost lost control more times than I want to admit."

"Have the infirmary patients been evacuated?" Sam asked.

Mills shrugged. "I don't know."

"What about the nurses?" I followed up. "Have you seen them?"

"Oh, yeah." The deputy nodded vigorously. "They're doing a great job. Hedy's taking care of the inmates, and the deputies and civilians go to Kentrisha. They could use some help, though. I don't think they've eaten or slept, either."

I looked him in the eye. "We'll get you supplies, but you have to promise to make sure Kentrisha and Hedy get food and water."

"You got it."

"I mean it!" I said again for emphasis.

Sam and I escorted Mills and the driver to the back porch. The kitchen worker I had defended yesterday was working the food tables again. He gave us all the MREs and water we could carry.

After we stowed the supplies, Sam and Mills went back for more, leaving the driver at the boat to guard the stash. I went to find a volunteer to relieve one or preferably both of the nurses. Hedy and Kentrisha had both been on the overpass for more than twenty-four hours. They needed some relief.

Kentrisha's friend Carol Evans agreed to go. She had "Nurse" written in black letters on her orange prison scrubs, but the driver still did a double take when she climbed into the boat.

"This is *Nurse* Evans," I said. "Take good care of her."

"We will," Mills answered as he loaded the last of the provisions.

I asked him to wait a minute, and waving Sam to follow, I bolted for the sheriff's office. We grabbed all the records and a couple bags of meds and raced back out. Mills started to object when we piled the bags into the boat, but I ignored him.

"That's it, Doc," he said when I started to go back for more. "The boat's already overloaded."

Thrilled that we were finally getting records to the overpass, I didn't press the point. I told Carol to send the bags to Hunt Correctional with the infirmary patients. If they had already been evacuated, she should send the bags on the next bus out.

As Mills's boat pulled away, Chief Bordelon arrived from the Intake Processing Center. He had been working without food or sleep for thirty hours and looked terrible.

"Doc, I sure could have used you this morning," Bordelon said after I greeted him. "An inmate ripped the vent fan out of the showers and climbed into the ductwork."

"He fit in there?" I asked.

"Hard to believe," Bordelon said, "but he was small enough to crawl through. He got to the roof and tried to jump down into the water, but he got tangled in the razor wire on top of the fence. We had to cut him free. Man, he was sliced from the top of his back to his butt."

I winced. "What did you do with him?"

"Cleaned him up, bandaged him, and sent him to the overpass." Bordelon sighed. "There wasn't anything else to do without power or water."

"The nurses on the overpass will take care of him." I hoped they'd put him on the next bus out to Hunt.

As soon as Bordelon walked away, I turned to his boat driver. "So everyone's out of Templeman 3 now?"

"Just about. A few inmates are still stuck in cells that won't open, but Maintenance is cutting them out with a blowtorch."

"What happened to the inmates that jumped from the pipe chase a while ago?" I asked.

"We probably caught them," the driver replied. "A lot of guys have tried to escape, but we tracked most of them down. I'm sure some got away, but not many."

When the deputy told me his next stop was the Old Prison, I got paper and scribbled a note for Jan Ricca. I wanted to reassure the nurse that her husband and son were safe with us.

A few moments later, the pregnant woman from Conchetta arrived. I instructed the two deputies helping her out of the boat to take her inside to the clinic.

Gary walked over when we entered the lobby, and I was glad to have the backup. "How are you doing, ma'am?" I asked the woman.

"My baby's coming." She slowly lowered herself into a chair.

"How far apart are the contractions?"

"Every couple of minutes, I guess."

"When did they begin?"

She shrugged. "About two hours ago."

"How many weeks along are you?"

"Thirty-seven."

"Is this your first baby?" I asked.

"No, I have four children."

I pulled Gary aside. "We're in trouble. This is her fifth child. She's going to go fast."

"If she's really in labor," Gary said. "We need to examine her. She might be pretending so she can get out of here faster."

The patient rested while Mike, Brady, Gary, and I moved a desk out of the computer room and hauled it across the lobby to a spot near the glass windows, where the light was better. Then I quietly asked Gary, "How's your OB?"

I hadn't done obstetrics since medical school, thirteen years ago. Internists didn't do obstetrics. Gary was five years younger than me, much closer to his OB training.

"I'm pretty rusty," Gary admitted. "We should ask Victor for help."

Why didn't I think of that? I asked myself. As an emergency medicine physician, Victor had substantial obstetrical training and experience.

Gary put a pillow and blanket on the desk while we cleared the area of curious onlookers and guided the woman onto the table. I hurried out to the front porch to find Victor and ask a couple of nurses for help. Victor was taking a break after working in the clinic all morning, but he was used to having his rest interrupted. Denise and Lillian, who had been an OB nurse for years, rounded out the team.

The nurses draped the blanket over the woman and helped her out of her pants. Then they supported the patient's legs and held a flashlight while Victor performed his examination. Gary and I did our best to block the view from the porch.

"She's about six centimeters dilated and seventy-five percent effaced," Victor announced when he finished. "She's not delivering now, but we only have a couple of hours."

We had to get the patient out of the jail. I did not want to deliver a baby in the mess at the Correctional Center. The environment wasn't sterile, and we didn't have the proper equipment. If there were complications, we'd be helpless.

"What were you arrested for?" I asked the woman.

"Possession of crack."

Gary scowled, obviously unhappy that the woman had been using drugs while pregnant. I was just glad she wasn't in jail for something more serious. We had to get her to a hospital, and I knew a deputy couldn't be spared to accompany her. However, I needed the sheriff's permission to release her.

On my way to speak with him, I saw Captain Devlin sitting up in the triage area. Still concerned about the deputy, I walked over to take a quick look.

"Guess you're feeling better." I glanced at the IV bag, the third we had hung. It was half empty.

Devlin swallowed a bite of MRE oatmeal cookie. "Much better. This is the first thing I've eaten since lunch yesterday when I had one of the sandwiches we took over to Conchetta."

"Turkey and cheese, I bet." I took his pulse.

"The flooding was so bad, we had to deliver food by boat," Devlin said. "We dumped racks of sandwiches into trash bags, but when we got to Conchetta, the water was above the first-floor doors."

I noticed that Devlin was coherent again.

"So some deputies inside went up to the roof and lowered ropes of sheets. We tied the bags to the sheets, and they hauled them up. The sandwiches were probably all smashed, but at least the people at Conchetta got food." Devlin stood up.

I moved to sit him back down. "Wait a minute . . ."

"Get this stuff off me so I can go." Devlin held up his arm, trailing IV tubing.

"You have to stay here and get some sleep," I insisted. "The fluids helped, but you need to rest."

"Sorry, Doc, but I'm leaving."

"You can't," I said more firmly. "You have to stay."

"Not gonna happen." Devlin pulled the IV out of his arm. Blood dripped from the wound. "Just bandage me up."

I didn't have time to argue. I asked Chuck to bandage Devlin's arm and went to find Sheriff Gusman. The pregnant woman needed to get out of here.

Chapter 52

While Lillian and Denise helped the pregnant inmate get dressed again, I conferred with Victor. The sheriff had agreed to give us a boat, and Victor assured me the patient wouldn't give birth before she arrived at the hospital.

Just as I was beginning to relax, Deputies Skyles and Brunet burst out of the stairwell and headed straight for me. Alerted by their grim expressions, I met them halfway across the lobby. Paul saw them too and joined us.

Skyles spoke quickly but in a hushed voice to avoid being overheard. "The inmates we locked on the roof broke out into the stairwell. Verret and the others chased them back up, but one of them fell. His leg is broken."

"Man, it's mangled," Brunet said. "It's all twisted sideways."

"Is the bone sticking out? Is he bleeding?" I segued into crisis mode without pause.

"I don't know," Skyles replied. "We were too busy holding the other inmates back. He's in the stairwell on the seventh floor."

We had to get the man to the lobby. Bleeding out or into his leg could be life threatening. Even if he wasn't bleeding, he could still lose the limb without timely medical intervention.

"We need to go get him," I said to Skyles.

Paul grabbed my arm.

"Didn't you hear him, Dem? There are hundreds of inmates loose up there. This is a really bad move."

I hesitated for a second. I appreciated Paul's concern, but I still had to do it. There was no other way.

But I'd need help carrying the patient down. Brady would be willing to come, but I needed someone with medical experience.

"Paul," I said, "I'm going. Get Duane Townzel. I just saw him out on the porch."

With his search-and-rescue experience, the brawny nurse was the perfect choice—strong and cool under pressure. While waiting for him, I went back to tell Victor we had to delay sending the pregnant woman to the hospital; the inmate with the broken leg would have to go, too.

"Okay," Victor said, "but you don't have much time."

I briefed Duane on the situation, adding, "We'll need a litter to carry the guy and stuff to splint his leg."

"We can use one of those cots," Duane said, agreeing to go without much discussion. He pointed to the collapsible cots we had set up in the clinic area.

Working quickly, the nurse and I ripped off the cot's wooden legs. The canvas attached to the wooden frame would serve as a litter.

With guns drawn and flashlights out, Skyles and Brunet covered us front and rear as we started up the steps. I carried the litter and splinting materials while Duane held his diving knife high, ready for action. Moving quickly up the stairs, we paused on every landing to make sure the next flight was clear. The scene was straight out of every cop TV show I had ever seen, heightening the tension and suspense.

On the sixth floor we could hear voices above us, and Skyles called out, "Verret! It's us!" He did not want to surprise an exhausted deputy and risk getting shot.

"C'mon up," Verret yelled. When we reached the landing, the acting warden looked at me. "Make it fast."

Nodding, I knelt to examine the injured man.

The inmate was wearing orange scrubs and sitting on the concrete landing surrounded by deputies. Other deputies faced upward with guns raised, poised to repel any attack. The familiar sounds of shouts, banging, and cracking concrete were louder than

I'd heard before, and the odor of smoke was strong. I didn't waste time.

Groaning, the inmate gripped his leg around the calf. His twisted foot stuck out at a bizarre angle.

I looked at Duane. "This is dislocated. It'll take too long to splint it here. I think we should just take him downstairs like this."

The nurse nodded and opened the makeshift litter. We carefully maneuvered the patient onto the canvas, trying to keep the injured leg as still as possible. The man screamed in pain with every movement, which triggered a louder, more raucous response from the inmates above. When the patient was finally in place, I told him to keep holding his leg so it wouldn't move.

"You've got the head," I told Duane. "So give the count."

"On three." He grabbed the front of the litter. "One . . . two . . . three!"

The patient shrieked when we lifted him, but he held his leg as we started down with our armed escort close on our heels. We moved fast, driven as much by concern for the patient as by fear of the rioting inmates. The man was very heavy, and I was glad I lifted weights and ran every day. Even so, the effort was taxing. Halfway down, when I really began to feel the strain, Duane shocked me with an unexpected compliment.

"You know why I like working for you, Dr. Inglese?" he said. "You're always right in there with us. Some bosses just sit back and give orders, but you're right there."

I didn't reply, but his words meant a lot and gave me a small burst of energy.

Sam and Paul jumped in to help when we reached the clinic. We placed the inmate on the mattress and cut the pant leg off his scrubs. Sam took a quick medical history while I examined the foot.

"Looks dislocated," Sam said over my shoulder.

"It's neurovascularly intact," I said. "He has good sensation and blood flow."

"We have to put it back in place." Sam didn't look happy about doing it himself.

Neither was I. Neither of us had much experience in ortho-pedics. For the second time in as many hours, I was tremendously grateful we had an ER doctor at the jail. I sent Sam to get Victor and gave the patient a hefty dose of Ultram to ease his pain.

Victor agreed that the ankle bones had to be repositioned before we could risk moving the man to a hospital. That would minimize his pain and decrease the chance of his losing the foot.

Victor had performed the procedure many times, but usually with the aid of muscle relaxants. Typically that meant Valium, but the controlled substance was kept at very few locations around the jail, and none of them were accessible now. As we discussed our options, I suggested phenobarbital instead. The drug would sedate the man and we had some in our makeshift pharmacy. Before we could get it, however, one of the nurses said that she had a Valium prescription to help her sleep. She had pills in her purse.

Everyone worked quickly, mindful of our limited time. Sam administered fifteen milligrams of Valium with a sip of water, while Chuck inserted an IV in the male inmate's arm. As we waited for the drug to take effect, Victor checked on the pregnant woman, and I touched base with the sheriff again. He told me to send both patients to the hospital and immediately put in a call for a boat.

Back in the clinic, the injured inmate was quiet, but when Victor pulled and twisted to relocate his foot, he screamed despite the painkiller. Once the foot was in place, though, he, too, was ready for transport.

A Department of Corrections boat arrived a few minutes later. As the medical staff loaded the two patients, I wrote a note for the doctors at the hospital, listing the meds we had given the man.

"I gave him one hundred milligrams of Ultram for pain," Sam said.

Victor looked up. "I gave him fifty milligrams, too."

"Oh, God . . ." I said. "I gave him a hundred milligrams when we first got downstairs."

Sam raised an eyebrow. "I guess he'll be sleeping for a *real* long time."

I wrote down the total dose, which was way beyond the typical dose, but not critical. Then, attempting to add some levity to a trying morning, I added: *"Yes, we know!"*

I handed the note to the boat driver, who had come from Baton Rouge that morning. There were no open hospitals in the city, he told me, but Ochsner Medical Center in Jefferson Parish was operating. He agreed to take both patients to the boat launch site and drive them to the hospital himself.

"There're two inmates in that boat and no deputy to guard them," Gary said as the driver pulled away.

I had already discussed that with the sheriff. It seemed safe enough. The woman had been arrested on minor charges and was about to have a baby. And the man wasn't going anywhere soon on his injured leg.

After we moved the desk back into the computer room, I headed for the front porch. It seemed the last two hours had been one emergency after another, and I needed a break before the next wave of patients hit.

The clang of the security door slamming open stopped me in my tracks. I looked back as Verret and his deputies rushed through.

"Out!" Verret ordered. "Everybody out, now!"

When the last man cleared the door, Verret shoved it closed and locked it.

I knew instinctively what was happening.

The inmates were out of control.

Chapter 53

All the terrors of the hurricane, the hazards of the flood, and the discomforts and emergencies of the last three days faded into nothing, compared to the horde of inmates we were facing now.

"Get the civilians out of here!" Verret yelled. "The inmates are coming down. Move these people out of the building—now!"

The deputies standing around the information desk sprang into action, but the civilians in the lobby needed little prodding. They rushed out the doors and onto the porch.

The noise exploding from the stairwell sounded like rolling thunder that rushed closer with every second. I started toward the clinic and the pharmacy to warn the doctors and nurses there.

"Get your staff outside, Doc," Deputy Skyles called to me. "There're too many inmates coming down and not enough of us to hold them off!" The fear I saw in his eyes was unnerving.

"I'm getting them now!" I shouted, but before I got to them, Mike, Gary, Paul, and Denise streamed out the pharmacy door.

"Outside! Hurry!" Skyles shouted as he turned around to back up Verret.

Gary, Paul, and Denise ran past me. Mike stopped.

"Have you seen Vinnie?" The psychiatrist's face was pale, and his eyes swept the lobby frantically.

"He has to be outside," I said, steering him toward the doors. I knew Mike felt responsible for Dr. Shantha's son. "We'll find him."

Mike followed the crowd that was moving to the sides of the

Correctional Center, still searching for Vinnie. I stayed near the doors, where I could follow the action inside.

Like a human wall, Verret and his deputies took up positions in front of the stairwell door. They raised their weapons—a few had guns, some batons, and one female deputy held a curling iron like a bat. They had grabbed whatever they could find to hold off the rioting inmates on the other side of the door.

Once again I was struck by the bravery of Verret and his crew. I'd seen them in action over the past three days, meeting danger and violence with unswerving resolve. But this confrontation could mean life or death for all of us.

Gary, Sam, Brady, and Mike came back to find me, their faces dark, reflecting the same terrifying thought. Desperate inmates bent on freedom were rushing down the stairwell, and we stood in their way.

We really could die here, I realized, before a new calm settled over me. It was clear what I had to do.

I reached for a mop standing against the front wall, broke it in two against the porch railing, and started back into the lobby with a club in my hand. Before I had taken more than a few steps, Gary came after me.

When he realized what I had in mind, he didn't hesitate. He picked up a wooden chair, slammed it against the lobby floor, and stood next to me, ready with his own weapon. Before I knew it, Sam, Brady, and Mike each followed suit, hefting pieces of furniture that were strewn around the lobby. Behind us, Victor, Paul, Chuck, Denise, and other nurses armed themselves with flashlights, brooms, and anything else they could find and stood outside. They, too, were prepared to stop the inmates' advance.

Gripping his rifle, Verret nodded when I joined the deputies. The commotion in the stairwell reached a peak; the inmates had finally made it down to the first floor.

I was scared but excited as the steel door shook, battered by a mob of desperate men.

BAM! BAM! BAM!

I raised my weapon.

Suddenly, the roar of motors filled the air. I turned around. Through the glass doors I could see several boats docking at the front steps of the Correctional Center. A cadre of state correctional officers disembarked, all wearing Kevlar body armor and heavily armed with automatic weapons or shotguns. They had attack dogs on leashes. The onlookers cheered as the Angola SWAT team rushed up the steps and into the lobby, like the cavalry in an Old West movie, arriving just in the nick of time.

The Corrections leader hurried toward Captain Verret, and his men quickly took up positions alongside the deputies. Weapons raised and laser sights on, the deputies and SWAT team officers prepared to go in. On Verret's signal, Sergeant Ross unlocked the door and swung it wide.

Chaos followed.

Inmates yelled. Dogs barked. Caught by surprise and faced with overwhelming force, the prisoners turned and ran madly back up the stairs.

The SWAT team moved as a unit, ascending the steps with practiced precision. Sheriff's deputies, led by Verret, moved in after them. They had held their ground against the odds and would not be left behind now.

After the last deputy stepped into the stairwell, Ross closed and locked the door.

I breathed a sigh of relief, turned to Gary, and laughed. "Man, I thought we were dead."

"Not me," Gary replied. "I felt pretty safe with you and your mop protecting me."

Sam was laughing, too.

"That was bad, real bad," Paul said grimly as he and Vinnie walked up to us. "We couldn't have stopped them if they'd gotten through."

He was probably right. A few deputies with pistols and people with clubs couldn't have held the inmates back. However, that reality was lost in our adrenaline high.

"Did you see the nurses?" Sam asked. "They were amazing. Deputies from other buildings moved away, but the nurses—they were right there. They were right there."

"Can you believe that?" Brady shouted. "Oh, my God, that was so incredible."

"I have to pee so bad," I said, laughing. My unexpected announcement broke the tension, and I *did* have to pee.

"You don't even want to try using these bathrooms," Mike said.

I laughed again. Mike was probably more afraid of the bathrooms than he had been of the inmates.

Chapter 54

Evening:
Evacuation of Conchetta and the Old Prison is complete.

For the next thirty minutes, the deputies kept the civilians safely out of sight, but the medical staff stayed in the lobby. Those of us who had taken a stand had gained a new respect from Security. When the sheriff's office deputies and the Angola SWAT team began bringing inmates down in handcuffed pairs, we watched with our weapons still in our hands.

The SWAT team had brought a supply of "flex-cuffs"—thin plastic handcuffs similar to trash bag ties. They used them to cuff the left wrist of one inmate to the right wrist of another. The men walked in pairs, free hands on their heads and linked hands raised.

Still armed, Captain Hammack stood guard at the stairwell door as the inmates were escorted down and lined up in front of the information desk. Then, slowly, with several guns trained on them, the pairs were marched out to the front porch and seated, ten inmates to a row.

Deputies wielding batons walked up and down, patrolling the prisoners, who were ordered to sit without talking or moving. My friends and I helped maintain order.

Major Beach took command. "Hands on your heads!" He snapped every time an inmate tried to scratch. It was bizarre to see the Food Service director enforce control over an angry mob.

The word of the attempted breakout spread quickly through the jail complex, and Captain Devlin and Deputy Sloan pulled up in a boat soon after the first rows were seated. I was amazed that Devlin was still up and moving after his bout of heat exhaustion, but then not many patients would rip out their IVs so they could go back to work evacuating criminals in a flood.

A large imposing man with black hair and a handlebar mustache, Devlin's presence had a subduing effect on the restless inmates. He could control the men with a sharp word or a glaring look, even though he just wore black shorts and a white Search and Rescue T-shirt and wasn't carrying a gun.

"No talking!" Devlin's eyes flashed a warning. "Keep your hands on your heads!"

The porch gradually filled with rows of inmates, fifty, then a hundred, as the deputies cleared each tier. Those guarding the men were wary of every movement and sound. If a rebellion began, it could start a chain reaction of violence that the overwhelmingly outnumbered deputies wouldn't be able to stop.

Many inmates asked for water.

"Quiet. No talking!" Devlin responded.

Some tried medical excuses. "I'm a diabetic. I need medicine."

"You'll get it later."

Some tried to shift their position.

"Stop moving!" Devlin ordered an inmate who was squirming with discomfort. "Hands on your head."

"But, I have to piss!" The inmate's expression was pained.

"Too bad."

"But I really have to piss," the man insisted.

"Then piss here." Devlin pointed over the railing, giving the man permission to urinate off the porch and into the water.

The inmate was shocked. "I can't in front of all these people."

"Then you'll just have to piss yourself 'cause you're not going anywhere."

The desperate man, still cuffed to his partner, went to the railing and clumsily relieved himself. Several others, one pair at a time, took advantage of the opportunity.

Another inmate cried, "I've got to go."

"Okay," Devlin said. "Over there by the railing."

"No, I gotta shit." The man winced.

"Hold it." Devlin shrugged.

"Oh, man, c'mon," the inmate pleaded. "I've really gotta go."

Devlin was unmoved. "And I'm telling you, you're not going anywhere, so you'd better hold it."

I felt sorry for the man, but it wasn't safe to let the inmates move around too freely.

Before the porch completely filled, Department of Corrections airboats began arriving, and Devlin directed the inmates to move from the porch to the steps, nearer the water. They were not allowed to stand up, though.

"Scoot on your butts," Devlin ordered as he and Major Beach supervised the loading. "Keep your hands on your heads."

The inmates slid on their bottoms across the porch and down the steps. When a pair reached the boat, they stood up with their hands on their heads and stepped aboard. Each boat carried a dozen men, and when a boat pulled away, full of inmates and armed officers, Devlin and Beach ordered the next few pairs to slide down the steps.

"Just keep your mouths shut, eyes down, and your hands on your heads," Devlin repeated over and over. "You don't want to play with me."

Meanwhile, the deputies inside continued bringing inmates down into the lobby and onto the porch. The slow, tedious process of evacuating the Correctional Center was finally under way.

Chapter 55

At sunset, when the Angola SWAT team, Verret, and his deputies finally came out of the stairwell, the porch was nearly clear of prisoners. I watched the SWAT team get into boats and depart. Then I walked over to Verret for an update on the situation.

"It's getting dark," Verret explained. "The Department of Corrections commander felt it was too dangerous to keep going. They'll be back in the morning."

"What are you going to do in the meantime?" I knew there were still inmates upstairs, and the tiers were unusable.

"We're going to finish bringing down the men on the seventh floor," Verret said. "There are four sheriff's boats that can move them to the overpass. Then we'll have to quit. Sheriff Gusman wants us to take the rest of the inmates to the roof for the night."

"How many is that?"

"The whole fifth floor, a little over three hundred." Verret signaled for Skyles, Boersma, and a few other deputies to follow him back up.

Still gripping my mop handle, I went out to the porch to stand guard. Every ten minutes or so, Verret and his men returned to the lobby with more inmates from the seventh floor, but the groups were smaller, and the inmates' hands were free. They had run out of flex-cuffs.

At one point, an uncuffed inmate fell to the ground as he came through the front doors. Duane Townzel ran up and bent over him, but held tightly on to a baton that SID had given him.

"What's the matter, Duane?" I asked, hurrying over.

"He says he can't breathe." The nurse warily eyed the man. "He says he's having an asthma attack."

Gary arrived as I leaned down to examine the inmate. When Duane explained the man's problem again, Gary scoffed. "He's full of it. I looked at him when he came out of the stairwell, and he was moving air just fine. There wasn't a wheeze in his chest."

I backed off, and Duane's face tightened with anger. "We do not have time for this," he said. Grabbing the inmate by the neck, he pulled him to his feet. "Quit playing games now!"

The inmate met Duane's hard gaze, then blinked.

"Just keep in line with your hands on your head," he ordered the man.

The inmate started to comply but suddenly turned and lunged at the muscular nurse. Duane adroitly sidestepped the attack, striking the man once in the ribs and once in the shoulder with the baton.

The inmate doubled over, then slowly straightened up, not seriously hurt.

"If you try anything again," Duane said in a menacing tone, "you'll be *very* sorry."

Eyes down, the inmate moved into his row and sat down.

Throughout the incident, I had studied the inmate's responses. His breathing was normal. He had been faking.

Over the next few hours, the inmates were taken away in an orderly fashion under Captain Devlin's direction, but there was an added measure of tension since the inmates weren't cuffed. As the prisoners waited for the boats, a few of them began to talk, swear, or push each other.

Devlin walked over to a particularly unruly inmate. "You see that guy?" He pointed toward Deputy Sloan, who was armed with a shotgun. "He just got back from Iraq. He won't have any problem shooting you."

Sloan threw the man a menacing glance, and the inmate settled back down.

Once all the seventh-floor inmates were downstairs, Sam, Gary, and I joined Victor in the clinic. The deputies had the prisoners under control, and people were waiting for care. Nevertheless, we kept our weapons close as we began seeing patients again.

Most of the problems were minor, complaints that were becoming routine: fevers, rashes, diarrhea, dehydration, fainting, cuts, and infections. Occasionally we saw more serious problems. One man had lacerated his leg in the water and required sutures. A deputy's husband came in with acute DTs. The man was a heavy drinker and had not had alcohol for too long. He was sweating and shaking uncontrollably, and Gary gave him a sedative. Several deputies who were not assisting with the evacuation came in for antibiotics.

Although sick children mingled with injured deputies while dangerous prisoners were being loaded onto boats a few feet away, we never gave a thought to the surreal scene. It was amazing how fast my staff and I had become numb to the extraordinary circumstances.

By 9:30, nearly 500 inmates had been evacuated from the Correctional Center. Once the inmates were gone from the porch, the boats returned to begin moving civilians to the overpass—and to buses out of New Orleans.

The clinic emptied immediately. The drive to leave the jail was stronger than the need for a Band-Aid.

Chapter 56

Sam and I followed the crowd back outside as boats pulled up to begin evacuating civilians.

Captain Devlin called for the sick, elderly, and parents with young children to board first, but his words had little effect. Neighborhood evacuees, family members, and derelict deputies rushed toward the empty boats—pushing, cursing, and shoving their way forward, determined to get out.

The medical assistant whose husband had a bad heart cut to the front of the line, insisting that her spouse needed to get to a hospital. He still looked fine, but I didn't protest. She had been no help at all during the last three days, and I was glad to be rid of her. They were on one of the first boats out.

"Isn't that a deputy?" Sam whispered, nodding toward a man elbowing his way to the steps. He pulled a woman behind him.

"I think so." I watched many out-of-uniform deputies shove children and elderly people aside so their own families could get through. We did our best to move the young, the old, and the infirm to the front, but the sight of so many selfish people infuriated me.

"I'm going to see if I can find some of the sicker patients," Sam said. He was especially concerned for those he'd treated the past few days.

A burly man stepped on a young girl's foot and then threatened to hit the child's father when he complained.

"Hey!" I yelled at the man, furious. "Leave them alone and wait your turn!"

"Go to hell!" The man snarled and continued toward the boats, pushing another woman out of his way.

"Take it easy! Watch out for those kids!" Devlin tried to restore control.

People ignored the warnings or yelled obscenities back. Hair-trigger tempers and stressed nerves had reached the breaking point.

A woman carrying a toddler stumbled up. Her husband, a deputy on the job in another building, couldn't be there to help her. Using my body as a wedge, I opened a path for her to the steps, and Devlin promised to get them out soon.

For the next hour, I helped him load the boats. Sam returned with a teenage girl—a dialysis patient he had been treating—and her mother. Although the sixteen-year-old was stable now, it had been five days since her last session, and she desperately needed a hospital.

Working together, Sam and I forged a path for them to the bottom of the steps. However, just as we were about to get the girl and her mom onto a boat, the driver told Devlin that the buses had stopped running. Everyone still on the overpass would be there for the night.

"We should stop sending people over there," Devlin said.

"Especially the sick people," I added. They would be better off at the Correctional Center, with mattresses, food, water, and medical personnel.

Sam sent the girl and her mother back inside and glanced at me with a sly smile. "It serves those worthless deputies right if they're stuck on the overpass till morning."

"Yeah," I agreed, "but I hope all the sick people got off before the buses left."

As the last boat pulled away, a new uneasiness enveloped me. The evacuation of inmates and civilians would be completed within the next day or so. Then it would be our turn. I had been so busy taking care of patients and dealing with problems that I hadn't given much thought to the world outside—or what waited for me beyond the jail.

I suppressed those troubling thoughts, however, when I heard Mike call Sam and me over. I wasn't ready to think about tomorrow.

"Pull up a spot on the floor," Mike joked, patting the tile.

Vinnie sat just behind the psychiatrist on the edge of the group, sipping water and listening to local news reports on a nearby radio.

Exhausted, Paul, Scarlett, and Chuck leaned against the wall, enjoying the break from the hectic clinic.

"The Old Prison is on fire," Chuck remarked casually. He stared at flames shooting out windows in the old building, which we could see from the porch.

"It looks like the whole city's on fire," Scarlett said. The darkened horizon was studded with pockets of smoke and flames.

"What's the matter, Mike?" Paul asked, noting the psychiatrist's glum expression.

"I'm worried about my dogs," Mike explained. "The boat drivers told me they're not taking any animals."

Scarlett nodded. "Some of the families wouldn't get on the boats because they refused to leave their pets behind."

With so much else to worry about, I hadn't considered the problem of evacuating—or not evacuating—pets. Moby and Georgie were like family to Mike, and one thing was certain: he wouldn't abandon them.

"Did you hear that? They're saying the city shouldn't be rebuilt." Sam nudged the man with the radio. "Could you turn that up, please?"

The civilian turned up the volume. We listened to a broadcaster argue that the expense of rebuilding New Orleans couldn't be justified. He said federal tax dollars shouldn't be spent on a city that was below sea level and could flood again.

The premise was so unexpected and extreme it caught me by surprise. Reality suddenly hit me like the proverbial ton of bricks.

I still didn't know what had happened to my house, but damaged or not, it would be worthless if there was no city. In an instant, I saw my life savings evaporate. If the St. Tammany Parish jail had been destroyed, I might lose both my jobs. No house, no job, no savings . . . I'd be starting my life from scratch at thirty-nine. I panicked.

"Oh, God! They're not serious, are they?" For the first time since the storm, I felt myself losing control. Now that the worst of the emergency was over, I finally let my defenses down.

Reeling, I mulled over various contingencies in a frenzy, rattling on without a pause. "You know, Sam, we could start our own private practice—you, Gary, and I. Or we could form a medical group that goes around the state delivering health care to the smaller sheriff's offices. God knows there's a need for it."

I didn't give Sam a chance to comment as I blurted out plans as fast as they popped into my head.

"Or we could just go back to work in a hospital. Charity in Baton Rouge will be screaming for doctors."

Sam tried to reassure me. "I wouldn't worry, Dem. They're going to rebuild the city, and we'll all be fine."

"Not if I'm broke and unemployed," I insisted.

"With your experience, you can find a job anywhere," Mike said, taking a sensible approach. "Why worry now?"

I wasn't convinced. The idea of being wiped out was a shock, and I couldn't sit still. It was as though all the tension of the past few days had exploded in my body, and I had to move around. "I'm going to see how Gary is doing."

I walked into the clinic just as Gary finished bandaging a deputy's arm. No other patients were waiting.

"How are things outside?" Gary asked.

"They're thinking about not rebuilding the city," I said, launching right into another tirade. "We heard them talking about it on the radio."

As I rambled on about potential personal disasters and career opportunities again, Gary stared at me. Unlike the others, who had tried to lift my spirits, Gary agreed with all my worst-case scenarios. He was certain we'd both end up homeless and destitute.

Thankfully, we were distracted when a deputy with diarrhea showed up in the clinic. Whatever Katrina and the flood had done to our property, families, and friends, we could do nothing about it now.

Chapter 57

When the boats stopped running to the Correctional Center, more deputies descended on the clinic. They had put off getting help for trench foot, lacerations, and other ailments during the evacuation. All the doctors and several nurses returned to duty, and we handled the problems quickly. When the last deputy left, Chuck and Denise volunteered to staff the clinic overnight and keep an eye on the pharmacy. The rest of us went back outside.

I had resisted sleeping on the porch before, preferring the privacy and comfort of Medical Administration. But Verret had declared the second floor off-limits, and Gary and I were resigned to a night outside. At least the air was cooler than inside the building.

"Anyone hungry?" Brady asked.

The response was unanimous, and we threaded our way through camped families to the back porch. Local evacuees had filled up every spare inch, and there weren't enough prison mattresses and pillows for everyone. Restless and noisy people jammed under the overhang. Snarling dogs and whining children punctuated the steady drone of conversation.

Major Beach had deputies posted at the food tables all night to guard the supplies, but they were happy to provide us with food and water.

I spotted Captain Hammack making his rounds. Every couple of hours, he toured the lobby and porch to keep an eye on things, and I joined him for a walk. As we turned the corner of the building, a loud argument erupted between a large man and a heavy-set woman. Within a few seconds, the disagreement escalated into an exchange of blows as the woman slapped the man and he punched her back.

"Hey!" Hammack pushed in between them. "Break it up! That's enough!"

The pair continued to swing at each other, trying to land their punches around the deputy. A circle of onlookers took sides, egging them on.

"Stop it!" Hammack ordered, but the couple continued to brawl.

Hammack pulled his gun, stepped back, and leveled the weapon. "I said, break it up. I mean it."

"He's got a gun," someone shouted.

I stood there dumbfounded, waiting for Hammack's next move. The man and woman looked at the weapon and stopped fighting.

Keeping them at gunpoint, Hammack asked, "What's this all about?"

"He's got my pillow!" the woman glared at the man.

"She's took my mattress and blanket," the man countered hotly.

"I did not!" the woman fumed.

"That's your stuff, honey," a woman in the crowd piped up. "Don't you let them take it away from you."

"It's not hers," someone else said. "She stole it!"

"Enough!" Hammack shouted. "Stop it now, or I'll throw the pillow, mattress, and blanket into the water."

The woman's head snapped around. "You wouldn't."

"Don't try me, lady," he warned her. His mouth was set in a hard line, and his stare was cold. No one could doubt he was serious. "I don't have a pillow *or* a blanket. I'm sleeping on the floor of my office with a rolled-up jacket."

The woman averted her gaze. The man started to speak, then thought better of it and walked away, cursing. Hammack sighed as he holstered his gun.

"You sure handled that well, Gerald." I didn't know if the

fighters were neighborhood residents, deputies, or family members, but he had certainly diffused the situation. "I'm so glad you didn't shoot anyone." I laughed.

Hammack shook his head. "Those people were ready to hurt each other over a pillow. It's so stupid."

"Everyone's tired and scared," I said. "They weren't thinking straight."

"I guess, but . . ." He gave an exaggerated sigh, then added with pointed sarcasm, "What more could they ask for? We've got clear skies. The stars are out, and we're camping on the peaceful waters of Lake New Orleans." He chuckled and continued on around the building.

As I started across the porch toward my friends, a roll of toilet paper landed at my feet. It was smeared with excrement. That wasn't the only present the inmates had sent down from the roof. Wads of urine-soaked clothing were strewn across the tiled floor, and a steady stream of trash rained down. What on earth was going on up there, I wondered.

"I'm not sleeping out here," I announced as I rejoined the staff. "The ground is filthy and too hard. It's too noisy and too crowded."

"Where are you going?" Brady asked. "The clinic?"

"And smell the bathrooms all night?" Gary grimaced.

"Medical Administration," I said. "If Verret okays it."

"Good luck with that." Sam stood up and stretched. "I'm staying out here with Victor and the nurses."

Gary, Mike, Brady, Paul, and Vinnie all liked my plan. They waited while I made my case to Verret.

"Sorry, Doc, but no way." Verret was firm.

"Why not?" I was not giving up until he relented. "The inmates are locked on the roof, right?"

"Yeah," Verret conceded.

"Then what's the problem?"

"We've been moving inmates in the dark," Verret confided. "We don't know if we got them all. And there's no deputies guarding the inmates on the roof."

"Why not?"

"The sheriff pulled us off," Verret said. "The deputies and inmates are both ready to pop, and he didn't want to chance the violence."

"Listen, Verret, last night you locked us on the second floor," I said. "What if you lock the foyer doors, too. Then there'll be two steel doors between us and the stairwell." All my energies were drained. I no longer cared about the danger. I just wanted to sleep away from the noise and the crowd.

Verret hesitated, but he gave in, once again, probably out of friendship.

The stairwell was quiet as Verret and his deputies escorted us upstairs. Despite the overpowering smell of dogs, Mike and Gary had no problem bedding down in Medical Administration.

The clinic where I had slept last night would be beyond the locked door tonight, so before Verret shut us in, we dragged an exam table into the foyer for Vinnie to sleep on. The boy curled up on it and fell asleep almost instantly.

"Don't forget to get us if there's a fire," I told Verret as he left. I was suddenly conscious of being trapped with no means of escape.

Brady and I moved into a large classroom next to Administration and found a piece of musty carpet big enough to share. As I lay down, I couldn't help thinking about the future. The inmates' ordeal would end tomorrow. But what, I wondered, lay in store for us?

Thursday, September 1, 2005

The Fifth Day

Chapter 58

Morning:
Evacuation of House of Detention inmates begins.

"Get up! Get up!"

I froze in the open doorway of Medical Administration.

I had woken up early that day—the classroom floor was no place to linger—and returned next door to the medical offices. My stash of food provided a quick breakfast. Then I had brushed my teeth, taken a sink bath, and changed into clean clothes. My burned chest had started to blister, but I felt refreshed and more hopeful as the new day began.

That good feeling shattered in a split second.

Three SID deputies stood over Vinnie, who was still lying on the exam table by the foyer doors. One of the men held a gun to the boy's head.

"Get up now," the deputy repeated. "I'm not going to tell you again."

Awakened abruptly, Vinnie didn't understand the commotion. The groggy teenager swatted the gun away.

"Stop! I'm Dr. Inglese! He's with me." My heart pounded when the deputy with the gun turned his gaze on me. I was terrified he would shoot the boy. Then I realized that if the deputy didn't recognize me, he might shoot me, too. "We're not inmates."

"Who are you, and what are you doing here?" the deputy asked.

"I'm Dr. Inglese," I repeated, "and he's Dr. Shantha's son. Ver-ret brought us up here to sleep last night. He locked us in."

After a few more tense seconds, the deputies slowly lowered their guns. Then they demanded that we leave at once. Inmates had gotten into the stairwell again, and it wasn't safe to stay.

The deputies waited while I rounded up Gary, Mike, Paul, and Brady. It took a while for everyone to dress, then Mike wouldn't leave until he fed and watered his dogs, which pushed the limits of the deputies' patience. As they finally rushed us out and down the stairs, the smell of smoke and urine filled the air.

Gary and I went straight to the clinic and found Sam and Victor already there. They had been up all night with a baby in severe respiratory distress.

"For a while there, I thought he wouldn't make it," Victor explained. "He wasn't moving much air. His respiratory muscles were straining, and he had nasal flaring, bad wheezing—the whole picture."

"We didn't have a nebulizer so we used blow-by MDIs," Sam added, referring to repeated puffs of asthma medicine blown into the baby's face. "It was touch and go for a while."

"But he's okay now?" I asked.

"He's out of danger," Victor said, "but we should get the family evacuated as quickly as possible."

"As soon as they start taking civilians again," I promised as I began treating patients.

There were fewer people than we had handled on previous days; the problems were less serious and the pace less hectic. When Captain Devlin entered the lobby, I had time to go see how he was holding up.

"I'm okay, Doc," Devlin said. "We started evacuating the House of Detention this morning."

"Did you get any sleep?" I asked.

"A couple of hours," Devlin said. "But I got an early call from Major Beach to help evacuate Templeman 5."

"Templeman 5?" I asked, puzzled. The new building hadn't been opened yet. "Who was in there?"

"Some work-release inmates and a bunch of kids from the Youth Studies Center," Devlin explained. The work-release inmates were employed in the community during the day and slept in the jail at night. And the sheriff's office had sheltered young teen offenders, both boys and girls, at Templeman 5 during the storm.

"Getting those kids out wasn't easy," Devlin continued. "The water's over six feet deep in spots. Most of them were too short to walk, and a lot couldn't swim."

"How'd you get them out?" I asked.

Devlin said he and his men had taken rope and life vests from the Search and Rescue supplies. They stretched the rope between the building's exit and a flatbed truck that had stalled in the street outside. Wearing life vests, the teenagers walked, swam, or floated to the truck using the rope to pull themselves along. Deputies and work-release inmates carried some of the smaller children on their shoulders. The truck then served as a loading dock for boats, which ferried the kids to the overpass.

"It was kind of heartwarming to see the deputies and inmates working side by side like that to save those kids," Devlin said. "One little girl had to be around twelve years old. She said, 'I can't die here! I got a baby at home.' Can you imagine? She's just a kid herself.

"This other little guy had his leg in a cast. He wasn't supposed to get the cast wet so Jack Bettis . . ." Devlin paused. "Do you know Jack?"

"Yes," I said. Captain Bettis was sixty-nine, and he'd been in the Marine Corps for thirty-nine years.

"Well, Jack wrapped the kid's leg in a trash bag to keep it dry," Devlin said. "Then he lifted the boy above his head and carried him all the way to the truck."

Devlin was smiling as he left to join the Department of Corrections boats that were docking at the Correctional Center once again.

Chapter 59

Captain Verret and his deputies were glad to see the Department of Corrections men return. The SWAT team had brought more personnel today, all of them armed and equipped with riot gear. With the extra manpower, it would only take a few hours to evacuate the remaining 300 inmates.

As the deputies started up the stairs with the Corrections officers, Verret paused to glance back. Captain Hammack stood in the doorway with his gun drawn, and in the lobby, the medical staff again carried makeshift weapons as they waited for the inmates to begin coming down.

As Verret climbed upward, he could hear movement above him. He knew inmates had escaped the roof into the stairwell during the night, but they hadn't been able to find a way out of the jail. Now, with Corrections officers and sheriff's deputies advancing, the inmates were retreating to the roof. Verret didn't anticipate any more resistance. Desperate for food and water, the men surely wanted to be evacuated.

As expected, the inmates were waiting when Verret reached the top. The deputies began to flex-cuff them in pairs and escort groups of ten down to the lobby. Verret stayed on the roof with the remaining inmates. Deputies guarded every landing, and more were positioned downstairs to control the evacuation. As soon as the escorts returned, they left with another group of ten.

The third group had just started down, when the Corrections SWAT team leader received a call.

"Our commander just ordered us out of the building," he told Verret. "There's a lot of smoke coming off the tenth floor."

With the inmates burning everything in sight, Verret had been afraid of a fire for the past three days. Still, the reality came as a shock.

Telling Verret they'd return when the fire was out, the SWAT team leader ordered his men off the roof.

Verret understood the decision. The Corrections officers didn't know the layout of the building. An officer could easily become trapped in unfamiliar, smoke-filled hallways, and one group risked shooting another by mistake.

But it didn't make his job easier. Designating two deputies to guard the roof, Verret warned the inmates, "This isn't the time to get smart. There's a fire, and we don't have time to fool around," he said in no uncertain terms. "We'll shoot anyone who tries anything."

Then he and Captain Boersma hurried down to find the fire.

On the tenth-floor landing, smoke poured from a hole the inmates had punched through the cinderblock wall. With Boersma close behind him, Verret opened the security door and ventured in. The smoke was thicker inside, and down the hall he could just make out a pile of burning debris. Coughing and choking, the two men dashed back out.

Deputies posted in the stairwell had raced up to help Verret. But the acting warden worried about having too many people on the floor. The windowless corridors were pitch-black, and the few remaining flashlights were useless in the smoky haze. He wouldn't be able to keep track of who went in and who came out.

And Verret couldn't tell how bad the fire was. He knew only that he wasn't going to let the building burn down or permit any of the inmates on the roof to die. He and Boersma would have to take turns going in to fight the blaze.

"I need every fire extinguisher you can find," Verret shouted to the deputies around him. There was an extinguisher just inside every stairwell door. While the deputies ran to get them, Verret grabbed the extinguisher on ten and moved alone into the smoky corridor.

Verret realized the terrible danger as he made his way toward the tenth-floor elevators. He had no oxygen, no protective gear, no water, and almost no visibility. The stairwell door was the only access to the floor. If the fire got behind him, he would be cut off and trapped.

He was coughing when he reached the pile of burning mattresses, toilet paper rolls, and trash. Forgetting about everything he didn't have, Verret aimed the fire extinguisher at the blaze. The spray reduced visibility even further, and the chemicals seared his throat. After a minute, the caustic fumes forced him to run back to the stairwell. Wheezing and eyes watering, he handed Boersma the extinguisher.

Verret struggled to catch his breath as Boersma went in next. The seconds dragged, until finally the captain stumbled out onto the landing and leaned against the wall, gagging. A deputy handed a new extinguisher to Verret, who raced back inside.

The two men alternated places—fighting the fire or recovering—half a dozen times until the fire was out. Coughing and gasping for air, they struggled back to the roof.

"Get everyone back in position," Verret told Deputy Skyles, who was watching the inmates. The acting warden's voice was no louder than a rasping whisper, and he continued to cough up charcoal-colored sputum as he instructed the deputies to resume the evacuation.

"We don't have any flex-cuffs," another deputy said. "Corrections took them downstairs."

"Then be careful," Verret said. He didn't want to delay getting the inmates out of the Correctional Center. "Corrections will come back when they know the fire's out." He paused, hacked, and then inhaled slowly. "Make sure they bring the cuffs back with them."

As the next group of inmates was taken downstairs, Boersma looked at Verret with a crooked grin. "That was a really stupid thing we just did, you know?"

Verret coughed—loudly—then replied, "Yeah, I know. But we only had two choices."

Boersma waited.

"Let the building burn or put out the fire," Verret said. "Not a tough decision."

"Nope." Boersma smiled. "I keep my motorcycle on the tenth floor. I wasn't going to let it burn."

Verret laughed. Boersma's Harley was his prized possession.

"With all the mattresses and blankets lying around there, it looked like some inmates slept on that floor," Boersma added.

They probably lit the fire so they could see in the dark, Verret thought. And when the inmates heard them coming up the stairs this morning, they ran to the roof and left it burning.

"I wonder if the smoke got to that inmate in the ductwork," Boersma said.

Verret shrugged. "We'll know soon enough."

Chapter 60

I had been in the lobby when the Department of Corrections officers ran down from the roof, yelling about a fire upstairs. Several of Verret's deputies had rushed up to help. Then, for the next twenty minutes I waited with fifteen or twenty sheriff's deputies for some shred of news. The deputies nervously fingered their guns, anticipating some movement in the stairwell—officers or runaway inmates. I still had my mop handle, and I was mentally prepared for anything.

Captain Hammack was among those crowding around the information desk. His gaze darted across the tense faces in the lobby.

"This isn't going to work," he told Sergeant Ross. "Somebody's going to get shot, Patrice."

He's not kidding, I thought. Too many excited deputies here were operating on too little sleep.

Unwilling to leave safety to chance, Hammack decided to take control. He posted two armed deputies at the door and ordered everyone else to holster their weapons. Then he took position at the bottom of the stairs, inside the security door.

"If I don't come out first," Gerald said from inside the stairwell, "shoot whoever comes through."

Ross closed and locked the door behind him.

Again the rest of us waited, counting the minutes until Hammack and several deputies shouted through the door that they had inmates with them. As they came out, the acrid odor of smoke was evident, but the fire was out, they assured us.

The deputies took the inmates to the porch, then hurried back for another group. Hammack again stood at the base of the stairs. "Sing out when you come back down," he warned the deputies, "'cause if I don't know it's you, we'll have a problem."

Outside on the porch, Corrections officers were guarding the rows of inmates as Captain Devlin, Deputy Sloan, and Duane Townzel supervised the loading of the boats.

"Slide on your butts," Devlin barked, overseeing the procedure he had established the day before. "No talking!"

I stood guard along with several other people on the medical staff, but the process went smoothly. The only disruption was a man who collapsed and began twitching on the ground.

"You think it's a seizure, Doc?" Duane asked me.

I'd witnessed many seizures over the years, but this was completely uncharacteristic. I was certain he was faking. "No, it's not."

"Are you sure?" the nurse asked.

"Absolutely," I answered.

Duane reacted by grabbing the inmate's neck and pulling him to his feet. The man was so shocked he just stood there for a moment, motionless.

"Don't mess with me!" Duane shoved his baton in the inmate's face. "Don't even think about it."

The man placed his hands on his head and sat down. Two hours later, Verret appeared and announced that all the inmates were off the roof. Soon after, the airboats finished taking the prisoners to the overpass.

As soon as the porch was clear, the Corrections officers headed to the House of Detention, the last building with inmates.

"All this standing around has made me hungry," Gary said as he finally tossed his chair leg aside. "Think there's any food left?"

"Let's go see," Sam said, leading the way to the back porch.

We lined up for MREs and Ensure—water was scarce—then we joined our friends to discuss the news. The radio reported that looters had set fire to the nearby Oakwood Mall, not far from the homes of many of the nurses. But on a brighter note doctors were performing dialysis at the Superdome. That was welcome information for Sam, who wanted to get his sixteen-year-old dialysis patient there as soon as possible.

The conversation waned as we ate. Everyone looked as depressed as I felt. I couldn't stop thinking about my house and my jobs or how worried my parents must be. This morning, I'd had too much to deal with to dwell on my own problems. Now, with the inmates gone, there were fewer distractions to take our minds off our troubles.

"I wish we could get word out somehow," I fretted. "My family must be worried sick."

"Lisa, too," Sam said. "At least I know she and the kids are okay."

"I'm really worried about my dogs," Mike said. "I keep hearing they're not taking pets on the boats."

We heard shouts from the House of Detention, but none of us paid much attention. The building was being evacuated, and there was nothing more we could do. But we couldn't ignore the cries for help from people in a house across the street. They begged for food, water, and someone to save them.

"How come they haven't been rescued?" Gary asked. "It's been four days since the hurricane hit."

A man on the porch overheard us. "There are too many people that need to be picked up."

"That's my house," another man said. "The sheriff sent food and water over to my family yesterday."

He appreciated the sheriff's gesture, but to me it seemed so small compared to how much still needed to be done. I felt completely helpless, which depressed me even more.

Chapter 61

Afternoon

As soon as we finished eating, the four of us returned to the front porch. Mike saw Verret and asked if he could go upstairs to get his dogs. The inmates were gone, and Moby and Georgie had been cooped up for days.

"Sorry, Dr. Higgins," Verret said. "We haven't swept the building yet. There could still be inmates up there we missed."

Mike wasn't happy, but he didn't argue. He had left the dogs plenty of food and water . . . for now. But thoughts of what might happen to them later were clearly playing havoc with his emotions.

Meanwhile the Corrections boats had begun taking civilians to the overpass again. The process was anything but orderly. As they had the night before, people cut in line, pushed, argued, and fought, trying to get on the boats, and the exhausted deputies could no longer deal with the mob of crazed people. The young deputy trying to coordinate the chaos was even-tempered and methodical, but he was nowhere near forceful enough.

Sam and I pitched in to help load the sick, the old, and people with young children before the others. For most of the crowd, however, it was "me first"—unless the boat filled before their whole family could board. I was unprepared for this new snag.

The airboats could carry ten to fifteen people. I had loaded two couples and a family of five into one boat, which left room for three more. However, the next couple in line had three kids.

"We can only put three more in this boat," I explained to the man. "Let your wife and girls go now. You and your son can go in the next boat."

"No way!" The man objected loudly. "We're not splitting up."

His refusal took me aback. "But the next boat is right there!" I pointed at the airboat idling a short distance away. "They're all going to the overpass."

"We're not splitting up, and that's that," the man said, glaring at me. "We'll go on the next one."

"Suit yourself." Annoyed, I looked at the next man in line. "I need three people. Are you coming?"

He shook his head. "There're four of us. We're all going together."

Frustrated, the driver looked at the man and then at me. "Somebody better get on this boat, or I'm leaving."

An older man and his wife came forward, and I settled for two to fill out the load. But we had the same problem with the very next boat. I needed three people to complete the load, and the families in line refused to separate.

"Just get on the boat!" Someone in the crowd yelled.

"Are you going to leave half *your* family behind?" The man in front shouted back.

The argument ended abruptly when the second boat left with three empty seats.

My patience was at an end. "All the boats are going to the same place," I shouted. "From now on, when it's your turn to get on a boat, you'll get on. Some families may have to split up, but we'll make sure everyone left behind gets on the next boat."

"We're not splitting up our families!" someone yelled back.

"You can't make us," said another voice.

I yelled louder, "You'll get on the boat when it's your turn, or you'll go to the end of the line."

More groans and protests rippled through the crowd.

"And you'll probably be stuck here until tomorrow," I added.

"Who put you in charge?" a woman called out.

"You don't have the authority to make us do anything," a man bellowed.

"Don't I?" I stared at the man. "Let's get Verret over here and find out."

He backed down, and we began loading the next boat, but tension and uncertainty hung over us all afternoon. In many ways moving the civilians was more difficult than evacuating inmates.

People asked questions we couldn't answer. They wanted to know where they'd be taken from the overpass. We didn't know; the boat drivers didn't know, either.

And the boat drivers refused to let animals on board. Pets weren't being allowed on the buses or on the helicopters, which had begun transporting civilians from the overpass. More than one person went back into the Correctional Center rather than leave their dog or cat behind. An elderly woman was distraught over having to abandon her tiny Yorkshire terrier. Whispering, I told her to put the little guy in her purse and not tell anyone. She thanked me over and over as we loaded her, her husband, and the hidden dog. But people with big dogs—like Mike's—didn't have that option.

Sam spotted his dialysis patient and her mother, and he pulled them aside until a smaller boat pulled up. When he told the driver that the girl needed dialysis, and that the Superdome was doing the procedure, the driver agreed to take them there. Just as they were about to pull away, I remembered that Charity Hospital was near the Superdome.

"Wait a minute," I shouted as I ran across the porch. "Victor," I yelled.

"Dr. Tuckler's over here!" Lillian waved from the corner where the nurses were camped.

"Victor, grab your stuff!" I shouted. "You've got a ride out of here!"

Victor scrambled to his feet and hurried toward me. The only thing he carried was the red backpack with his family photos.

The driver was anxious to get going, but Victor made him wait as we said good-bye. "I want to tell you, you held everyone together," he said to me. "You made sure we got the job done."

I was as grateful as he was. "I couldn't have done it without you," I said, giving him a bear hug of farewell. "The pregnant lady, the guy with the leg—thank you so much for all you did. Take care of yourself. Be safe." I waved as the ER doctor boarded.

I felt a pang as the boat pulled away. Victor was headed into a city where criminals roamed the streets, shooting and setting fires. I hadn't known him well before the storm, but I was definitely going to miss him.

Chapter 62

As Thursday wore on, and Sam and I helped load boat after boat, news of events in- and outside the jail helped break the tedium of dealing with squabbling families. We heard that deputies had finished evacuating Conchetta and the Old Prison on Wednesday night. If the inmates in the House of Detention were gone by sundown, the boat drivers would have moved almost 7,000 inmates in seventy-two hours.

The sheriff's boats had been running 24/7 since early Tuesday morning, and a couple of them were having serious mechanical problems. The small trawling boat ran on battery power. Most of the others, however, used gas, which was in short supply. To keep the evacuation going, deputies at Detention had siphoned gas and taken batteries from cars parked in the adjacent police department garage. The need to get everyone out trumped all other considerations.

When Deputy Mills came back to the Correctional Center from the overpass, Sam and I took a break to talk to him. Twenty-four hours had passed since the young deputy had left with food, water, and Nurse Evans. Now he was even more sunburned and dehydrated, and he seemed on the verge of collapse. Mills belonged in bed, not cruising the city's flooded streets, but he refused to quit.

"I just came for more supplies, Doc," Mills said. "Deputies are passing out, but they won't leave the overpass while there're inmates to guard. Oh, and Hedy Hartzog wants some sunscreen."

Sam gasped. "Hedy's still there?"

Mills nodded and held up his radio. "Do you want to talk to her?"

"Please." Sam took the radio when a deputy on the overpass put Hedy on. I stood close enough to hear both sides of the conversation.

"Why are you still there?" Sam asked the nurse.

"They wouldn't let me on the bus with the inmates," she said. "I don't know why. Kentrisha and Carol went earlier."

Sam looked at me, stunned. Hedy had been on the overpass for two days. She probably hadn't slept much, and there was no relief from the sun or heat during the day.

"Have one of the drivers bring you to the Correctional Center," Sam said. He wasn't asking.

"No, Dr. Gore. They need me here. I have to stay."

Sam decided against trying to change her mind. "Can we send you any supplies?"

"The bridge would be nicer with cars," the nurse said, "but they won't run without food."

"What?" Sam asked. "I didn't get that, Hedy. What's wrong?"

"Sorry . . . it's hard to think," she replied. "I haven't had water in over a day, and I'm a little dizzy."

It was clear that Hedy was slightly delirious from dehydration and heat exposure. "We'll get some water," I told Sam, as I motioned for Mills to come with me. Then I called Brady, who was sitting on the porch railing nearby, and drew both men to one side.

"Does the kitchen still have water?" Mills asked.

"Not much," I said, "but I know where there are several five-gallon bottles. Gary and I found them in some administrative offices on Sunday night. We took one bottle to Medical Administration and left the others upstairs."

"There's one in Medical Supply, too," Brady said.

"Then let's go get them," Mills said.

"Verret isn't sure all the inmates have been accounted for," I cautioned. "Some might still be free up there."

"I've got a shotgun," Mills said, cradling his weapon.

He was reading my mind.

"Okay, this is what we need to do." I proposed that Mills find another armed deputy to escort Brady and me upstairs. He could take whatever water we found to the overpass as long as he swore to give plenty to Hedy.

Mills promised to personally deliver the water.

Brady and I waited until Mills returned with another deputy, then we asked Sergeant Ross to unlock the security door. At first she refused. Verret had given strict orders not to let anyone up.

But when I explained that the deputies on the overpass needed water desperately, Ross relented and gave us the keys we needed. Once we stepped into the dark stairwell, she locked the door behind us.

Indistinct noises sounded far above us. We couldn't tell if they came from inmates or deputies doing sweeps. Nervous, I turned on my flashlight and aimed the beam ahead of Mills, who led the way with his shotgun raised. The other armed deputy covered the rear. We stayed tight together as we ascended one flight at a time, calling out loudly at each landing to avoid being shot by an overzealous deputy.

"Those guys sure made a mess," Brady said. "It smells like a sewer in here."

"Pigs," Mills said as we passed a pile of burned garbage and stepped over a blanket on the stairs. Clothing, empty MRE packages, and other trash littered the floors. Urine and feces had been smeared on the walls.

"Look at this hole!" Brady paused on the seventh-floor landing and beamed his flashlight through an opening in the steel fire door. The reinforced glass in the window had been smashed out. Then, as though suddenly remembering that inmates could still be lurking in the shadows, he pulled back and quickly caught up.

We reached the eighth floor without trouble, and I unlocked the stairwell door. Brady let us into Medical Supply, and we quickly collected the five-gallon jug of water and some sunscreen for Hedy. Then we hurried down to Medical Administration and picked up the second jug.

Brady and I carried the water and flashlights, leaving Mills and the other deputy unencumbered, in case they had to use their weapons. The bottles were heavy, and it was hard to keep the flashlights aimed. The beams bounced off the floor and walls, adding to the tension as we rushed out of the medical offices.

When we stepped back into the stairwell, we could hear more noise on the higher landings, and we ran down the last flight of stairs. My heart pounded as hard as Mills's fist on the door, and I stumbled into the lobby when Ross let us through.

After we loaded the water onto the boat, we added MREs the kitchen staff gave us. As Mills set off, he slipped the sunscreen into his shirt pocket and promised again to make sure Hedy was taken care of.

I knew the supplies would be a godsend to the nurse and the deputies, but the sight of the boat disappearing plunged me into a funk. Hedy had risked her own health to help inmates and strangers on the overpass, and no one but Mills, Sam, and I knew or cared.

I glanced toward the steps where Sam and a deputy were still loading hostile men and women and unruly children onto boats. Gary moved through the crowd, looking for sick and elderly people who needed assistance. They, too, were doing what needed to be done. None of them expected glory or praise, but had anyone even thanked them?

Chapter 63

There were no civilians waiting for care when I walked back into the clinic. Mike, Brady, Chuck, and Scarlett were giving deputies antibiotics and tetanus shots. We were running low on vital medicines, and I told them to save the last few bottles of tetanus serum for high-risk cases.

"Have you heard when they're going to get us out of here?" Scarlett asked. With her tangled hair, cut-off scrubs, and dirty legs, she looked like she had fled a war zone.

"Or where they're going to take us?" Chuck had bags under his eyes, and his shaved head was covered with fine fuzz. His orange scrubs clung to his sweaty back.

Mike and Brady didn't have to say a word. We all wanted to cash in our get-out-of-jail-free cards.

Promising to fill them in as soon as I could, I went to the sheriff's offices, where wardens and officers had gathered after their buildings were evacuated. I found Chief Bordelon. He looked rested, but he had been in the water a long time, and I told him to be sure and get a tetanus shot and antibiotics from the clinic. Bordelon had heard that the jail staff would be taken to the evacuation staging area in Gonzales, Louisiana, but he didn't know if the information was reliable.

Chief Belisle heard us talking and said we're going to Baton Rouge, probably tomorrow. His source was a Corrections boat driver. Everyone in the office had a different idea about our destination. The only thing they agreed on was that none of us were going anywhere today.

Frustrated, I wandered onto the front porch. I had no news for my staff, no idea where we'd end up or when. Trying hard not to feel despondent, I went over to talk to Warden Lacour when I saw him getting into a boat.

"How are things at the Old Prison?" I asked. "We saw fires in the windows last night."

"Nothing major. No real damage," the warden explained.

"Are the nurses still there?"

"Yeah," Lacour said. "Our staff isn't being evacuated until tomorrow."

"Tell Jan Ricca that I'll keep her husband and son here tonight. She can meet them on the overpass tomorrow."

The warden agreed to deliver the message and waved as his driver cast off. Just then a loud argument broke out on the far side of the steps. A large man picked up his dog, pushed past Sam and a deputy, and boarded a boat.

Sam just threw up his hands. He couldn't enforce the no-pets order, and the driver decided not to press the issue either. I suspected the buses and helicopters were a lot stricter, however. The man and his pet would probably be stranded on the I-10 overpass.

Along with Mike, I thought. I told Sam and the deputy to take a break while I stepped in. Staying busy was the only way to take my mind off my problems.

Chapter 64

Evening:
Shooting increases in the neighborhood around the jail.

My mood hadn't improved by the time I joined my friends for dinner. Since Sunday, meals had been the high point of our days, not just for the food and drink but also for the opportunity to laugh, cry, and complain among friends. Tonight, we sat wallowing in our troubles.

"There's a crime wave in the city," Paul said as he absently swirled a can of Ensure. "Murder and rape, gangs terrorizing people on the streets and in the Superdome."

"Maybe I shouldn't have sent that girl and her mother there." Sam looked distressed.

"She needed dialysis," I reminded him, "and the Superdome was the only place she could get it. You didn't have a choice."

"Was all that water stashed here in the Correctional Center?" Brady glanced at numerous five-gallon jugs that had recently appeared behind the food tables.

"I don't think so," Gary said. "The deputies raided the Kentwood water plant."

"That's the rumor anyway." Mike hesitated, then mumbled, "Guess I won't run out of water if I have to stay here with my dogs."

I listened halfheartedly. I couldn't stop worrying about the staff at St. Tammany. Did they have enough food and water? I felt as though we'd been stranded on an island in a never-ending night-mare. Exhausted, sore, and tired of feeling down, I decided I had to do something proactive. I could try to help others feel better.

I went to the pharmacy and grabbed a large bottle of vitamins. Systematically making my way around the porch, I gave a red pill to each person I encountered.

"What's this?" a female deputy asked.

"Vitamins," I answered. "For energy."

The people accepted the pills enthusiastically. Some even asked for two. Everyone was burned out and looking for any antidote to their grueling ordeal. I realized, of course, that the vitamins were of little real benefit, but the psychological effect was star-tling. People perked up the moment they swallowed the pills.

I spent an hour distributing vitamins and listening to people vent and then joined the others in the clinic. With sick people, locals, and most family members gone, we treated a leisurely in-flux of deputies. In between patients, we traded stories and lis-tened to a portable radio.

One news report caught my attention. The uptown area was relatively dry, the broadcast said, especially between St. Charles Avenue and the river. I lived near that area, and so did Sam and Mike.

"Did you hear that, Sam?" I asked.

"I can't believe my house didn't flood," Sam said, smiling.

"You know *my* house is underwater," Gary groused.

When I took a few minutes to step outside, the early evening sky glowed with light from fires all over the city.

Deputy Skyles overheard me ask a group of his colleagues if they knew anything about the St. Tammany Parish jail.

"They're fine, Doc," Skyles said. "My wife works at St. Tam-many. I just talked to her, and she said they had very little dam-age."

"You talked to her?" I was relieved to hear about St. Tam-many, but my attention was riveted on Skyles' communication with his wife. "How?"

The deputy held up a cell phone. "I have a signal."

I stared at the phone. "Could I use that for a minute?"

Skyles pushed me into a secluded corner of the porch and spoke quietly. "Just for a minute, Doc, okay? The battery's almost dead, and everyone will want to use it."

"I'll be quick," I promised.

My hand shook as I took the phone and dialed my parents, but all I heard was a recorded message: "All circuits are busy. Please try your call again later." I tried again, then dialed my grandmother, but couldn't reach anyone. Afraid of draining the battery, I reluctantly returned the phone to Skyles. But the mere possibility of outside communication, coupled with the good news about my house and the St. Tammany jail, had bolstered my spirits tremendously. By the time I got back to the clinic, I felt renewed and energized. There was no time to celebrate, though. Civilian evacuation had ceased for the evening, and patient traffic had picked up again.

As we realized our hardships were almost over, deputies, doctors, and nurses began to joke about situations that had been matters of imminent peril just a few hours earlier. Everyone had something they wanted to do first—as soon as they were back in civilization. Reunions with spouses and children topped the list, along with hot showers and pizza. Occasionally, though, we could see that the strain of the ordeal had taken an enormous emotional toll.

"Maryanne! Maryanne!"

Deputy Calvin Jones wailed and swayed as he stumbled in, steadied by a deputy who gripped his arm.

"I love you, Maryanne!" Jones cried, his speech slurred. "I just want to talk to my wife. I just want to talk to my wife."

"You'll see her soon," the deputy said.

Jones broke down sobbing. "Maryanne! Maryanne!"

I directed the deputy to lay Jones on a mattress and asked, "What's going on?"

"Jones has been loading boats for three days," the deputy explained. "He has carpal tunnel, and his hands were all cramped up. He's been taking Motrin, but it didn't help so he took something called Flexo . . ."

"Flexeril?" I asked. The drug was a powerful muscle relaxant often prescribed for spasms.

"Yeah, that's it." The deputy nodded. "His fingers were really hurting so he kept taking more and more. Then a little while ago, he just started bawling."

"I love my wife so much," Jones sobbed.

I took the patient's vital signs and asked more questions as I examined him. "Has he had any sleep? What about food and water?"

"Nothing," the deputy replied. "None of us have. We've been working round the clock. Is he going to be okay?"

"I'm sure he'll be fine," I said. The man appeared uninjured. "It's probably a combination of stress, dehydration, exhaustion, and sleep deprivation, along with too much Flexeril."

I instructed Chuck to start IV fluids and then called Mike over to take a look. This was the worst case of emotional breakdown we had seen, and I wanted the psychiatrist's opinion.

As the hours passed, and the inmate evacuation at the House of Detention neared completion, more and more deputies from other buildings arrived at the clinic. Some had rashes and infected cuts they had neglected for days. Most were exhausted and dehydrated.

Finally, at almost eleven we had finished seeing everyone. It struck me then how much we'd gone through in the past four days. Besides the fury of the storm, we had swum through floods of sewage, rescued a heart attack victim, faced grave threats from rioting inmates, helped pregnant patients, and reset a dislocated leg. We had seen countless instances of heroism and cowardice, been terrified, exhausted, and exhilarated, sometimes all at once.

Now, for the first time since Sunday, we could finally begin to relax.

Chapter 65

Night

The mood was light on the side porch, where Gary, Sam, Mike, and I joined the nurses to kick back. We would be leaving tomorrow, and we all felt like celebrating.

"Maybe we should sleep out here tonight," Gary suggested. "It's a lot cooler."

"I don't care where I sleep as long as the wake-up call doesn't involve guns," Mike said.

"Yeah, once was enough." Vinnie grinned.

"We have to get our stuff," I said, though I wasn't sold on the idea. The cool breeze felt pleasant, and there was more room now that so many civilians had left. However, the deputies were noisier than the families had been.

"They're getting a little rowdy, aren't they?" Paul stared at a group of six men and two women twenty feet away, who were hooting and talking loudly.

"It's been a rough couple of days," Brady said. "Can you blame them for letting off a little steam?"

This was more than exuberance, however. The men started clapping, and one of the female deputies launched into a risqué dance that quickly degenerated into a striptease.

Using a sheet to cover herself, the woman took off her clothes and tossed them into the cheering audience. People on the periphery shouted encouragement and lewd comments as she dropped the sheet to reveal herself dressed only in her bra and underwear.

Shocked with disbelief, we watched for a few minutes as she began kissing an eager deputy. The display wasn't even remotely sexy. It was shameful.

"The sins of Babylon," Chuck muttered.

"I've seen enough." Mike stood up. "C'mon, Vinnie. Let's go walk the dogs."

One of the men with the dancer held a megaphone, which amplified the obscenities he exchanged with another group of deputies nearby.

"Hey!" A man lying on a mattress by the wall yelled. "Keep it down. We're trying to sleep."

Both groups shouted insults at the man.

"Shut up!" another sleeper demanded.

Laughter and more cursing drowned him out.

Not all the families had been evacuated. As the deputy with the megaphone continued shouting indecent remarks, a mother with two children gave the man a nasty look. Incensed, Gary and I walked over to him.

"It's late," I said evenly. "Tune it down a little, will you?"

"You know what you can do to yourself," the deputy shot back, making himself clear in precise expletives.

"Don't bother," Gary said, pulling me away. We went to sit on the front steps. Staring out over the placid flood, we didn't say anything for a moment.

"I can't believe how these people are behaving," I finally blurted out as Sam sat down beside us. "They're sheriff's deputies, and there are families with kids around. It's been like that all week," I continued. "The storm brought out the best or worst in people. People like Verret, Denise, Devlin, and Bordelon are real heroes. Some of the others are cowards or just plain lazy."

"Like the Templeman 3 deputy who swam off with the keys or the guys on the overpass who quit working," Gary added.

"And look at the deputies who came to the Correctional Center and sat around for days doing nothing," I went on. "When it was time to leave, they pushed ahead of children and sick people to get on the boats."

"I hate to say it," Sam said, "but a few of the nurses aren't behaving any better. Some got here and refused to work, and last night one of them was caught stealing from the others."

"What?" Gary and I exclaimed in unison. We were stupefied.

"She was taking food and clothing," Sam explained.

It's like something out of *Lord of the Flies*, I thought. Without normal social controls, some people simply turned into animals.

The scene with the deputies convinced Gary and me to sleep inside one more night. We ran into Verret at the information desk, and he assured us that the building was secure. The stairwell door was propped open again.

"We did a thorough sweep," the acting warden said. "We never found the inmate who was crawling through the ductwork, so he probably got out."

"What if he didn't?" Gary asked.

"Then we'll smell him eventually." Verret laughed.

It was good to hear him relaxed.

Paul, Brady, Mike, and Vinnie were already in Medical Administration with bottles of warm water and snacks. Gary and I took the time to wash up using Paul's trash-can water, and then we changed clothes. The skin was peeling off my chest, but the burning sensation was nearly gone. After raiding our personal food stores, we joined the midnight party.

Bored and restless, Vinnie got up to stretch his legs. When he saw a picture of a motorcycle in Paul's office, he asked about it. The rest of us paled. We knew from experience not to get Paul started on cars or motorcycles. He'd never shut up. But Vinnie was genuinely interested, and Paul was delighted to have an audience as the two walked to his office.

"That was close," Gary whispered with a grin.

I made an exaggerated pretense of mumbling thanks to heaven. Gary laughed, but Mike just stared at the floor.

"I'm not leaving without them," he said as he scratched each of his dogs behind the ears.

"And I'm not leaving you." I looked him in the eye. "We'll get them out somehow, Mike. If we need to, we'll swim them back to your house. It's dry uptown."

"But *how*?" Mike persisted, still distraught. "Georgie can barely swim, and Moby can't swim at all. He'll just sink and drown."

"Look," I reminded him, "if they could get the nurses out in laundry carts, we can get your dogs out. We'll wait at your place until the others come back for us."

"As soon as I get to Baton Rouge, I'll drive back and pick you guys up," Brady offered.

"I'm not leaving you, Mike." I stared at him until he was convinced I was serious. "But it's not going to come to that. Trust me. We'll find a way."

Reassured, Mike seemed to relax.

But my anxiety kicked in again. What had I just promised? I remembered the dire predictions before the storm—there would be no water or power for weeks. And I might not be leaving tomorrow after all.

Friday, September 2, 2005

The Final Day

Chapter 66

Morning:
At 9 a.m., 1,000 National Guard troops take control of the
   New Orleans Convention Center.
Evacuation of staff from the Old Prison and Conchetta is
   under way.

Late Thursday night Gary and I had finally gone up to sleep in
Infection Control, where we had left our bedding three days earlier. When we woke up on Friday morning, we were hot, sweaty—
and ecstatic. Sometime today, we'd be leaving the jail.

Anxious to get going, we hurried down to the second floor to
wash up and change. The biting odor of urine and wet ashes filled
the stairwell, and garbage, broken glass, and soiled underwear littered the steps. Gary had been too tired to notice when we came
upstairs, but now the damage was inescapable.

"They really trashed this place," Gary said.

"They sure did," I replied, avoiding a burned blanket as we
walked down.

Mike was in Medical Administration when we walked in. Despite our midnight discussion, the psychiatrist was still worried about
getting Moby and Georgie out. As he and Brady left to walk the
dogs, I told Mike again that I was serious about staying with
him.

"Would you really stay here?" Gary asked when they were out
of earshot.

"If Mike's staying, so am I," I said as I went through my food stores for breakfast.

Down in the lobby the ambience was relaxed and joyful. Everyone was ready for our captivity to end. Deputies and the remaining families smiled and joked, in dramatic contrast to the belligerent crowd we had loaded onto boats during the previous two days.

Gary and I headed straight to the clinic, but there was only one patient—Deputy Jones, who was calm and coherent again after a good night's sleep. When Jones left, I followed him out to the front porch.

The sheriff's boats still came and went, and Sam asked the drivers for the latest news. The last inmates in the jail had been moved the night before, they told him. Today, the boats were evacuating employees and the remaining family members from the Old Prison, the House of Detention, and the Correctional Center. The deputies also suggested that when we finally did get to the overpass, we should get on buses rather than helicopters. The helicopters would be taking evacuees to the airport, where the passengers would leave with the general New Orleans population. The buses would take employees to a specific destination. Where? That was still a mystery, but the current rumor was Baton Rouge.

The drivers had one last piece of information: pets were not being allowed on the boats.

"If Mike can't take his dogs, he's not going." Sam shook his head. "What's he going to do?"

"It'll work out," I said. I had to believe that Mike, Moby, Georgie, and I would be leaving with everyone else—on schedule. "Are the nurses ready to go?"

"More than ready, but they're thirsty," Sam said. "The kitchen's rationing water in little cups."

"Why?" I asked, surprised. "They have all those five-gallon jugs?"

"They *had* them," Sam clarified. "Deputies took most of them to the overpass last night. The people over there really needed it."

"We can get the nurses more water," I said. "Gary, Mike, and

I brought gallons to the jail. The bottles are just sitting up on the second floor."

Gary and I brought down the water, and the rest of the morning passed quickly. Loading boats was no longer a hassle, and the clinic patients consisted of deputies who had been too busy evacuating others to take care of themselves.

At noon, Sam, Gary, and I headed to the back porch, hoping the kitchen was serving lunch. We weren't sure how the imminent evacuation was affecting Major Beach's operation.

"Apparently, they still have plenty of MREs," Gary remarked as we passed an obese deputy.

The man weighed at least 350 pounds. He sat on a chair, swilling Ensures and ripping open one MRE after another. He'd eat the cookies and desserts, sample the entree, and then drop the package. A pile of empty cans and half-eaten meals surrounded his chair.

"What a jerk!" Gary remarked as we rounded the corner. "You know he won't clean up that mess."

We picked up our own MREs and Ensures from the food table and sat down with the rest of the medical staff. Quiet and pensive, Mike perked up when Sam and I related the boat drivers' advice about evacuating.

"Any more word about pets?" Mike asked.

I hesitated for a moment. Before I could answer, an outburst of shouting across the street diverted everyone's attention.

Chapter 67

Marcus Dileo, several nurses, and a handful of deputies were yelling and waving at us from the second-story porch of the House of Detention.

I couldn't make out their words, but I was relieved to see that the medical staff was all right. This was the first contact I'd had with the people at Detention since Monday.

"What are they saying?" Gary listened closely. After a moment, his eyes widened. "They want food."

After days of work and worry, my mischievous side took control. I walked up to the railing and held up several MREs. When I pointed to the packages, the nurses shouted and waved their arms furiously. Clearly they wanted the food. Still having fun, I took a bite of my meal and rubbed my stomach in an exaggerated pantomime of satisfaction.

My audience screamed louder, but I still couldn't hear what they were saying. A deputy nearby asked if I wanted to talk to them. When I said yes, he pulled out his radio and called a deputy at Detention, who put Marcus on the channel.

The doctor told me they had not eaten for two days. I was speechless. We had assumed the building had gotten supplies from the kitchen and warehouse just as the Correctional Center had. I promised to send provisions over immediately.

"We need medical supplies, too," Marcus continued. "I have two really sick people here."

"How sick?" As far as I knew, the other clinics hadn't had any serious problems aside from the pregnant inmate from Conchetta.

"One of the deputies has emphysema," Marcus explained. "Inhalers aren't working, and we're out of oxygen."

The other man, a dialysis patient who hadn't had a treatment since the previous Friday, looked all right, but his potassium frequently rose to dangerous levels when he missed sessions—a potentially fatal complication. I told Marcus the man should be sent to the Superdome if possible, where he could receive dialysis.

Before signing off, I reassured the doctor that we'd send oxygen and the medications he needed. Then I began snapping orders. I sent Brady to get oxygen bottles from the pharmacy. Paul left to get more oxygen from the second-floor clinic. I remembered seeing Kayexalate, which lowers potassium, among the infirmary medications. Vinnie took Mike's dogs upstairs, and the psychiatrist went to find the drug.

Everyone else got MREs and some of the scarce water from the kitchen staff and carried it to the front steps. When everything was assembled, we hailed the next boat and loaded the supplies. As a precaution against someone else taking the food and water, one of the deputies radioed Marcus to have medical staff waiting.

As the boat pulled away, Sam shook his head. "Why would anyone bring a relative who needed dialysis to the jail?"

"Or babies?" Gary said.

I didn't have family in New Orleans, but I would never have brought my mother or grandmother to shelter at the jail. And they were healthy! Common sense should have told people to take children, the elderly, and anyone with serious medical conditions elsewhere.

As Mike walked up, the deputy with the radio told us that pets were being abandoned in the police department garage attached to the House of Detention. People had left food and water everywhere, and the parking structure had turned into a huge kennel with animals roaming loose. It was, in his words, heartbreaking.

"I can't listen to this," Mike said. He turned on his heels and went back up to Medical Administration. Gary, Paul, Brady, and I all followed.

"I'm not leaving them," Mike kept repeating as he refilled his dogs' water bowls. "I don't care what anyone says. Moby and Georgie are going with me, or I'm not going."

"If you stay, Mike, I'm staying with you," I reassured him. "But we're going to need a plan. If we can't get the dogs out, then we'll take them to your house—in a laundry cart. It's only four miles, and the two of us can float them there."

"Uptown's dry," Gary said. "After a mile or two, you'll probably be able to walk."

"I have two bathtubs full of water," I continued. "And Sam filled his tubs, too."

"I've got plenty of supplies at my place," Mike said. "We just have to get there."

"But that's only if we *don't* get evacuated." I insisted. I wasn't ready to give up on leaving the area *with* the animals today. "Believe me, Chief Hunter isn't going to leave Lucky behind. If he can get his dog out, we can get Moby and Georgie out."

Mike shrugged. "Maybe."

"Hey, if the worst happens, we won't go hungry or thirsty," I said. "Between all our houses, we have enough supplies to last for weeks. We'll be fine until someone comes back for us. But I still don't think it'll come to that."

Just then, Sam walked in with a camera. "Anyone want to explore?"

We needed the break, and we accompanied Sam down the hall. Brady grabbed his camera, too, and ran to catch up. The mounds of garbage, shattered glass, and burned debris I'd already seen were just a prelude to the massive damage on the inmate floors. The prisoners had battered large holes through cinderblock walls. The security spaces between tiers were in shambles: Monitors and wires had been torn out, and windows were smashed. Pipes dangled from the ceiling, ductwork littered the floor, and everything combustible had been burned. The wreckage was beyond belief.

Brady and Sam took lots of pictures. Riots that were sources of terror hours ago were now only images to preserve.

On the roof, in addition to broken glass and crumbled concrete, the inmates had left messages. "Please, help us!" they had written on windows. Large letters on the rooftop declared, "Man down! Man dead!" Thinking they had been left to die, the inmates had tried desperately to signal helicopters.

But the inmates have been evacuated, I thought. We're still here.

Chapter 68

Afternoon

By three p.m. all the families were gone, and so were most of the deputies. We still didn't know where we were headed, but I told the medical staff to pack so they'd be ready when it was our turn to leave.

Up in Medical Administration, the possibility that Mike and I might be staying at the jail toned down everyone's excitement. We each packed a bag of clothing, toiletries, cell phones and chargers, and ample food and drink. Wherever we ended up, we had no idea how long we'd be there or what resources would be available. Then we pooled our remaining food and water—leaving some aside, just in case—and took it downstairs with our bags and Mike's dogs.

The kitchen staff had finally left, and several boxes of supplies lay unguarded. We grabbed those, too, and joined the rest of the medical staff on the front porch. The nurses made playful grabs for the breakfast bars, candy, and cookies we had brought down, and though everyone was sick of MREs, they took them anyway, along with the water.

When the food rush ended, I told the group that special transportation had been arranged for employees. However, they needed to board buses at the overpass—not helicopters. With all they'd been through, I didn't want anyone getting separated in the confusion. And before we left, I had to say a few words.

"I just want to tell you how amazing you've all been. It's been an honor and privilege to be here with you." I paused, clearing my throat to cover a rush of emotion. "I have never worked with a finer group of people. Your courage and dedication humbles me. After today, we may not see each other again, but I will always remember what an incredible job you did."

There were tears and hugs but no time for long good-byes.

"Medical!" A deputy called. "Time to leave."

A wave of excitement swept through the group as everyone scrambled for their stuff. They assembled on the steps and boarded the boats, a few people at a time. I hung back, though, with Paul, Sam, and Gary. I wanted the other staff members to leave first. And I wanted to keep a close eye on Mike and the dogs as they gradually moved to the front of the line.

"Well, we'll know in a second if they're going to take the dogs," I told Sam.

Suddenly several gunshots rang out.

"That sounded awfully close," I said.

"That figures." Gary threw up his hands. "We made it through a hurricane and inmate riots, and now we're going to get shot."

"We are not going to be shot," I responded. "No one is going to come *into* the jail, not with all the deputies."

"Think about it," Gary said. "There are only a few deputies left, and everyone knows there are drugs here. This is a prime target."

Too worn down to argue, I just grinned and shrugged. Gary could find the downside for just about any situation. As he started to add something, I saw Chief Hunter step into a boat, holding Lucky in his arms.

"Mike!" I called out. When he looked back, I pointed frantically. "Follow Chief Hunter. Get in the next boat. They can't take his dog then tell you yours can't come."

"I'll take Georgie," Gary said, walking to the steps. "He can't handle them both."

I held my breath as I watched them get on. The dogs were quiet and well behaved on their leashes, and the driver didn't protest at all.

Sam, Paul, Brady, and I were the last people to leave. As the boat pulled up for us, Paul looked at me. He was sad and serious. "We've spent the last six years building this department, Dem. This is the end of an era."

I turned for one last look at the Correctional Center. When I came here six years ago, the medical department was in disarray. My staff and I had worked tirelessly to create an outstanding medical program, the best I'd seen at any jail. Now, with the jail all but destroyed, I didn't know if we'd ever be back. All our hard work, everything we built, was gone, finished. In a strange way, the parting reminded me of the final episode of a much-loved sitcom: you spend years getting to know the characters and caring about their lives, and then it's simply over.

I shuddered as I turned my back and climbed onto the boat.

Chapter 69

Silence prevailed when we first pulled away from the steps, and I succumbed to a moment of melancholy. However, as the boat sliced through the flood, my sadness quickly dissipated. The wind on my face was as invigorating as the realization that I was headed toward freedom and an unknown future.

The boat dropped us off at one end of the I-10 overpass, which looked like an inverted U, rising out of the water to a central hump of roadway. As we walked up the slope to the top, I could barely believe my eyes.

The interstate—also elevated on pillars above the flood—crossed thirty feet below the arc of the overpass, then connected to dry land. The highway below us was packed with buses and people. Rescue workers had built three stories of scaffolding between the overpass and the road, and everyone had to climb down the metal framework in order to board the buses.

"Drop your bags over here!" A Department of Corrections officer directed our attention to a pile of suitcases, backpacks, duffel bags, and trash bags stuffed with belongings. Officers were lowering the luggage to the interstate with ropes so people could reclaimed their belongings after they climbed down.

I heard muttered objections as staff placed their packs on the pile—not surprising since those bags contained all the clothes and food people had brought, and in some cases, the only things they had left in the world. Despite their reluctance, everyone complied.

The need for the system became apparent as I watched the

staff navigate the scaffold. Many of the deputies and nurses were overweight and had trouble with the long descent. It was dangerous enough without trying to carry baggage, too.

It was also clear why the boat drivers had refused to take pets. Animals were not permitted on the helicopters, and there was no way to carry an animal down the scaffold.

I looked around for Mike. I hadn't considered the possibility of being stranded on the overpass with the dogs. However, the psychiatrist and Gary were nowhere in sight, and contrary to reports, no animals roamed loose on the roadway. Sam, Brady, and I dropped off our luggage and opted for a sightseeing walk till the line diminished.

Both sides of the overpass were lined with cars that people had parked there to keep them out of the flood. That had worked . . . sort of. The cars were dry, but they had all been vandalized. Windows were broken, radios were gone, and glove compartments had been forced open.

"How could they loot the cars?" Sam laughed aloud. "The whole place is surrounded by water."

"Did they swim here?" I asked, puzzled.

"Getting here wasn't the big problem," Sam said. "How did they get all the stuff off?"

"And there have been deputies here since Tuesday," Brady pointed out.

Every time I thought I had seen it all, something new astonished me. The city of New Orleans had just experienced the greatest natural disaster ever to hit the United States, and thieves had still found a way to loot cars.

As we walked the length of the overpass, I was amazed that Hedy, Mills, and the other deputies had toughed it out here for almost three days, with no shelter from the sun. We had only been on the overpass for thirty minutes, and we were dripping with sweat.

The surrounding devastation was also difficult to assimilate. My regular route to work had become an unrecognizable landscape. Roofs had been sheared off buildings, exposing rafters and attics to the elements. Cars and trucks were barely visible under the murky water, and familiar trees and billboards had disappeared.

Every few minutes a helicopter landed on the overpass, and civilians swarmed aboard. I hoped my staff remembered to take the buses.

Sam and Brady snapped picture after picture to capture the once-in-a-lifetime images. After they finished, we returned to the end of the scaffolding line. I still hadn't seen any sign of Gary, Mike, or the dogs.

Twenty minutes later, it was Brady's and my turn to climb down. Two people could descend the scaffolding at the same time, one on each side of the structure.

I glanced at Brady. "Ready?"

A devilish grin lit up his face. "Are you?"

My challenge was unmistakable, and he didn't back down. "Go for it."

We started out fast and picked up speed as we foolishly flung ourselves downward. Like kids swinging from monkey bars, we moved with reckless abandon. The Corrections officers shouted at us to slow down, but after a week of perilous confinement, we needed to have some fun.

We flew.

I reached the bottom first—by milliseconds—and laughed. My actions were half-crazed, but I had been in charge and in control for too long. Brady seconded that with a wild shout. It felt good to cut loose.

Chapter 70

When I got down to the highway, the nurses were searching for their luggage in the large mound of belongings Corrections had sent down. Some employees had begun boarding the buses, which stretched in a long line down the road. Bottles of water, MREs, and boxes of fruit littered the highway, and apples had rolled all over the road. The waste annoyed me; so many people at the jail had gone without food for days.

When I saw Mike, Gary and the dogs, though, I forgot my irritation.

"Mike! You're here!" I exclaimed with a wide smile.

"Yeah, we made it. The driver took us to the overpass first, but when the Corrections guys saw the dogs, they told us to get back on the boat. The driver was really great, though. He brought us around to the interstate, right by the buses."

"'Cause Mike *demanded* to be brought here," Gary clarified.

"Yeah, but then I saw the sheriff," Mike said. "He told me to put the dogs on a bus for Angola and get on a different bus with the employees."

Mike looked down. Moby wiggled his hind end, and Georgie's tail thumped on the pavement.

"If he thinks that I'm leaving my dogs now, he must have heat stroke," Mike added.

"Go find Chief Hunter," I told him, pointing up the line of parked buses. I had seen the chief waiting with his dog up near the front. "He's not leaving without Lucky, and I think the sheriff's dogs are up there, too. Just get on the same bus they do, and you'll be fine."

Gary went with Mike and the dogs, while Sam, Brady, Paul, and I found our luggage and got on a bus. The sun beat through a window on my side, and with the air-conditioning off, it was unbelievably hot. For thirty minutes we sat and waited, until everyone was boarded and nothing remained on the interstate but litter. Finally, as the bus pulled out, the word filtered down the rows. We were going to Houma, Louisiana.

I had no idea where that was or what we would find there. There were still so many questions—about homes, loved ones, and our future. Yet I couldn't help thinking about the way the entire medical staff—and my friends—had come through in the last week. Sam had been a pillar of support during the crisis. Gary, whom I never doubted, was always there. Mike never quit working; in fact, he had surprised us all by the way he threw himself into danger. And Brady, who was new to the jail, turned out to be strong and selfless, a real hero.

Yes, there were still uncertainties ahead, but we had survived. We were finally on our way.

Epilogue

~~~~~~~~~~

The trip to Houma, about sixty miles southwest of New Orleans, turned out to be a long, hot, three-hour journey fraught with unexpected waits and frustrations.

For those of us who had been cloistered in the jail for five days, with minimal contact with the outside world, it was also an eye-opening ride.

We had heard that the roof had been torn away from the Superdome, but as we passed the stadium, the sight of huge, gaping holes in the massive dome prompted gasps and comments from nearly everyone. In the central business district the hurricane had toppled small buildings and blown the glass out of skyscrapers. Furniture and bedding hung out of hotel windows. Reports that whole rooms had been swept clean by the fury of the storm suddenly seemed more plausible.

And along the interstate, which had been vacant of traffic when the buses set out, we began passing groups of people walking. Some pushed shopping carts or pulled children's wagons or luggage with wheels. Mostly, they carried food, water, and clothing. Occasionally, the carts contained less practical items, such as television sets.

Gradually, the number of people on the road increased. Individuals, couples, and families sat next to piles of belongings. Many men went shirtless, and several women wore swimsuit tops to cope with the heat. Others wore long-sleeve shirts and pants to block the sun's rays. Almost every head was covered with a hat or scarf for added protection. The rag-tag bands of refugees, dressed in wild garments and set against the backdrop of a demolished city, were a post-apocalyptic scene straight from a Mad Max film.

Toward the edge of the city, we passed the New Orleans Convention Center. Heaps of trash had turned the parking lot into a dump. Given radio reports of murders and rapes there, we expected to see police, the military, and throngs of evacuees, but the complex appeared deserted.

Around 7:30 we finally pulled into the Houma Evergreen Cajun Center, a large hall filled with tables and chairs but woefully lacking in showers and food. The closest airport was in Baton Rouge. Still, nothing could detract from the elation of the several hundred jail employees—wardens, deputies, and medical staff—who were gathered there. For almost everyone, the next few hours were a blur of phone calls to friends and family and attempts to arrange rides and alternate shelter.

Though pets were officially barred from the Center—two local deputies actually threatened to take Chief Hunter's terrier, Lucky, into the woods and shoot him—Mike and Gary managed to sneak in Moby and Georgie and keep them hidden until a friend arrived to drive them to Baton Rouge.

Some members of the medical staff experienced their own adventures on the way to Houma—or never got there at all. Marcus Dileo and the nurses at the House of Detention missed the buses and ended up on large helicopters that took them to the New Orleans airport. They were assigned to travel to northwestern Louisiana. Instead Marcus somehow met a local hooker, whose pimp transported the group of sixty jail employees and family members to Houma—for the bargain price of a hundred dollars in cash and the doctor's personal check for $400.

Kentrisha Davis and Carol Evans, who had been evacuated from the overpass on Wednesday, were bused to Hunt Correctional Center outside of Baton Rouge. There they hand-delivered the inmates' records and meds to the Department of Corrections staff, who gave them a hero's welcome. Kentrisha's uncle picked up the two nurses and took them straight to Wal-Mart, where the salespeople embraced the bedraggled women, and the manager told them to pick out new clothes, shoes, underwear, and toiletries—all at no charge.

Later on Friday night, Sam and I got a ride with a friend to Baton Rouge; the following day he flew to meet his wife in Louisville, Kentucky. I spent the next two days with friends until I could get a flight out of the city. Then, after another day of weather delays and missed plane connections—and a night of sleeping on the floor of the Dallas airport—I finally made it to Atlanta, where my parents picked me up.

The twelve months after Katrina hit were a year of change, readjustment, and evolution for all of us. The St. Tammany jail survived relatively undamaged by the hurricane, but the staff was decimated. Some employees had quit; others lost everything and had to rebuild their personal lives. Still, eager to return to work, I drove back to New Orleans and returned to my job at St. Tammany on September 9, 2005.

The New Orleans jail had, of course, been devastated, but renovations began within weeks, and by the end of September we started the long process of rebuilding the medical department there, too, so it could function in the crippled city. Personal and professional considerations forced each doctor, nurse, and medical staff member to make difficult choices about the future.

Sam Gore came back to work at the New Orleans jail almost immediately; though his house had been severely damaged by wind and rain, his wife and children joined him in the city in mid-December. Gary French chose to take a job at the St. Tammany jail; miraculously, despite massive flooding nearby, his house stayed dry . . . and not one tree fell on his new roof.

Mike Higgins reported to duty at the New Orleans jail on September 22 and spent twelve-hour days cleaning, removing debris, and salvaging supplies to rebuild the medical department. He moved back to his home in October—with Moby and Georgie in tow—and, because of layoffs, has staffed the jail's mental health unit alone, seven days a week since that time.

After staying with friends in Baton Rouge for a few weeks, Brady Richard returned to his New Orleans apartment. He turned down a position at St. Tammany and instead went to work for FEMA, helping others rebuild their lives.

Paul Thomas refused to go back to the New Orleans jail, voicing strong criticism of Jail Administration. He accepted a nursing position at St. Tammany. Sadly, in December 2005 he fell and fractured his kneecap. A week later Paul developed a blood clot that traveled to his heart, killing him.

Victor Tuckler reunited with his wife and daughter in Beaumont, Texas, and a week later came back to New Orleans. At first he worked at the military field hospital set up inside the Convention Center, then he returned to Charity Hospital, which had established a temporary tent facility. Marcus Dileo lost his home and car but is nevertheless back at work at the New Orleans jail. His arm recovered completely from the paralysis.

The nurses, too, endured many cases of personal dislocation, damage to homes, and loss of cars. Denise Sarro was stranded in the Cajun Center for four days; she recuperated in Florida for a while, then made her way back to New Orleans and her job at the jail at the end of September. Duane Townzel, who had been reunited with his wife in Houston, also came back to work in October, followed by Lillian Ford a month later. Lillian replaced Paul Thomas as director of nursing services. Kentrisha Davis is also once again a member of the staff. Her good friend Carol Evans lives with extended family in Texas, where the nurse works in a mental health facility. Her husband did escape from their house, which was completely destroyed.

Chuck Perotto and Scarlett Maness were united with family and friends who had evacuated to Tennessee and been "adopted" by a local Baptist church. Late in the year both nurses joined the staff of the St. Tammany jail, as did Jan Ricca, who finally reconnected with her son and husband by accident at the New Orleans airport.

As for me, my house had significant roof damage and five feet of water in the basement and was unliveable. For weeks after I returned to Louisiana, daily living was a struggle. Accommodations were scarce. Phone service was spotty, and restaurants and grocery stores were closed or crowded. Initially I commuted to the New Orleans jail from Baton Rouge, but I often slept in my St. Tammany office. By the end of the year, however, I had renovated my house and sold it, and am still planning to move into the condo I found what seems like a lifetime ago.

The New Orleans jail is once again functioning, but the facility is smaller and more primitive than it was before the storm. Housing 2,000 inmates, the jail now offers only basic medical services, rather than the comprehensive health care programs available before Katrina. In July 2006, I made the difficult decision to step down as medical director, though I continue to work there part-time. And I still serve as medical director of the St. Tammany jail.

Writing this book with Diana Gallagher has been my way of acknowledging the men and women of the New Orleans jail—ordinary people who found themselves in extraordinary circumstances and rose to meet the challenge. They became heroes in every sense of the word.

Author's Note

The events described in this story are real, based primarily on my recollections and in-depth interviews with other key participants. I have made every effort to keep the account as factual as possible. The dialogue was, by necessity, recreated. However, the conversations are consistent with the spirit of the situations and the actual personalities. The names of the inmates were changed to protect their identities. Similarly, the names of certain jail employees were changed when specifically requested by the individual or to prevent embarrassment.

The media has given considerable attention to events at the jail during and after Hurricane Katrina. The decision not to evacuate the jail prior to the storm, as well as the treatment of inmates in the course of the evacuation, has been heavily scrutinized. *No Ordinary Heroes* does not try to explain or justify those decisions. Instead, my goal was to chronicle the actions of the medical staff and selected jail employees throughout the storm and subsequent five days. I tried to honestly depict our struggles, showing both our strong points and faults. I hope I have shown the courage and heroism of this amazing group of people and done their stories justice.

There have been a number of books that effectively document the events surrounding Hurricane Katrina. What I felt was lacking, however, was a first-person account that tried to convey to the reader what it was like to be in the middle of the storm and its dangerous aftermath. Many of the outside responders have been rightfully praised for their roles in helping the citizens of New Orleans. However, the doctors, nurses, and deputies at the jail were in a unique position. While they unselfishly fought to assist others, they were, at the same time, themselves victims of the storm. Many of them lost loved ones, houses, and other property, yet they continued to do their jobs.

I wish to apologize to persons omitted from this book. It was impossible to include everyone in the narrative. Many dedicated deputies guarded the overpass, drove rescue boats, or assisted with the evacuation of buildings. They worked diligently to ensure the safe movement of more than 7,000 inmates, staff, and civilians. Similarly, many nurses assigned to clinics other than the Correctional Center or the infirmary were not specifically named.

I would also like to thank the many generous people who opened their hearts and homes to residents after the evacuation. Finally, I want to thank everyone who assisted in the evacuation or helped with the rebuilding of the city, including the New Orleans Police Department, the Red Cross, the Department of Corrections, other sheriff's offices across the state, the Louisiana National Guard, police and fire departments from across the country, and the U.S. military.